Managing
Computer System
Projects

THE TOUCHE ROSS MANAGEMENT SERIES

Managing Computer System Projects

John C. Shaw

Partner, Touche Ross & Co.

William Atkins

Principal, Touche Ross & Co.

WITH CONTRIBUTIONS BY
Arnold E. Ditri and Howard J. Peterson

McGRAW-HILL BOOK COMPANY

New York   St. Louis   San Francisco   Düsseldorf   Johannesburg   Kuala Lumpur
London   Mexico   Montreal   New Delhi   Panama
Rio de Janeiro   Singapore   Sydney   Toronto

Sponsoring Editor   Dale L. Dutton
Director of Production   Stephen J. Boldish
Editing Supervisor   Linda B. Hander
Designer   Naomi Auerbach
Editing and Production Staff   Gretlyn Blau,
   Teresa F. Leaden, George E. Oechsner

MANAGING COMPUTER SYSTEM PROJECTS

34567890 MAMM 75

THE TOUCHE ROSS MANAGEMENT SERIES

This book is part of the Touche Ross Management Series, an open-ended library dedicated to presentations of techniques for managing the challenges of change faced by business and government executives.

Each book in this series is dedicated to the bridging of a portion of the gap in management techniques which inevitably associates itself with new problems or technologies. Change itself can be said to have achieved the status of a constant in today's environment. Thinking of change in this light, it becomes an environmental factor presenting management challenges to policy-level executives of business and governmental organizations. Change becomes both a challenge and an obstacle. In particular, problems result from the time lags between the identification of a technologically generated problem and the evolutionary development of management techniques to cope with it.

This series, then, is dedicated to abridging the time lag between recognition of an emerging technology and application of working methods for its realistic application and control.

Individual volumes within this series address themselves to the management levels where needs exist. Each book is directed primarily toward two specific audiences, policy-level executives and operational executives responsible for the function.

Each volume deals with some aspect of change-related technology. Each addresses itself to the methodology for making the new techniques work on behalf of management. Each book in this series uses management-level language. Emphasis is on the requirements for management control rather than technical involvement. Similarly, the philosophical or theoretical aspects of each new technology are treated in terms of management "need to know" only. As quickly as feasible, each book moves from the philosophical to the practical—concentrating on the "doing" aspects of the specific subject at hand.

As sponsors of this series, Touche Ross seeks to guide the content of each volume along the general lines followed in its own consulting practice. Specifically, the aim of the firm, and the dedication of its people, lies in the area of doing—leading the transition for each management skill from the realm of art to science.

Traditionally, doing and writing have tended to be separate—unfortunately unrelated—areas of management endeavor. With this series—and with the blending of skills which have gone into its creation—Touche Ross hopes to fill a need by presenting practical solutions in an understandable form—on a timely basis.

In summary, we at Touche Ross feel that the work we do is dedicated toward helping others in what should be done, and, more importantly, how to do it. This series of books is dedicated toward that end.

DONALD W. JENNINGS
National Director, Management Services
Touche Ross & Co.

Preface

Electronic data processing (EDP) is an area of growing professionalism. The decade of the sixties witnessed a transition in system development techniques. For want of a better analogy, it can be said that the transition was from art to science. This transition applied to the management of the EDP function as well as to the technology itself.

At the beginning of the sixties, computers were technological marvels which held management people in awe. By the end of the decade, technology was being formalized for controlling and applying computers as workaday management tools. Profitable application of this technology, then, carried forward as a major management challenge of the seventies.

The methodology behind this transition utilized a project approach: Each computer system to be developed was defined fully and specifically at the outset. Objectives were stated and programs mapped for their achievement.

The methodology itself is a management staple. Project approaches have been used in areas as diverse as putting a man on the moon, designing and producing an automobile for a given model year, electing a public official, or revising educational curricula.

While the principles of project management are universal, special adaptations and applications were necessary in applying them to EDP. That is what this book is about. It presents philosophies, approaches, and proven techniques by which project management methods have been used for the controlled, effective development of computer-based data processing and information systems.

Within the context of this book, the emphasis has been placed upon the practical. The authors and the contributors are working consultants. They are versed in and work regularly in the theoretical areas of data processing and management. But, without exception, they are also dedicated to successful implementation and realization of projected results from computer systems—as distinct from a limited interest in design only. The resulting work, it is hoped, will have a valid application as a working guide toward successful achievement of profitable EDP systems.

The authors and contributors have structured this work in the hope that it will be of interest to a cross section of readers, including:

- Executives of corporate and governmental organizations whose activities interrelate with the systems function
- Directors or managers within systems departments responsible for system project implementation
- System project leaders who are actively "doing" project development for computer systems
- Systems analysts and assistants to project leaders whose career paths lead in the direction of computer system project management
- College students at the upper-level undergraduate or beginning graduate level who have had courses in programming

It is hoped that this book will serve as either a primary or supplementary text for courses in system planning and development.

The ideas and techniques which make up the methodology offered in this book represent a cross section of effort by contributors too numerous to name. Credit belongs, primarily, to those business, industrial, and governmental organizations which have successfully managed the Planning, Development, and Implementation of EDP systems. Individuals involved include literally scores of EDP professionals, systems managers, and practical-minded consultants.

This book itself has had several generations of predecessors, including standards manuals used at individual EDP installations and a series of working manuals covering EDP techniques created and implemented by the consultants of Touche Ross.

Without meaning to slight any of the people or organizations who worked long and hard to bring the project management technology covered in this book into existence, the authors feel that a few people have contributed at a level which demands special recognition.

In particular, the collaborators whose contributions are acknowledged on the title page should be identified further.

Arnold E. Ditri, a Principal in the Management Services Division of Touche Ross & Co., was a prime mover in bringing this technology into existence. It is gratifying to be able to acknowledge both the intellectual and technical leadership which he applied in the creation of the methodology and in making this book a reality.

Howard J. Peterson, CPA and a Partner in the Management Services Division of Touche Ross & Co., was a vital conceptual leader in the creation of the project-management techniques which form the basis for this book.

Another member of the original, dedicated group which initiated the methodology for the project-management techniques outlined in this book is John DeJong, a former Manager in the Management Services Division of Touche Ross & Co.

A pioneer in bringing the project management methods presented in this book into being is Roger C. Guarino, Director of Systems and Data Processing of The Kelsey-Hayes Corporation in Detroit. During the trying, early days of project management development, Roger was an invaluable sounding board, a contributor of valuable ideas, and a management innovator who was one of the first to make these concepts work in a "real world" environment.

JOHN C. SHAW
WILLIAM ATKINS

Contents

Section 4   IMPLEMENTATION PHASE

SECTION ONE

Overview

CHAPTER ONE

Organization for Effective System Development

EARLY FAILURES

Collectively, computers have been an overwhelming success. But, individually, most computer systems have failed in some respect.

Failure incidence has been particularly critical as corporate organizations have applied computers first to routine paper work, then to operating functions, and, finally, to management-oriented information-processing systems.

Failure, as the term is used here, has been relative. Specifically, a failure exists when any stipulated objective or operating goal set for a new system is not achieved. Such a goal can be operational savings (for example, improved customer service, reduced inventory costs, lower production costs, personnel cost reduction). Other goals can include development costs, schedules, reliability, or the ability of a system to make itself accepted within the user organization. Both surveys and practical experience have indicated overwhelmingly that most computer systems installed during the fifties and sixties failed in at least some important respect.

With failure, many management and computer people alike have experienced frustration. On the one hand, operating management found itself hamstrung by the inability to control costs or results of data processing activities. On the other, technically qualified data processing people tended to feel they were being treated as outcasts or, at best, tolerated as a necessary evil.

RATIONALE EMERGES

Without going into the minute details or relative merits of success/failure ratios of computer installations during the fifties and sixties, it can be said that, gradually, a rationale developed. People on both sides—management and electronic data processing (EDP)—learned to cope with their new tools and new roles.

Common denominator organizational and management philosophies began to emerge. The EDP or management information system (MIS) function began to achieve a recognized place in the operations of the average company—and in its organization chart.

Also important, management began to integrate the MIS function into the planning side of the business. During the early EDP years, planning for computer operations tended to be divorced—virtually completely—from overall corporate planning. As a result, it was fairly typical to find situations where top-level company planning and developmental programs worked out by computer people were completely out of phase. Even worse, it was not uncommon to find that operating management had made sweeping decisions which could not be supported by EDP people who did not know what was going to be expected of them.

END OF THE BEGINNING

An analysis of the status of computerized management sciences was published in 1969 in a paper prepared by Arnold E. Ditri and Donald R. Wood of Touche Ross and Company. The status of computerized information systems at that particular point was summarized in the title of the paper "The End of the Beginning." The authors saw computerized management techniques in a state of transition. One era was seen as coming to a close, another beginning.

The closing era was characterized by a condition of failure for most system development efforts—attributed largely to a lack of communication and understanding between EDP and operating management people. Reasons cited included:

Lack of Tradition In the early EDP days, there were no established standards which could be applied by either data processing or management people. Management men were not used to thinking of computers as essential tools. EDP people did not know where they really belonged.

Impact of Change Computers, inevitably, changed business operations with which they became associated. With enforced change came suspicion. It was extremely difficult—in some cases impossible—to establish the needed working rapport between EDP professionals and users of EDP systems within a company.

EDP Mystique A "gee whiz" aura was built up around computers. People who did not understand them were reluctant to adopt computerized methods. This applied at all levels—from management on down through the organization.

Language Barrier Almost overnight, computers spawned a baffling new vocabulary. Communication obstacles developed between EDP people and management of user groups.

Lack of Direction During the formative years, it was recognized that large companies needed computers. However, acceptance tended to be grudging. Management people swallowed the medicine to cure specific symptoms, but there was no overall plan. Computers were not management sponsored, they were management tolerated.

Managerial Competence Because managers tended to look at computers in terms of technical and functional differences in comparison with other aspects of their business, established techniques which had proven themselves elsewhere within an organization were not applied to EDP operations. Standard techniques for budgeting and delegation of responsibilities were not used as they would normally have been in a company which, for example, was installing a new manufacturing process or undertaking marketing of a new product.

Abdication of Concern Having failed to cope with or control EDP operations, many management people tended to abdicate responsibilities. Management reporting channels were set up to establish control of EDP operations at comparatively low levels. EDP people, in turn, were generally not in a position to impact corporate decision making or planning.

DEFINITIONS

Before getting into a necessary review of the MIS environment as it is unfolding today and promises to continue to develop, let us establish a basis for this discussion—and for future references throughout this work. Specifically, some key terms should be defined within the specific context of this work.

System   A *system* is an ongoing activity encompassing people, procedures, materials, and equipment coordinated to provide an identified, coherent service or end product.

The existence of a system presupposes the presence of an organization within which it functions. Within the larger organization, however, each system must have its own identity and structure for coordination and communication.

The principles of system development and management are basic. They are the same whether the end result will be a walk on the surface of the moon, the delivery of finished products from a manufacturing plant, or the utilization of a computer. An understanding of the similarities between computerized systems and other complex, coordinated activities is vital to effective management and control of the MIS (EDP) function.

Project   A *project* is a time-oriented activity with functional objectives and constraints. It has definite starting points, an organized functional pattern, specific budgets, established responsibilities, and completion schedules. As is true for systems, the principles are basic, applying to any type of developmental activity within an organization.

Systems Management   *Systems management,* today, is recognized as a first line function of a corporate or governmental organization. Typically, the departmental identity carries a designation of MIS or some other information-related title. The systems manager, as a rule, will have a stature at a peer level with a manager of manufacturing, purchasing, engineering, finance, and so on.

The systems management function itself needs a multiple-responsibility type of organization. Project management is one of the functional and staffing requirements. The MIS department also has production-type responsibilities for the operation of ongoing business and information systems. The MIS organization also needs an integral staff function for support of both ongoing and developmental activities. In this area, staff support is largely of a technical nature.

Acceptance of this multifaceted concept for organization of the systems management function has been important to successful integration of computerized techniques within corporations or government agencies. The structure is designed to facilitate communication between the MIS department and management of user organizations. Within this organizational structure, highly technical people are at a staff level. Their dealings are chiefly with peers within their own department. This approach eliminates the problem of communication between technical specialists and management generalists. In the past, the inevitable communication bottlenecks between EDP technical people and line or general management people have plagued system development efforts. Through an interdisciplinary approach to organization of the MIS department, personnel assigned to project management of production service responsibilities can be selected for their ability to interrelate with users of EDP services.

Systems (MIS) Manager   This man is a new breed of the executive. He is a qualified technician/manager capable of operating at the vice presidential —at lowest, the assistant vice presidential—level within a corporate organization (with commensurate recognition within governmental agencies). His special capabilities and/or training qualify him to deal with and direct professional and technical people responsible for the implementation of EDP functions and operations. He must provide the caliber of management which will enable the company to hire qualified creative and technical talent in the EDP field. He must provide the direction which molds a group with normal tendencies toward individualism into a working entity.

Underlying all these tasks, the systems manager must, himself, build and maintain a technical awareness of the computer field as a whole. A systems manager who does not keep up with developments and innovations in computer technology and applications will find his background becoming obsolescent within two to four years. A continuing awareness of developments, trends, and techology is necessary for the recognition of valid new approaches and techniques which are the lifeblood of an effective systems organization.

This technical competence must be exercised continually through involvement in each system development project under the manager's jurisdiction. That is, technical competence alone is not enough. The systems manager must be involved in and cognizant of the progress, quality, and problems of each system development project for which his department is responsible.

Involvement in specific, individual projects is one of the chief methods by which the systems manager develops the top-flight people he has been able to attract into an organization. Professional growth is vital to the spirit of a systems organization. Close association, in turn, is necessary for this growth.

Projection Management   This is a technique for isolation and individual management of projects and the series of tasks leading to their completion. For most companies (or government agencies) and most management people, the basic project nature of EDP system development has posed new requirements, new problems.

The typical business or governmental organization is geared toward management of ongoing, or flow-type, operations and responsibilities. A manufacturing firm, for example, has scheduled quotas of product deliveries to meet. The products are established. Procedures for their manufacture are firm. Management deals with known quantities basic to the primary business of the organization.

A system project, on the other hand, deals with unknowns. The unknown quantities inherent in system projects are twofold. First, where an EDP system is involved, it is, basically, foreign to the established activities and involvements of most management people. Second, a project terminates when defined objectives have been met.

Learning to cope with project management requirements has been one of the major new skills which successful management people within organizations using computers have had to master. Special communication and control techniques which are valid on a "need to know" basis at both technical and nontechnical levels have had to be devised and implemented.

In particular, since a system development project, by definition, deals with elements of the unknown, special attention must be paid to monitoring progress — checkpointing — and to budgetary and staffing controls. End products, milestones for review, and standards for measurement and evaluation must be inbuilt if a project is to be carried forward successfully.

Further, size and scope of projects must be kept within manageable limits. To illustrate, as a general rule of thumb, Touche Ross consultants recommend that project definitions, goals, and working plans be restricted so that, insofar as it feasible, any individual project for development of a computerized system would have outside limits in the area of $100,000 in expenditures — 4 man-years of systems analysis effort.

This guideline, of course, is not universal. Exceptions are inevitable. For example, a project set up to develop a nationwide airline reservation system clearly could not be implemented within these boundaries. Similarly, far-reaching manufacturing control or governmental systems involving extensive use of computers would require activities and budgets in excess of this general rule of thumb. However, the basic principle is still valid: A system project should be budgeted and staffed within manageable limits, with controllable organizational structures, missions, and budgets. Where a defined job is larger than the scope of a single, manageable project, several projects, or subprojects, can be established utilizing the same basic methodology.

System Project Leader This person functions at a middle-management level similar to that of a project engineer within a research or manufacturing organization.

Typically, he holds a bachelor's (or master's) degree in business, mathematics, industrial engineering, or another quantitative science. His work experience probably includes programming and systems analysis.

As a rule, he will have four to seven years of EDP experience. He must have both a level of technical competence and a personality which inspire confidence. This combination is critical because the system project leader is charged chiefly with managing and relating to people. On the one hand, he must have enough technical depth to understand the problems of and supervise his own staff. On the other, he must be able to present and "sell" concepts to user organizations and other executives.

The system project leader must understand problems of user groups, convince them that the system under development will provide the logical solution, and supervise adaptation of system elements to their satisfaction.

The system project leader must also be dynamic enough to keep enthusiasm for his activity both stimulated and directed. It is not unusual for a project to stretch out for periods of one to three years. At the outset, everything is in sharp focus. The need for the new system is apparent. Responsible managers are anxious to realize the projected benefits. But, six months later, attention spans begin to sag. It is at these critical times that the personal drive of a system project leader spells the difference between continuity and faltering.

Systems Analyst *Systems analysts* are the people with the primary working and functional responsibility of carrying out the activities of a system project. In terms of system project accomplishment, systems analysts are the staff professionals. They handle the bulk of surveying, specifying, designing, developing, and implementing tasks associated with a system project.

Most systems analysts have done computer programming. They retain a level of proficiency in this area so that they can interact effectively with programmers assigned to a project. However, the primary professional skills which they contribute to a system project lie in surveying existing systems, formulating proposed new systems, documenting operations and/ or plans, interacting with system users at all levels, and assisting with the training of system users.

User This is a term which, literally, can be applied to anybody, almost anywhere. For the purposes of this discussion, a *user* is any individual who functions outside the EDP area and is affected by a data processing system. A user can also be a department, a group, or even automated equipment which relies on or interacts with a data processing system.

Users exist and must be dealt with at every level of a company's operations. At any given time, a user interacting with system project personnel can be a clerk, a worker in a manufacturing area, or a top-ranking vice president.

At whatever level he is found, a user holds the ultimate key to the success or failure of a data processing system. Simply stated, if a user "buys" a data processing system, it is virtually a foregone success. This is because all systems, ultimately, are judged by results realized by the user. Therefore, it is possible to have an EDP system which is technically superior but which fails for lack of user acceptance. On the other hand, a system which is technically marginal can be highly successful if it enjoys enthusiastic user response and cooperation.

System Project Team   This is a full-time organization set up to staff and carry out the business of the system project. Except for a core group of a few top, project-level, full-time people, the team is dynamic in its makeup and nature. On an as-needed basis, personnel with requisite skills are assigned to the system project team for the duration of project requirements at their own level of usefulness.

Full-time members of the team include the system project leader and, as a rule, at least one other systems analyst on his staff. There can, of course, be other systems people, depending on the scope and complexity of the individual project.

System users provide the other full-time membership for the system project team. At least one key, working-level user employee represents his group as a full-time member of the system project team. As a rule, this user representative will be backed up by at least one other full-time team member from the user department. If the system is interdepartmental in scope, each user department may be represented on the team. Assignments in such cases depend on the nature of the system and the type of involvement of user personnel.

Within the scope of a system project, the full-time members of the team —and their administrative and clerical and support people—provide the necessary continuity.

On an as-needed basis, additional user personnel become members of the system project team during critical surveys associated with planning and development. Further, such key activities as System Test and Conversion are carried out by users functioning as self-sufficiently as possible.

Depending on the nature of the project, programmers may also become full-time members of the system project team during the critical activities where their technical experience is needed.

Conceptually, the important thing to recognize is that technical people cannot handle system development projects on their own. It is true that many computer-inclusive systems have been developed entirely by technical people. But the likelihood and opportunities for success are, truly, infinitely greater when users are involved in the planning, development, and implementation of systems which they will be expected to operate, support, and live with.

THE SYSTEMS MANAGEMENT (MIS) ORGANIZATION

By the late sixties, most major corporations and governmental agencies had worked out structures and methods for integrating information-processing operations into the mainstream of their organizations. By this time, of course, the concept of information processing was gaining wide acceptance. Management information systems were beginning to happen. Other information-processing techniques were being applied successfully to mainstream operations of business organizations—as distinct from earlier applications to accounting and paper-work routines. Inventory management, manufacturing scheduling and control, and financial information systems were being implemented with regularity. Computer manufacturers and software houses were making support materials readily available for file processing information systems.

As the scope of information processing expanded, business and government organizations began to structure themselves to absorb and manage this potential. Typically, all data processing operations within an organization were brought under the cognizance and/or control of a single, central MIS department.

At the head of this group, the systems (MIS) manager functioned as a top-level corporate executive. In many instances, he reported directly to the chief operating officer of the company—executive vice president or president, as the case might be. In some companies, the systems manager actually held the rank of vice president. In other cases, he reported to a vice president responsible for either finance or administration.

Even in such cases, the systems management function has been elevated considerably from its comparatively lowly stature of the fifties. The old tabulating supervisor had, traditionally, run a shop in the basement of his company's offices and enjoyed similar stature on the organization chart. Today, however, it is fairly safe to assume that the systems manager is either one or two steps removed from the chief operating officer of the company.

A typical organization chart under which an MIS department might be structured is illustrated in Figure 1-1. Briefly, this depicts a systems manager, in this case titled director, MIS, reporting to the operating head of his company. Under the systems manager are three group-level managers who are responsible for: (1) systems and programming, (2) technical services, and (3) computer services (operations).

The illustration of this concept with a single organization chart should not be construed as indicating there is only one way to relate an MIS department to its organization. Rather, this is one typical method. Many other alternatives are possible. Further, there are many alternatives open in the organization of the MIS function itself. Again, it should be stressed that the intent is to provide an example for the purposes of discussion in this book, not to suggest rigid structures. Organization concepts for the MIS function are discussed in greater depth in a companion work, *Managing the EDP Function.*

Note that the department is organized for close interrelationship: The

ORGANIZATION FOR SYSTEM MANAGEMENT

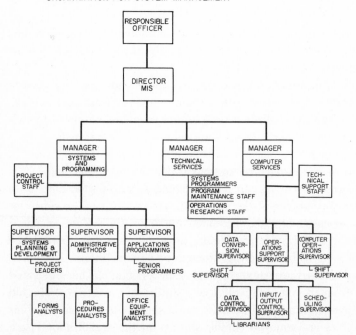

Figure 1-1

systems and programming group has a staff function for project control. This group or individual manager maintains close liaison with the other two organizations within the department.

Similarly, the operations group has a technical support function which dovetails closely with the technical services organization. Typically, the technical support people in a computer operations group would be responsible for maintaining the operating system, equipment planning, maintenance of job control specifications and run documents, and so on.

The technical services group, as indicated, has general responsibility for system software and program maintenance. In practice, the technical services group acts as a filter or quality assurance checkpoint between the system development staff and the computer services group.

Under the manager of systems and programming are three groups, each headed by a supervisor. Responsibilities are for systems planning and development (the area of concentration for this book), administrative methods, and applications programming.

Similarly, the computer services section of the MIS department has three groups headed by supervisory-level people. Responsibilities are for data conversion, operations support, and actual computer operations.

The MIS/User Relationship

An implicit requirement for the total operation of the MIS department is sensitivity toward and coordination with EDP users. This is particularly true in the system project area. System project development is done on a team basis. The user organization has full-time members on each system project team working in close coordination with systems analysts and the system project leader. Therefore, systems analysts assigned to a project must be politically, as well as technically, adept.

It should be stressed that user involvement and coordination plays a positive role in system development. In the past, there has been a tendency on the part of many systems analysis people to regard users and user coordinators as unavoidable burdens. In the modern system development environment, this is not the case at all. At least three good reasons can be cited for coordination with and participation by users on the system development task force.

1. Only users have full knowledge of departmental operations within which the system will exist. Application of this knowledge to the functional features of a system is indispensable for its success.

2. Without user participation in system development, probability of failure in the acceptance of the new system rises geometrically. Con-

versely, if user people have had an active hand in developing the new system, acceptability to their peers is enhanced many times.

3. After a system is developed, involved user personnel are necessary for its successful implementation, ongoing operation, and continuing updating and improvement.

To a smaller, but nonetheless important, extent, interaction between computer operations personnel and users is also critical to system success. Users are customers for computer operations people. Procedures within the EDP operations function should recognize this status. Mechanisms for service and interaction should be built in.

Position and Role of the MIS Department

Figures 1-2 and 1-3 diagram alternate positions and relationships indicating the interaction between the MIS department and other areas of an organization.

As shown in Figure 1-2, the MIS function falls under the vice president for finance and administration. In such an organization, the MIS group would be on the same line as the corporate controller and treasurer.

As diagramed in Figure 1-3, the MIS function is headed by a vice president positioned on the same reporting line as vice presidents responsible for marketing, engineering, manufacturing, personnel, and finance/administration.

Variations, of course, can be infinite. The main point to be made is that

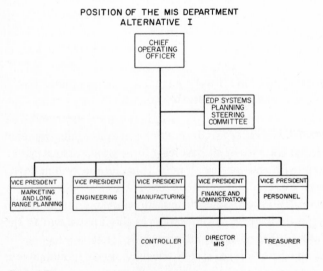

Figure 1-2

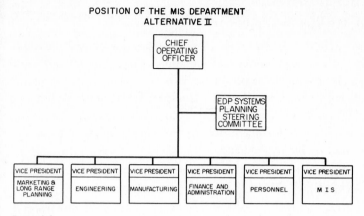

Figure 1-3

the data processing function is now firmly established in the organizational mainstream of most well-run corporations.

Management Cognizance and Control of the MIS Function

From a general management standpoint, system development poses a special problem: It is extremely expensive. During the fifties and early sixties, many organizations experienced painful write-offs and cost over-runs as a direct result of failures to structure themselves for management of the system development function.

THE EDP SYSTEMS PLANNING STEERING COMMITTEE

One approach to establishing corporate control over system planning and development which has proved feasible for a number of organizations and, at this writing, appears to be gaining wide acceptance, is the formation of a top-level EDP Systems Planning Steering Committee.

Membership of such committees is generally at the vice presidential level. This assures the ability of the committee to reach and implement decisions. Also, an executive group at this level serves as a true committee in that it is not charged with "doing" responsibilities. Rather, it reviews requests for action, arrives at decisions, resolves conflicts, and monitors the development and implementation of system projects. It also serves to oversee user performance in determining that objectives and benefits agreed to at the inception of a system development project are, in fact, realized.

Steering Committee User Participation

In practice, membership on or attendance at steering committee meetings can vary with projects under consideration. One generally accepted rule, however, is that the vice president with management responsibility for the organization which will be the primary user of a new system is a key member of the steering committee. He should be a party to all discussions and agreements involving development and implementation of a system to be used by his department.

PROJECT MANAGEMENT CONCEPTS

In effect, the EDP steering committee serves as an overseer of corporate interests. With continuing surveillance by an operating management group, system planning and development can be implemented in minimum stages of effort and expenditure. Putting it another way, management does not make any decisions without having commensurate supporting information.

Under this approach, systems are developed in stages. The process is analogous to strip mining techniques. The system planning and development effort digs into successive layers of information the way mining equipment scrapes away levels of soil and rock. At any point, a strip mining effort can be terminated because the ore uncovered does not justify further expense. Similarly, in a staged approach, system planning and development activities move in successive layers of research and detail. At established checkpoints, available information is examined. Only then are commitments made to go to the next level of expense and effort or to terminate the project.

In other words, management is no longer asked for a blank check in the development of a projected system. Management commitments are limited —not irrevocable. However, a standing steering committee is a necessity for implementation of this type of "creeping commitment." This committee must interact with system planning and development task forces on a scheduled basis, at established checkpoints. In other words, the EDP Systems Planning Steering Committee and the task force developing a new system must be mutually responsive.

Project Implementation Techniques

The ability to manage system development and implementation on a project basis stems directly from the evolution of an applicable body of knowledge and the parallel accumulation of experience. Project management is an established, recognized discipline with structured patterns and methods which, in turn, provide a basis for control.

Specifically, system projects can be divided into three clearly recognizable elements:

1. Planning
2. Scheduling
3. Control

The project management process is outlined schematically in Figure 1–4. As the diagram shows, each project element has several separate components.

Project Planning

Components of the planning element of project management include the following.

Job Guidelines   The guidelines for a system project are equivalent to a road map. They consist of a series of documents incorporating:

- *A summary of the job and its relationship to other projects.*   This is a general definition of what is to be accomplished and how the projected system will fit in with other operating elements of the company.
- *Statement of objectives.*   This is a specific statement of what will be accomplished.   It identifies end products and benefits.
- *Statement of job scope.*   This defines organizational areas to be covered in planning studies — bearing in mind that, under the creeping-

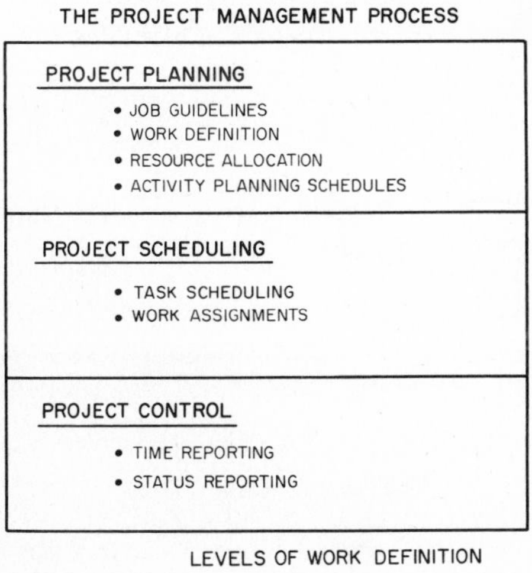

THE PROJECT MANAGEMENT PROCESS

```
┌─────────────────────────────────────────┐
│ PROJECT PLANNING                         │
│      • JOB GUIDELINES                    │
│      • WORK DEFINITION                   │
│      • RESOURCE ALLOCATION               │
│      • ACTIVITY PLANNING SCHEDULES       │
├─────────────────────────────────────────┤
│ PROJECT SCHEDULING                       │
│      • TASK SCHEDULING                   │
│      • WORK ASSIGNMENTS                  │
├─────────────────────────────────────────┤
│ PROJECT CONTROL                          │
│      • TIME REPORTING                    │
│      • STATUS REPORTING                  │
└─────────────────────────────────────────┘
```

LEVELS OF WORK DEFINITION

Figure-1-4

commitment principle, project activities are subject to checkpoint and control by the EDP Systems Planning Steering Committee.

Work Definition The overall project is broken down into measurable work units. The skills and levels of experience necessary to perform all work are identified and documented. The definition includes estimates of the amount of time required to complete each work unit. Job breakdowns within the work definition are handled one level at a time, as illustrated in Figure 1-5. Examples of how these work-definition levels might be applied in a business data processing environment are:

- *Projects:* Accounts receivable, inventory control, etc.
- *Activities:* System specifications, programming, user training, etc.
- *Tasks:* Record layouts, run programming, etc.
- *Subtasks:* Record layouts—inventory, record layouts—open order file, subroutine programming, etc.

Resource Allocation This includes determination of requirements in terms of manpower, facilities, equipment, software, funds, and so on.

Activity Planning Schedules At this level, resource allocation is broadly time related. That is, taking into account such elements as personnel availability, equipment installation schedules, software completion forecasts, and so on, general time frames are established.

Project Scheduling

This segment of project management takes the broad activity schedules established within the planning function and breaks them down to a task level. Typically, project planning would be done by the systems manager.

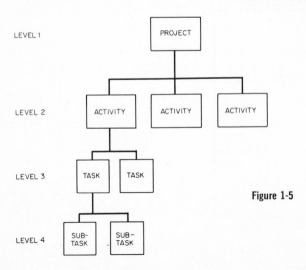

Figure 1-5

The next level, then, is carried out under the direction of the system project leader. Activities include:

Task Scheduling Specific work functions relevant to activity completion are established for each task and subtask necessary to get the overall job done. At this level, indentification is according to job description. Schedules, however, include specific start and completion dates for each job to be performed.

Work Assignments This activity involves the assignment of specific people to tasks and subtasks previously described and scheduled. Work assignments are closely coordinated on a task force basis. They involve systems analysts, programmers, and user staff people.

Project Control

This is a monitoring and decision function within the project management process. The emphasis is on project reporting in terms of time expended by task force people. Activities include the following.

Time Reporting All personnel assigned to a project fill out time reports. These must be accumulated and summarized regularly. Information on time expended, in turn, serves as input to the next activity.

Status Reporting On a regular basis, as determined under project schedules, reports are prepared for steering committee review on actual progress against the working plan for the project.

Project Control Techniques Within the general project framework described above, graphic display and reporting techniques can be adapted to the scope and working requirements of the individual situation. Any method which does the job to the satisfaction of the system project leader and persons to whom he is responsible can be judged adequate in a given instance.

Standard techniques which can be applied to project control in the development of computer-oriented systems include:

- Critical path method
- PERT
- PERT/time
- PERT/cost
- Gantt charts
- Line of balance

In addition, combinations of these methods or special adaptations are suitable—as long as they gain the confidence of the system project team and the EDP Systems Planning Steering Committee.

To illustrate another potential approach: Some computer manufacturers have developed and made available machine-processed scheduling pro-grams. These are available for implementation either on an exception basis or through full status printout.

A full discussion of the techniques and applications for project scheduling is beyond the scope of this work. Several books have already been written on such subjects as critical-path-method scheduling. In addition, standard industrial engineering handbooks are recommended as workable guides in this area.

CHAPTER CONCLUSION

This discussion has covered the general concepts and approaches of project management. It cannot be emphasized too strongly that these prin-ciples are basic to any type of project. With these as a basis, the next chap-ter will review the specific application of these techniques to EDP system projects.

CHAPTER TWO

The System Development Process

SYSTEM DEVELOPMENT APPROACHES

As information systems themselves have come of age, so also has the system development process. The late sixties marked a period of transition, with the project management approach emerging and system development itself going from art to science.

During the comparatively short history of integrated man/machine business and information-processing systems, two basic approaches to system development have been enunciated and applied.

1. System development has been attempted through a series of free-form study/design activities. Projects have been undertaken without specific goals in mind. Rather, the idea has been to dig in and see what was to be found. One study activity led to the next in a series of "successive approximations." In effect, this approach applies behavioral learning theory to system development. Functional guidelines and working discipline for the personnel involved were minimal.

   Where the object of the study was relatively unknown and where the purpose at hand was chiefly the performance of research, this

approach has had considerable merit, and it still does in such circumstances. However, in a practical business environment, such methods
prove both difficult to manage and virtually impossible to budget
realistically.

2. More commonly, information system development for business, industry, and government has tended to become results-oriented —
structured. System development, under this approach, begins with
the stipulation of the end product to be achieved. Then a series of
orderly steps — projects, activities, tasks, and subtasks — is followed.
Each step is fully documented; each is reviewed and approved. Both
progress and expenditures are checkpointed at each key activity or
phase in the development effort.

In other words, under the approach which will form the subject matter
for the remainder of this book, system development has become a structured professional discipline. Predefined activities have been established,
tested, altered, and ultimately, proved. These form a basis for an orderly,
continuing process under which system development is carried out by an
interdisciplinary system project team which includes participation by users,
systems analysts, programmers, computer operations personnel, operating
management, and others.

PROJECT MANAGEMENT BENEFITS

This disciplined approach incorporates a number of important characteristics and potential benefits which are worth reviewing:

- The methodology which will be discussed in this work is fully self-
documenting. All the information needed to develop an operational
system is specified on forms which serve as working guides for analysts
and other project personnel. Properly used, these forms become a
repository of information — a complete, cumulative systems library.
People can be assigned to projects according to the best interests of the
company or other sponsoring organization. No project becomes dependent on one person or a few individuals. At any point, a system
development project can be expanded or personnel assignments rotated
with assurance that new people will be fully briefed as they come upon
the scene. In other words, with the document-as-you-go principle of
this technique, all participating people and their managers know the
status of a system development project at any time.
- Discipline is established so that communication features are built in.

Forms and work assignments are tailored to the skills, specialties, and capability levels of the people involved. There are, for example, specific functions where the presence of user personnel is critical. Other jobs can be done by analysts without recourse to programmers. In other situations, programmers, technicians, or operations personnel must be on hand. In all cases, activity levels and documentation are structured for communication which will be comprehensible to all participants and to operating management. Basic documentation, therefore, is at a nontechnical level. Technical depth and detail are added only as needed and only in those activities and phases to be performed by technicians. The idea, in short, is not to get too technical, too soon.

- The system development process, through activity planning and documentation, calls for a step-by-step, controlled learning process. Information gathering takes place throughout the planning and development stages of a project. The cumulative principle, in effect, is not to get too smart, too soon, but to put information together on a building-block basis, level by level, for absorption by personnel and integration into the system.

- Above all, the defined activity approach to system development eliminates the historic overemphasis on computer programming which has been so costly in the past. There has been a tendency to consider programming and system development as somewhat synonymous. Actually, the term programming has been used frequently where the intent was system development. Nontechnical people, in particular, tend to think of programming as what system development is all about. In stressing that this is not so, there is no intent to downgrade the importance of programming. Obviously, it is essential to the development of computerized systems. However, in true perspective, it is one of a number of vital activities which must be kept in balance. This emphasis, incidentally, also serves to remove undue pressure from the programmers themselves. In a programming-oriented environment, pressures tend to build for getting coding on paper almost immediately at the inception of a project. Too frequently, programmers have been forced to start writing coding before they have had enough information to guide them. With preprogramming documentation built into the development project, programmers are relieved of unwarranted pressure and also have the advantage of working with specifications describing the results they are to attain.

- The scope of each activity within the system development process is defined to dovetail with the background and experience of the people who will be doing the work. Thus, people of many types and levels can be used effectively. No one is extended beyond his area of competence or capability. Yet, because of the building-block approach, total requirements are met by available people.

- Quality assurance for each system development project is built in through a stipulated series of review points and management commitments by a high-level group such as the EDP Systems Planning Steering Committee discussed in the last chapter. The recurring review and approval checkpoints, in themselves, tend to apply a discipline which assures effective self-documentation during each system development project.

- All activities are in a stipulated sequence. Where work should be done in parallel, this condition also is specified. This approach allows for effective work scheduling, budgeting, expenditure control, and efficient utilization of personnel resources.

- The structured approach lends itself particularly well to the assignment and management of subcontracted activities. Particularly with the advent of hardware-software "unbundling," more and more application programming is being subcontracted. The self-documentation inherent in the disciplined approach to be described in this book serves, in effect, to provide—routinely—all the written specifications needed in dealing with outside vendors of programming packages or software services. At the very least, relationships with software houses are greatly facilitated by the self-documenting approach.

- For file processing and data base–oriented systems, the nontechnical approach to documentation places emphasis where it belongs—on information content. Data elements are specifically defined and agreed to by management and user people as part of the system development process. End products are more likely to be what management wants because management has had a hand in the actual definition and approval of results to be delivered.

- Indoctrination and training are implicit and cumulative. This applies both to data processing personnel and to users. The building-block approach avoids a situation where a total system has to be superimposed on a group of people. Rather, everyone concerned is involved in the building and learning process. User management grows into the system rather than having it loaded upon the system in one big end-product lump.

MEETING ESTABLISHED OR NEW NEEDS

In the development of computer-oriented business information systems, some established, ongoing methodology will frequently be in operation within the organization. Existing procedures may be more limited in scope than the proposed new system. But, where an organization is functioning, basic transaction and control records are necessary for every facet of the business. The technology under discussion in this work is designed to cover the full scope of planning, development, and implementation requirements where a transition from an existing to a new system is involved.

At the same time, however, it should be pointed out that the approaches and techniques to be covered in this book will apply equally in instances where no previous system exists.

Within a business context, the creation of totally new systems is a common occurrence with the formation of new companies—or in cases where new dimensions of information processing are introduced—as happens with the creation of MIS systems. The consulting group whose work forms the basis for this book has had personal experience, for example, with meeting wholly new system requirements in the area of retail credit-card services and central information files in the banking field. Specifically, a credit-card operation performed by a commercial bank will generally represent a totally new venture for the institution. System development proceeds from scratch. The same obviously holds true for information system development. Actual experience has shown the project management techniques under discussion equally applicable whether or not existing procedures are in force.

EVOLUTION OF THE SYSTEM DEVELOPMENT PROCESS

As already stressed, the process under discussion represents a standardized approach which is workable in any system development situation. Therefore, it is, for all intents and purposes, universal.

This, in turn, becomes a way of saying that there are common denominators in the system development discipline which transcend industry or application requirements. This position—and the standardized technique being described here—evolved through solid experience. That is, the consultants at Touche Ross whose experience forms the basis for this book did not set out to develop a theory of system development. Rather, a gradual dawning took place.

Over a period of years, a number of widely divergent systems were developed for a broad range of industries and situations. In each case, the approach was to prepare a series of questions to be posed and a series of forms to be executed as a guide for information gathering by systems analysts. Gradually, it became apparent that there was a basic similarity between all this special-purpose documentation. The same general information requirements and working rules were found to apply equally to situations as diverse as banking, hospital management, manufacturing, government, retailing, and transportation.

A standard series of forms and associated procedures emerged for use on all system development projects. These were revised and refined over a five-year period. The versions now in use—including the forms and flow charts reproduced in this work—have been applied in literally hundreds of "real world" system development projects.

Experience, then, has proved that there are certain common denominators involved in planning, developing, and implementing a computerized data processing system. These common denominators, as far as can be determined, apply to virtually all system development situations.

The feasibility of this type of approach is witnessed further by the fact that several manufacturers, software houses, and computer education firms have developed and offered techniques designed for the same general purpose. Most commonly, such methodology has concentrated in the areas of feasibility studies or specification development for programming. Typical examples include IBM's SOP (Study Organization Plan) and NCR's ADS (Accurately Defined Systems). The approach discussed in this work applies the same basic philosophies and techniques to full project scope.

THE PROJECT APPROACH

The system development process as it will be covered in this book is diagramed in Figure 2-1. As this flow chart shows, the project is divided into three phases: Planning activities, Development activities, and Implementation activities. Thirteen activities are delineated.

Each of these activities delivers specific end products. This is an important part of the concept: The basic idea behind the project structure is a results orientation. It takes results to measure progress and values. Each activity within a project, then, must deliver tangible results, usually in the form of structured documents, which serve as the basis for evaluation and commitment decisions.

Note particularly that five separate management approval checkpoints

THE SYSTEM DEVELOPMENT PROCESS
PLANNING ACTIVITIES

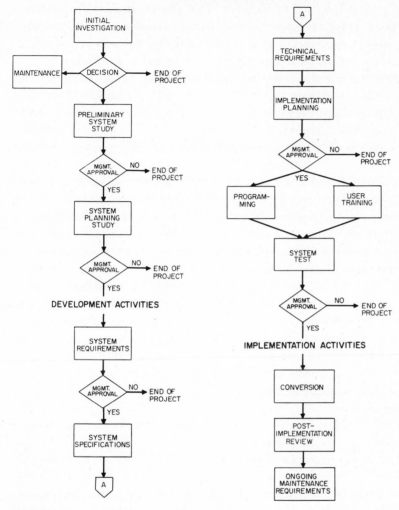

Figure 2-1

are specified and that the project can be terminated at any of these points. These recurring checkpoints are the devices used for making the creeping-commitment concept workable. They are positioned within the project following nontechnical, decision-appropriate activities.

For example, each of the planning activities is followed by a checkpoint. This means that a complete review and management decision takes place at each level of information accumulation and design involvement. Remember, one of the basic concepts of this technique is that the scope of each activity is specified in advance. Thus, the effort goes to a predetermined point, is fully documented and summarized, then reviewed by users, system project personnel, and management before the next step is taken. Time and money commitments can be discontinued at any time.

Further, because all efforts are fully documented, rescheduling can also take place at any of these checkpoints if new priorities present themselves within the sponsoring organization. Thus, if a decision is made to table rather than drop a project, nothing is lost. All the information and documentation assembled to the point of this decision can be picked up at any time.

Since project documentation is specifically decision-oriented, it follows that cost considerations are incorporated within the basic structure and methodology of the project. In fact, costs are part of the considerations for each activity within the project structure, from inception to conclusion.

Note in Figure 2-1 that checkpoints beyond the Planning phase are commensurate with the technical depth of users and the management committee. For example, a review has been specified after System Requirements are stipulated. Then, three highly technical activities are indicated —System Specifications, Technical Requirements, and Implementation Planning. There would be no point in reviewing equipment or technical specifications with a general management committee until a total Implementation Plan, complete with costs and projected results, can be put together. This happens in the review which follows the Implementation Planning activity.

It should be pointed out that Figure 2-1 diagrams only approval activities which will go to the EDP Systems Planning Steering Committee. In fact, however, further discussion of specific activities will show that review and approval is part of each step in the process. For example, during the Development activities involving System Specifications and Technical Requirements, "buy off" reviews are performed and confirmed with actual signatures by the technical services section within the EDP department. In Chapter 1, this group was described as serving as a sort of filter between systems and operations people. As further discussion will show, the technical services group also acts somewhat like an internal auditor/reviewer within the EDP area.

Note also that total management approval is implied at the conclusion of the Development phase. Following Conversion, review and revision are incorporated in succeeding activities. However, by this time, a system will have moved ahead beyond the point where an abort decision can be considered realistically.

SYSTEM PROJECT ACTIVITIES

The remainder of this chapter will provide a brief review of each of the thirteen system development project activities shown in Figure 2-1. Following this introduction, a separate chapter will be devoted to each of these activities. In the individual chapters, the special forms and working techniques devised for carrying out each activity will be covered.

Planning Activities

The Planning phase of a system development project is chiefly at a nontechnical or very low technical level. It is highly interdisciplinary, calling for continuing interaction between users and systems analysts and management. The reviews and commitments during this phase of the project are most critical. The general idea is to determine feasibility, establish firm objectives, estimate costs, determine reliability, and orient the project toward development.

Initial Investigation   An Initial Investigation should be considered a routine step any time a request or requirement surfaces within an organization using computer systems. This applies whether the situation at hand is of major importance or whether it calls for a seemingly minor alteration to an existing system.

A request for an Initial Investigation activity can originate anywhere in the organization—from a user group or from within the EDP department itself.

Within the system planning and development group of the EDP function, all such requests are routed to the system project leader with cognizance over the affected area. The initial response to such requests is generally a meeting between the system project leader and the initiator. The main purpose of this meeting is to provide the system project leader with an idea of the scope of the request.

Should the request cover a minor point—the changing of a heading on a report, for example—the matter can be referred immediately for system maintenance. Should a further look be indicated, an Initial Investigation will be arranged.

Typically, Initial Investigation is a short activity, involving one to three days of systems analysis. Its purpose is to define the scope of the request more formally and to determine, on closer examination, whether the problem can be handled with maintenance, whether actual system development is necessary, or whether no problem exists. In summary, Initial Investigation can result in any of three alternate courses:

1. Maintenance activity for the existing system
2. A new system development project
3. No action because the problem is not of sufficient magnitude or because a solution may be incorporated within a system development project already in process

Preliminary System Study This activity is designed to take a next-step-deeper look at the problem. The objective here is to come up with enough information so that the EDP Systems Planning Steering Committee can be briefed realistically. This is what the creeping-commitment concept is all about. The expenditure to this point is still minimal.

The Preliminary System Study addresses itself to the existing system as it is currently being carried out. If a new system is involved, the study deals with the affected areas of operation or information sources. It is conducted chiefly through interviews with users of the present system and/or prospective users of the new system. The end product of this activity is a *Preliminary System Study Manual* incorporating a management summary which provides the basis for a continue/terminate decision by the EDP Systems Planning Steering Committee.

Figure 2-2 illustrates implementation of the creeping-commitment concept in simplified chart form. This shows that the project management approach recommended here provides for a major review and a management commitment at a point where only 5 percent of the time and effort needed to develop a new system has been expended.

System Planning Study The System Planning Study activity incorporates the area traditionally assigned to a feasibility study. But, it takes in considerable additional scope. This point in the project marks the beginning formation and full-scale activation of the system project team. Users are closely involved in the System Planning Study. They will generally devote as much time to this activity as systems analysts.

The main fact-finding technique remains interviews. But, they are carried to far greater depth than in the Preliminary System Study. Where applicable, the present system is defined in terms of its files, inputs, out-

THE "CREEPING COMMITMENT"

Project Activity	Degree of Risk of Proceeding to Project Completion Without Further Checkpoints	Degree of Organizational Commitment to Project	Cumulative Expenditures
Initial Investigation	100%	0%	0%
Preliminary System Study	90	10	5
System Planning Study	75	25	15
System Requirements	50	50	25
System Specifications	40	60	30
Technical Requirements	30	70	35
Implementation Planning	20	80	40
Programming	15	85	70
User Training	15	85	75
System Test	10	90	80
Conversion	5	90	99
Post-Implementation Review	0	95	100
Ongoing Maintenance			

Figure 2-2

puts, and controls. In each case, the proposed new system is defined within the same functional areas.

In addition, preliminary computer system configurations are determined. Preliminary programming specifications are also worked out. This information, however, is not developed in great depth during this activity. The chief purpose here is to come up with preliminary cost estimates for hardware and software. Operational benefits are also identified.

The end product of the System Planning Study is a *System Planning Manual* incorporating all the basic documentation which will be needed to initiate the Development phase of a system project. This includes a summary evaluation of economic and operational considerations — including projections of the cash flow and return on investment factors associated with the projected new system.

The *System Planning Manual* includes a Management Summary which serves as the basis for steering committee consideration and a decision on whether to terminate or continue the project. Significantly, the presentation to the steering committee is done by its user member. As part of this presentation, the user stipulates, for his organization, which benefits have been identified. He commits his department or group to attainment of these benefits — at least on the basis of data available up to this point in the project.

The System Planning Study marks the conclusion of the Planning phase of the system development project. The steering committee is asked to make a key commitment at this point, since proceeding into the Development phase will involve stepped up expenditures and time outlays.

Development Activities

With the System Requirements activity, the project enters its most critical, and expensive, phase. Technically and moneywise, this is a make-or-break area. As Figure 2-2 illustrates, about 65 percent of the expense of a project will be encountered in this phase. Therefore, this is the stage of greatest commitment and, automatically, of greatest risk.

System Requirements System Requirements is a heavily user-oriented activity. This is the point in the project at which user background, working situations, and requirements are delineated as a basis for actual developmental activities. Studies deal almost entirely with the user organization, calling for close coordination between user members of the project team and systems analysis.

The information gathered is nontechnical, in a data processing sense. Initially, analysis centers around establishing output criteria. Documentation or display requirements which will be the end products of the new system are specified first. Tracing back from there, the effort covers input, information flow, files, and clerical functions. This activity also marks the beginning of a compilation effort for a glossary of terms which will apply specifically to the environment at hand and which will be used in conjunction with documentation of the new system. Functionally, this glossary of terms becomes a series of data element designations which serve as a foundation for the new system's data base.

The end product of this activity is a *System Requirements Manual* which incorporates elements of the *System Planning Manual* but goes far beyond. Again, a Management Summary is prepared as the basis for a major commitment by the EDP Systems Planning Steering Committee.

System Specifications Up to this point, study activities have been largely nontechnical—except for the gathering of necessary data on existing computerized systems. With the System Specifications activity, analysis and documentation move to a middle level of technical depth. Specifically, emphasis is on how operations will be performed by computer equipment without descending to really minute detail. For example, processing requirements are forecast according to computer run/module and processing time estimates are developed.

The impact of the new system on existing processing work loads is considered. Several alternate processing approaches and file organization techniques are hypothesized and evaluated.

Outputs from this activity include report layouts of a technical nature (as opposed to conceptual layouts developed during the System Requirements activity), file layouts, file definitions, input/output definitions, processing functions, processing decision tables, overall computer processing charts, definitions of technical constraints, and stipulated controls (including descriptions of these controls and how they will be applied).

This activity is carried out chiefly by EDP professionals, though it does call for reviewing output, input, and data flow specifications with users. Within the EDP function, the activity calls for interaction between systems analysts, programming, operations, and technical services personnel.

Technical Requirements This activity is chiefly a technical extension of the work done in System Specifications.

Flow charting and supporting documentation are developed to a run/module detail level.

Depending upon the specific situation, this activity might also extend to functional logic. As a rule, decisions about functional logic are left to the programmers. However, where special, complex requirements are involved—as might be the case in operations research projects—the system project group could even stipulate logical algorithms to be utilized.

Where previous development carried file definitions to a master-file level, this activity goes on to specify working, run/module, and transaction files.

Specifications are developed for transaction codes and decision rules which affect these codes. Where required, operating system control language specifications are prepared. Also prepared are sort, print, file, merge, and other functional system specifications.

This activity is carried out either by the system project staff, if this group possesses the necessary technical qualifications, or by high-level programming personnel. Computer operations and technical services people are also involved in this activity. They verify that the system being specified will use available (or planned) equipment and software resources efficiently.

Implementation Planning This activity is, in effect, a pause for evaluation and review. The full project team—including users, EDP operations, technical, programming, and any other system project people—get together to examine documentation created to date and to map steps which will be taken and schedules which will be adhered to in the implementation of the project.

The end product of this activity is a detailed Implementation Plan. This plan covers schedules, work assignments, and end products for all remaining activities of the project.

The Implementation Plan, in turn, is presented to and closely reviewed by the EDP Systems Planning Steering Committee, which either terminates the project or authorizes a major commitment covering system implementation at this point. The importance of this decision can be brought into realistic perspective by looking at the last column in Figure 2-2. The next four activities within the Development phase account for 40 percent of the total expenditure for the system project.

Programming As illustrated in Figure 2-1, the Programming activity runs parallel with User Training. This is feasible because, for the most part, different people are involved. Parallel completion is desirable because of the obvious advantages of having users trained when the programs begin running so that they can perform System Test operations, making these as realistic and meaningful as possible. Actual work schedules, of course, can be adapted to individual situations.

In terms of project management principles, the Programming activity does not call for direct involvement of the system project leader or his staff. Rather, the project leader must be cognizant of what is happening. He influences the end product through his specifications. He utilizes his department's required documentation to measure results of Programming. The system project leader also retains quality assurance responsibility. In particular, he must be in continuing communication with the programming group to interpret his specifications and to clarify any questions which arise.

The system project leader receives progress reports at a minimum of three key points during the preparation of each run/module:

1. Logic
2. Coding
3. Testing

User Training Frequently, User Training does not take place until after a system is operational. It is not at all unusual for systems personnel to install a new system and get it running before User Training even begins.

Such practices invoke automatic penalties where user involvement is concerned. If users have had nothing whatever to do with implementing a system, there can be no pride in making it work. Ultimately, all systems belong to their users. The sooner identification and a feeling of possessiveness can be established, the greater the likelihood of success.

Functionally, a big advantage of sequencing User Training at this point in the project lies in the fact that users perform the actual System Test. Therefore, the System Test itself is more valid. It provides a truer reflection of operability and benefits for the new system.

This activity is carried out chiefly by user members of the system project team.

System Test   Although this is one of the most important activities in a system project, it is also the one which is most frequently abridged or skipped over. Where schedule slippage occurs, system project teams seem inevitably to be tempted to go right into Conversion rather than taking the time and expending the effort for full System Test. Almost inevitably, this proves to be a costly omission.

System Test is a milestone activity. It should be emphasized accordingly. The system project leader should be in full control during this activity. The objective is to bring together all components of the system—personnel, procedures, materials, equipment, and live data—to verify that they will fit together and operate smoothly. The activity takes place under test working circumstances and in a test environment. But all situations should be as realistic as feasible.

One of the underlying philosophies of System Test should be to make the system fail. This is done by overloading, by entering logically inconsistent data, by consciously entering operator mistakes, and by doing things in combinations which represent a hypothetic worst possible condition under which the live system might be forced to survive. By determining in advance where a system is likely to fail, the project team can take the design, training, or other steps necessary to reduce failure probability under live operation.

At the conclusion of System Test, all documentation and procedures should be established for operation of the final system.

Following System Test, the EDP Systems Planning Steering Committee hears a major presentation by its user member. On the basis of test data, the user executive stipulates that operating objectives and benefits projected at the conclusion of the System Planning Study can, in fact, be realized.

The steering committee makes its most critical terminate/continue decision at this point. Approval of System Test reports authorizes the project to move forward into its Implementation phase. Should any problems at all remain unresolved at the conclusion of System Test, approval to proceed should be withheld pending their solution. Invariably, unresolved problems in System Test will be multiplied into far greater difficulties following Conversion. The need for caution at this point cannot be overemphasized.

Implementation Activities

During this phase, the new system "goes live." Close supervision and evaluation are necessary, particularly during Conversion.

Depending on controls exerted by the project team, the activities in this phase can lead either to gratifying success or the most miserable type of failure. If preceding Planning and Development activities have been carried on effectively, Conversion runs smoothly. The effect is something like putting a pipeline on stream. Valves are opened gradually and flow is absorbed smoothly. However, care is continually necessary to avoid overloading or shocking the system prematurely.

Conversion Conversion actually is the orderly process of bringing the new system on stream. The activity is initiated with the development of a final Implementation Plan. In effect, this is a detailed review and update of the documentation created during the Implementation Planning activity in light of realities which have emerged since its completion. The system project leader, at this point, works directly with users to firm up final schedules and conditions under which the system will be considered operational and accepted. This is important. Failure to establish these criteria could keep a project leader on the scene indefinitely. By definition, a system project has a termination point. This is the place where it should be established.

The end product of this activity is a system buy off by the user group. This generally takes place at least ninety days after a new system goes into initial operation—allowing time for alterations or revisions in the system which come to light during Conversion to be implemented.

Post-Implementation Review This activity, clearly, takes place after the project has been completed and the project team disbanded, at least nominally. Therefore, a special responsibility or working team is generally assigned for this activity. Two basic approaches are feasible:

1. The EDP group within a company can have a special team which performs this function, in cooperation with selected users. In this respect, the activity would be similar to the internal auditing function performed by accounting groups.
2. The steering committee can form or appoint a special group for the Post-Implementation Review.

The objectives of the review will, generally, be threefold:

1. Review accomplishments of the system as compared with requirements and objectives stated at the outset of the project
2. Review project costs as compared with initial estimates

3. Review ongoing operating costs and results as compared with forecasts

It is generally a sound idea to provide for two Post-Implementation Review activities. One would normally take place six months after initial cutover—or about three months after user acceptance of the system. The second would be six months later—about one year after initial cutover.

Ongoing Maintenance Requirements   This activity marks a changing of the guard. Once a system has been through Conversion and Post-Implementation Review, it is considered fully operational.

Ongoing maintenance, under the organizational outline cited in Chapter 1 of this book, becomes the responsibility of the technical services group within the EDP department. This group has the resources and responsibility for maintaining operational systems. This is the group, for example, which would receive the assignment directly if the Initial Investigation or Preliminary System Study indicated that the problem was of a maintenance rather than a system development nature.

Because the commitment and responsibility of the technical services group is for the life of the system, an orderly transition of all documentation and files to its care is considered as a vital, final step in the system development process.

The succeeding chapters of this book, as indicated earlier, will deal with documents and techniques for carrying out each of the thirteen activities identified within the system development process.

SECTION TWO

Planning Phase

CHAPTER THREE

Initial Investigation

THE PLANNING PHASE OVERVIEW

This chapter and the two which follow will discuss the activities which make up the Planning phase of a system project. It begins, therefore, with an overview/review of the significance and functions performed within the Planning phase.

To assist the reader in relating the Planning phase to the total project, Figure 2-1, which outlines the project cycle, has been repeated here with the Planning phase activities highlighted in relation to the others.

The Initial Investigation activity marks the initiation of a system development project. It also marks the beginning of the first of three phases within the project management technique to be described here—Planning. As discussed in the last chapter, the other phases of a system project are Development and Implementation. There are two other activities within the Planning phase: Preliminary System Study and the System Planning Study.

The Planning phase of a system project can be compared directly with the research and development function within a business organization. Typically, the R&D department would be charged with analyzing what

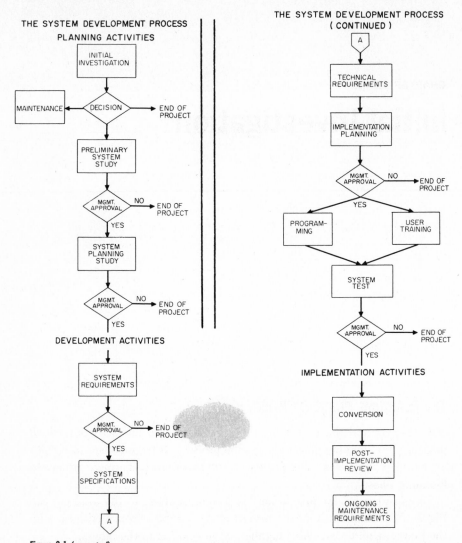

Figure 2-1 (*repeated*)

products can profitably be developed. This group would usually establish technical and economic feasibility for new products. It might even carry its efforts into pilot production and test marketing.

For example, a well-managed corporation would not be likely to enter right into manufacture, distribution, and marketing of a product without having established feasibility through research and development. Similarly, the Planning phase of a system project establishes its feasibility, its profit potential, its schedule for development and introduction, and its impact on the organization and its operations.

The end product of the Planning phase is a *System Planning Manual,* which serves as the basis for a decision on whether or not the project should move forward into the Development phase. Within an overall management context, the planning function implies a weighting and decision-making process aimed at determining what systems are to be developed and what operational systems will be used within the organization's management.

A definite distinction will be established within the project management methodology discussed here between *planning* activities and *doing* activities. Specifically, planning is a study-type function. It implies information gathering and decision-alternative identification at a level which does not impact or change the *status quo* as it may exist at any given moment within the sponsoring organization. Doing, in a system development context, involves preparation for or implementation of change.

Within the Planning phase, the decisions on system development and associated priorities derive from the problem identification and investigation efforts to be described in this and the succeeding two chapters.

EXTENT OF PLANNING ACTIVITIES

The magnitude of Planning activities should be proportional to the risk or exposure associated with the individual project. As a general rule, the smaller the risk, the less extensive planning has to be. Conversely, the larger the risk, the greater the time, investment, and detail which should be devoted to planning.

Even these rules of thumb, however, are not ironclad. For example, a large-scale project with little likelihood for early adoption would not be planned to the same depth as a project of similar magnitude with a high probability for development and implementation.

Similarly, a comparatively small system with a high degree of interaction with major associated systems should be subjected to greater planning detail than one of the same scope which stands on its own.

This chapter and the others dealing with Planning activities will not go into great detail about the magnitude or depth of Planning activities. Rather, emphasis will remain on general, guiding principles.

PROJECT INITIATION

Every organization utilizing and developing EDP systems must have a mechanism for both encouraging and dealing with the initiation of requests for system development activities, services, or full-scale projects. When the

EDP function is firmly established within an organization, such requests can come from almost any level:

- Typically more than half the suggestions for system development projects come from within the EDP systems group itself. This is natural. Systems analysts and system project leaders are professionals charged with spotting possibilities and formulating opportunities for system development. Suggestions at this level will derive chiefly from two general types of sources:
  1. Observation of existing operations and requirements
  2. Information gathered at professional meetings or from professional literature on what other organizations with similar structures and problems are doing
- General operating management personnel will uncover many needs and instigate many requests. Again, these will be based partly on information about what other organizations in similar circumstances are doing. At this level, system development requests will also be impacted by overall executive planning, new business development activities, government regulations or practices, legal requirements, and other factors which affect organization leadership.
- Users—as individuals or groups—will frequently come up with system development requests. In a proportionally greater number of cases, requests initiated at this level will involve revision or modification of existing systems, particularly where an already-computerized application is involved.

In any case, the organization's EDP (or MIS) department should have standard procedures for receiving and acting upon requests for system development project initiation. Typically, system project leaders within the department's systems group will have assigned areas of responsibility in relation to the organization as a whole. If this is the case, initial requests are routed routinely to the responsible system project leader.

TYPES OF INITIAL REQUESTS

The same basic procedures for receiving, acknowledging, and processing requests should be applied to all levels or types of situations which might arise. Anyone in the organization should feel free to submit a recommendation and should be accorded the same courtesy no matter how large or small the scope of his request may be.

In practice, requests may range from simple suggestions that a heading be changed on a report through recommendations for development of full-scale, on-line management information systems. Realistically, the majority of requests will fall into a middle ground between these extremes. Some examples:

- A manufacturing manager indicates an interest in integrating an existing customer order processing subsystem into his inventory management system. This approach, he feels, will incorporate demand data into his finished goods inventory control system and provide better control over back orders.
- A user of an existing system may want to add a data element to the data base for possible inclusion in system reports, output documents, or display formats. Depending on the extent of the proposed alteration, such a request might be a candidate for either maintenance or project development. For example, a simple substitution of one data element for another within system files might be handled through maintenance. However, if extensive alterations are required in processing, output, or inquiry, the request might be a candidate for a system project.
- An on-line user might report that service levels are deteriorating at given times of the day. In such a case, the Initial Investigation would be aimed at identifying the problem. Disposition would depend on the nature of the individual situation. For example, it might be determined that the duration and extent of the problem are such that it is solved with a simple memo to users asking those who do not have urgent business to transact at critical times to withhold their inquiries during these hours. On a maintenance basis, the problem might be subject to solution by reordering processing priority schemes to downgrade some batch jobs during the critical periods. However, if equipment reconfiguration, software alteration, or communication network changes were necessary, a system project would be required if the Initial Investigation decision favored further study.

ACTIVITY WORK FLOW

The procedures followed within the Initial Investigation activity are diagramed in Figure 3-1. The steps indicated in this diagram include:

- A request is prepared and routed to the responsible system project leader. He, in turn, arranges a preliminary conference with the initiator.
- The Initial Conference, first, establishes a dialogue between requester and system project leader concerning the prospective project. Once

this preliminary briefing has been imparted, the project leader's second responsibility is to take an initial look at the scope and nature of the request to determine whether it should be referred for system maintenance or considered as a potential new project. If maintenance referral is indicated, this is arranged immediately and the request is terminated for project consideration purposes. If project potential is agreed upon, the leader schedules an Initial Investigation.

- An Initial Investigation, if authorized, will be a short task. It is handled by an analyst who delves just deep enough to determine whether the next project activity, a Preliminary System Study, appears justified.
- Following the Initial Investigation, the project leader and requester confer again, as necessary.
- Out of the conferences and study comes a Request for Systems Service document, which serves as the basis for the continue/terminate decision of the Initial Investigation activity.
- Based on this initial documentation, a preliminary decision is made from among three alternatives:
  1. The project can go forward into the Preliminary System Study activity.

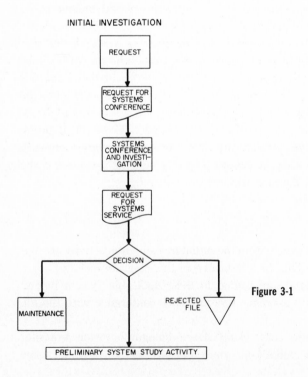

Figure 3-1

2. The situation can be referred for maintenance or modification of existing systems.

3. The request can be rejected because system development is not warranted, because closer inspection has shown that an imagined problem really does not exist, or because the problem is already being handled within another system project.

HANDLING INITIATION REQUESTS

The handling of requests for the initiation of system projects is an important customer-service responsibility of the systems and programming group. It should be given appropriate stature. Specifically, all initiation requests should be logged in as part of the working control of the department. Within the department, accountability for prompt and courteous handling of these requests should be part of the normal working procedures.

For their part, initiators of system project requests should also realize that they have a responsibility and that such requests are serious matters which deserve careful thought.

Therefore, some formalization of request procedures is advisable. It should be stressed, however, that request procedures should not inhibit members of an organization nor be so stringent as to become inflexible. The basic principle is: Systems analysis personnel should be highly accessible to anyone in the organization with potential need for their services.

The relationships between users and systems analysis personnel established at this initial point of contact are of far-reaching importance to the overall success potential of the project itself. It is at this point that the tone is set for the relationships between users and the EDP analysis staff. User participation and attitude patterns can be oriented toward system success at this point. It is important for EDP professionals to recognize, in every one of their activities, that all operational data processing systems belong to their users. Without user involvement and active participation, really successful systems cannot be developed.

INITIATING PROJECT DOCUMENTATION

Right from the Initial Investigation activity, documentation of system development should be cumulative. It must be complete up to any point to which a project has advanced.

The system documentation responsibility should be assumed by systems analysts and system project leaders.

Even with this stated requirement, great care should be taken to avoid situations—even where standard forms are used—in which procedures become so rigid that they are inhibiting or that they discourage potentially valid suggestions. Therefore, a request for an Initial Investigation of system development potential should be accepted and acted upon in any form in which it is encountered.

However, all Initial Investigation request factors should be committed to writing at an early point in the relationship between the requester and the system project leader. The statement of these request factors should actually form the basis for discussion during the Initial Conference.

Initial Investigation documentation can be as formal or informal as management of the systems function feels necessary. The request elements can, for example, be handled in an informal memo handwritten by the system project leader. Or, procedures manuals within the EDP department may require that they be typed, filed, logged, and/or distributed.

In other cases, a working document like the one shown in Figure 3-2 can be made available within the systems group and elsewhere within the organization, as appropriate.

Note that the form in Figure 3-2 is loosely structured. It can either be typewritten or handwritten. In some cases, the system project leader can choose to fill out a form while he is handling the initial request, face to face or on the phone. With such application, the form would serve as a guide to structure the conversation and to help the system project leader draw out specific information. As still another alternative, the form could be executed by the requester and forwarded through internal mail channels.

In any case, the form in Figure 3-2 serves to illustrate the type of information which should be available to the system project leader at the outset. Once this information is in hand, the system project leader should contact the requester and set up an Initial Conference to discuss the request.

INITIAL CONFERENCE

As indicated, the system project leader should take note of, log, and acknowledge each request for project initiation. He should also make it his business to give each initiator full opportunity to discuss his problems, requirements, and ideas.

At this initiation point, the system project leader's need-to-know requirements include:

REQUEST FOR SYSTEMS CONFERENCE

DATE *10·14*

Requested By: *B.BROWN*   Org. *ACCOUNTING*   Ext.

Problem/Services Requested:

A COMPUTER GENERATED SET OF LABOR DISTRIBUTION REPORTS.

Reason For Request:

TOO MUCH MANUAL WORK AND ANSWERING OF THE TELEPHONE TO SUPPLY INFORMATION TO LINE DEPARTMENTS.

Benefits/Expected Results:

SMALLER WORKLOAD FOR ACCOUNTING DEPARTMENT.
MORE ACCURATE AND TIMELY INFORMATION FOR LINE DEPARTMENTS.
LESS PHONE CALLS BETWEEN ACCOUNTING AND OTHER DEPARTMENTS.

Approval: *W.WHITE, SUPV. SYS. PLANNING & DEVEL.*   Date: *10-15*

Figure 3-2

1. Origin of the request, including identification for the individual and his department.
2. A description of the problem which was stated or the services requested.
3. The reason, or background, behind the request.
4. The results or benefits which the initiator anticipates. This element should be cost related. That is, at the outset, emphasis should be placed on establishing realistic cost estimates and justification bene-

fits for proceeding with system development. Even though such factors cannot be stated exactly at this point, it is important to implant a consciousness for these requirements.

JUSTIFICATION PRINCIPLES

Where possible, system projects should be economically justifiable. Even so-called intangible benefits, such as increased accuracy or the delivery of more decision-related information to management, should be given economic values as part of the justification process. The effort which should be expended in quantifying intangible benefits should be related to the size and prospective cost of development for the new system. That is, since the object is to assign values to benefits to determine whether a system project is worthwhile, the effort in establishing what these benefits are should be proportionate to the size of the business decision to be made.

However, it should also be borne in mind that there are many other reasons for the development and operation of information systems—over and above cost savings or quantifiable benefits.

In one obvious case, an entirely new activity might be contemplated within the sponsoring organization. Where start-up is involved, there are obviously no cost comparisons with any existing methods.

In other cases, management may want new levels or types of information not previously available. In such instances, expressions of value for the system are important. But, at the same time, justification cannot be entirely on a cost basis.

In still another type of situation, competitive factors may mandate a system project to a level where costs or other constraints do not enter the picture.

Still another consideration might be customer service. On-line processing of savings transactions by banks is a good example here. No money is saved for the institution. But the expense is easily justified on the basis of elimination of waiting lines at teller windows during busy lunch hours or on paydays in congested metropolitan areas.

PREPARATIONS FOR INITIAL CONFERENCE

In preparation for the meeting with the requester, the system project leader should review and gather information on the possible relationship between the new or modified system which has been proposed and existing systems or projects under development.

This preparation is important.   The system project leader must be able to win the respect of any other individual or group within the organization if his own operation is to run effectively and project assignments are to be performed successfully.   Toward this end, preparation for the Initial Conference should serve to establish or reinforce background information on the organization's existing systems or development projects which could relate to the new request.

Examples of the types of information the system project leader should have at his fingertips for this meeting include:

- The potential effect of the proposed system or system modification on existing systems or development projects.
- In general terms, the system project leader should be able to evaluate and discuss the efficiency and/or feasibility of the proposed new systems or modifications within the specific environment of the sponsoring organization.
- Insofar as possible, the system project leader should be prepared to describe and discuss any constraints which would apply to the request under consideration.   Constraints which could affect a new system at this point could come from virtually any source—company policy, legal restrictions, available resources, equipment limitations, and so on.
- The system project leader should make an effort to find and be ready to discuss any redundancies or conflicts of interest between the request under consideration and existing procedures or pending projects.

INITIAL CONFERENCE—STRUCTURE AND LENGTH

The structure and length of the conference itself will depend largely on the scope of the request and the level of sophistication of the initiator.   For example, if the requester is an experienced systems analyst, rapport will exist in advance.   Further, a data processing professional who has been advised in advance on what will be expected of him will almost surely have the requisite documentation and information available.   In such a case, a relatively complex situation can be discussed and resolved quickly.

Top-level executives, even if their requests are comparatively complex, are likely to state their requirements in simple terms and delegate further information-gathering or definition responsibilities to subordinates.

User personnel who have little direct contact with computers may require additional time and patience.   A user who has never been involved in a system development project simply may not be aware of what type or how much information is needed.   He may not know how to go about accumulating it.   Assistance to such persons is particularly vital for the good name and respect which the EDP department should cultivate within its organization.

INITIAL INVESTIGATION

If the Initial Conference serves to convince both the initiator and the system project leader that the request is worth a further look, an Initial Investigation is undertaken.   The extent of this task will depend, obviously, on the scope of the project at hand.   As a general rule of thumb, the Initial Investigation for a project with a scope in the range of 4 man-years of systems analysis ($100,000 in expense) would involve 1 to 3 man-days of study time.

The comparatively small size of this initial effort serves to illustrate the creeping-commitment concept described earlier.   This is made feasible, in part, by the cumulative documentation approach which utilizes and adds to all efforts performed during each successive activity of a project.

The subject area for the Initial Investigation takes in the full scope of the proposed system, but at an overview depth only.   For example, this investigation would concern itself with general information flow patterns, file organization, file magnitude, transaction volumes, interfaces with other systems, a preliminary review of benefits, an evaluation of the consequences of rejection of the request, and so on.   Information gathering for the Initial Investigation is confined chiefly to interviews with user personnel at the supervisory or management level.   This, in itself, indicates that detail requirements are minimal at the outset.   For example, a request from a senior systems analyst could possibly be discussed and documented sufficiently at a single conference so that no Initial Investigation is needed; the decision can be based on data provided by the requester.   In such a case, the initial conference would constitute an Initial Investigation.

In other situations, there may be no formal Initial Investigation.   Rather, this requirement may be met by moving right into a Preliminary System Study and incorporating an Initial Investigation as the first step in the following, more detailed activity.

If persons other than the requester are interviewed during the Initial Investigation, the project leader should schedule a follow-up meeting with the initiator to review findings.

In any case, the general rule that every request is worthy of an Initial Investigation should apply.   Further, response to requests should be as prompt as possible.   Conferences and, if necessary, Initial Investigations, should be carried out as quickly as is reasonable in each individual situation.

INITIAL INVESTIGATION DECISION ALTERNATIVES

As previously indicated, three alternatives are open to management at the conclusion of the Initial Investigation activity:

1. Refer the request for routine system maintenance and/or modification
2. Terminate the request because the problem has not materialized, does not warrant special system development, or is being taken care of through other project activities
3. Recommend that the project be carried forward into a Preliminary System Study

As appropriate to the individual case, the alternatives should be reviewed with and understood by the requester during conferences or the Initial Investigation.   It is the responsibility of the project leader to present and clarify all pertinent information bearing on each request.

REQUEST FOR SYSTEMS SERVICE

No matter what decision is made, a report on the conference and/or Initial Investigation must be prepared and distributed as the circumstances require by the system project leader and/or members of his staff.   If the request is to be referred for system maintenance, the conference report will serve as initiating documentation for members of the technical services group within the EDP department.

If no further action is to be taken on the request, minimum supporting documentation should still be reviewed by EDP management and incorporated in activity files.

The report can be documented in any form convenient for and compatible with the EDP department of the sponsoring organization.   Figure 3-3 illustrates a Request for Systems Service form which the authors have recommended on a number of occasions.   It is readily adaptable as Initial Investigation activity documentation.

Note that this form provides spaces at the bottom to indicate which of the disposition alternatives has been selected.   The form itself is unstructured except for requests in the heading asking for specific information:

1. The system project leader is asked to list conference participants.
2. A summary of the initial request should be included.   This content item illustrates, at an early point, the cumulative documentation ap-

REQUEST FOR SYSTEMS SERVICE

PAGE ___1___ OF __2__

PROJECT NO ___036___

ORGANIZATION ___ABC COMPANY___   PREPARED BY ___W.SMITH___

APPLICATION TITLE __LABOR DISTRIBUTION__   DATE ___10-21___

A. CONFERENCE PARTICIPANTS   E. RELATIONSHIP TO EXISTING OR PLANNED APPLICATIONS

B. DESCRIPTION OF REQUEST   F. WHEN NEEDED

C. SYSTEMS ACTION REQUIRED   G. EVALUATION

D. POTENTIAL BENEFITS

A. CONFERENCE PARTICIPANTS

      W.SMITH   - PROJECT LEADER

      W.WHITE   - SUPERVISOR, SYSTEMS PLANNING AND DEVELOPMENT

      B.BROWN   - SUPERVISOR, ACCOUNTING

B. DESCRIPTION OF REQUEST

      B.BROWN WISHES TO AUTOMATE THE GENERATION OF LABOR DISTRIBUTION

      REPORTS AND DISTRIBUTION OF INFORMATION TO LINE DEPARTMENTS

C. SYSTEMS ACTION REQUIRED

      THIS REQUEST WOULD REQUIRE THE DEVELOPMENT OF A COMPUTER SYSTEM

      TO CAPTURE, STORE AND REPORT LABOR DISTRIBUTION INFORMATION

D. POTENTIAL BENEFITS

      THIS COMPUTER SYSTEM WOULD PROVIDE:

          - A DECREASED WORK LOAD FOR THE ACCOUNTING DEPARTMENT BY ELIM-
              INATING MUCH MANUAL POSTING AND COMPUTATION

          - MORE ACCURATE AND TIMELY INFORMATION FOR LINE DEPARTMENTS

          - LESS NEED FOR PHONE CALLS BETWEEN ACCOUNTING AND OTHER DEPTS.

DISPOSITION: MAINTENANCE ☐   PRELIMINARY PLANNING ACTIVITY ☒   REJECTED ☐

DISPOSITION BY: W.WHITE   Date: 10-23

Figure 3-3

proach recommended for system projects. It summarizes documentation to date and serves as a transmittal or reference for previous documentation. The Request for Systems Service lists the project action which will be required if this report is acted upon favorably by EDP and user management.

4. A summary of potential costs and benefits should be included.

5. The relationship of the proposed system to others which exist or are under development should be summarized.

6. Schedule factors should be summarized. At this point, schedule information will obviously be general and approximate. However, an estimate should be included on a target date for putting the new system into operation.
7. The system project leader should give a brief professional recommendation for the potential values, impact, and/or ramifications associated with the proposed system.

INITIAL DECISION

The decision alternatives for the Initial Investigation activity do not have to be referred to the EDP Systems Planning Steering Committee. The decision on whether to reject the request, refer it for system maintenance, or go into a Preliminary System Study activity is made, on the basis of recommendations by the initiator and the system project leader, by the manager of the EDP (or MIS) department and the manager of the user function involved.

Satisfaction with the outcome of this activity by the initiator, user (if he is not the initiator), and the system project leader is important both to the project at hand and to the position and image of the EDP function within the organization.

The situation is particularly sensitive if a request should be rejected. When this happens, the reasons for the rejection should be clearly documented and understood by the requester. Should the initiator want to present his request again, perhaps in a different form or in a more specific scope, he should be invited to do so.

Where a decision is reached to proceed into a Preliminary System Study, the Request for Systems Service document becomes the basis for initiating this next activity.

CHAPTER FOUR

Preliminary System Study

ACTIVITY SCOPE

The Preliminary System Study is the first really formal activity within a project structure. Even though the Initial Investigation was documented with a Request for Systems Service which carried forward into this activity, the Initial Investigation tasks were loosely structured, consisting chiefly of meetings between the initiator and the system project leader as well as an informal investigation on an as-needed basis.

The formality of the Preliminary System Study is oriented chiefly toward the fact that this will be the first activity subjected to a review and decision by the EDP Systems Planning Steering Committee. If the recommendation to the committee is for project continuance, documentary output from the Preliminary System Study activity will require the formality and completeness necessary to support further, deeper probes toward system development.

The end product of the Preliminary System Study activity to be covered in this chapter is a *Preliminary System Study Manual* which includes:

1. A Management Summary to serve as the basis for the decision by the EDP Systems Planning Steering Committee
2. A Systems Planning Work Plan, which incorporates the survey information needed to carry the project forward

ACTIVITY RESPONSIBILITY

The Preliminary System Study activity is carried on entirely by systems analysts. It is designed to develop a level of information deep enough for a decision-relevant presentation to the EDP Systems Planning Steering Committee without requiring the more extensive (and expensive) action of forming an interdepartmental, interdisciplinary project team. This activity structure keeps the project flexible and the commitment minimal. It is a good example of the application of the creeping-commitment concept.

Systems analysis people who carry out this activity will be charged with probing deep enough to gather information which will support a management decision, but not so far that a terminate decision by the steering committee will lead to out-of-line, unproductive costs. By way of comparison, where an Initial Investigation for a project calling for 4 man-years of effort might run 1 to 3 man-days, the Preliminary System Study within the same project could occupy between 2 and 4 man-weeks.

ACTIVITY WORK FLOW

Figure 4-1 is a flow chart covering the tasks and documents within the Preliminary System Study.

Note that the primary information-gathering task is interviewing. During the Preliminary System Study, these interviews are conducted chiefly at a supervisory and/or management level. This is in keeping with the limited commitment intended for the activity. The systems analysts gathering information will normally not be looking for a degree of working detail which requires interviews below the supervisory level. However, if any contact among clerical or operations personnel is needed, this should be done only with the approval and coordination of responsible supervisors.

The point to be made in this connection is that there is still no active user involvement in system development. When it does take place, detailed information gathering on user operations will be done by groups which include user personnel.

Note that the symbols in Figure 4-1 indicating tasks and documents associated with the Preliminary System Study are divided, for the most part, into two distinct streams of effort.

One of these groups of tasks and documents leads to the compilation of a summary report for management consideration. The other is concerned with information flow and requirements from a system development standpoint. This activity/document stream leads into the Systems Planning Work Plan portion of the *Preliminary System Study Manual.* The resulting documentation in this case will support further project activity if the steering committee decision is affirmative.

It should be pointed out that the term "manual" is used here in its reference context. The document compilation manuals which will be described in this text are accumulations of data and documents generated

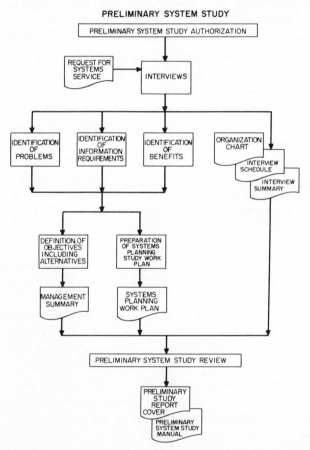

PRELIMINARY SYSTEM STUDY

Figure 4-1

during a given activity. These documents are generally index-tabbed and bound for use as a convenient reference base in succeeding activities.

STUDY PREPARATION

The systems analyst (or analysts) assigned to carry out a Preliminary System Study should be thoroughly familiar with the environment and operations of the organization under review. If a company already employs qualified analysts with applicable background, they should be assigned to this activity if feasible.

It should be made clear, however, that this is an activity for an experienced systems analyst. The project leader should, under no circumstances, agree to assign people of lower-level professional stature, even if they do have the required background knowledge. If available systems analysts with the proper professional qualifications do not have the knowledge they need of the operations to be studied, separate research should be undertaken before the actual interviewing tasks begin.

As a general guide, the analyst handling a Preliminary System Study should be thoroughly versed in all pertinent areas of the subject organization, including history, organizational structure, markets, products, budgets, facilities, and financial condition. Even though the background needed is extensive, it can be acquired far more readily than the training and experience of a senior systems analyst.

STUDY AREAS

During Preliminary System Study interviews, systems analysts will concern themselves with developing three types of information:
1. Identification of as many problems and/or opportunities as can be uncovered through interviews at the management level and supervisory level
2. Identification of information requirements of prospective users of the proposed system
3. Identification of potential benefits of every type—economic, informational, operational, customer service, and so on

As indicated in Figure 4-1, the findings become input to a separate task aimed at defining objectives and alternatives for the proposed system.

STUDY LEVELS

This sequence of tasks—information identification leading into definition development—highlights the fact that a systems analyst involved in a Preliminary System Study should have the capabilities and experience to apply skills at two separate levels:

1. Analysis: During the analysis segment of data collection, the analyst must apply the necessary system design skill, sensitivity, and responsiveness to interview subjects to uncover as large a body of relevant facts as possible. At the same time, he must have the judgment to avoid going to such levels as to clutter up the activity with so many facts which are irrelevant at this point that the information which is really needed will be obscured.
2. Interpretation: Having gathered information, the analyst must be able to weigh the stated, the unstated, and the implied to develop a realistically balanced evaluation of conditions, situations, requirements, economics, operations, and so on.

PERFORMANCE CONSEQUENCES

In the completion of the Preliminary System Study activity, success or failure hinges very largely on the expertise and judgment of a single individual or a few carefully chosen people who must possess the experience, the skills, and the native intuition to be able to determine where to go, how much time to spend, and to what level to delve during information gathering. Data gathered during this activity will generally not be quantified or structured the way it can be later in the project, during the System Requirements activity, for example.

If too much information is gathered, costs will soar out of line, schedules will be overrun, results will be off-target. This is particularly true because the Preliminary System Study is a comparatively generalized, preliminary-level activity. Thus, the time expended must be directed productively on the basis of experience.

To illustrate, an analyst performing a Preliminary System Study on a manufacturing operation would know, from experience, that he is more likely to find information pertinent to the isolation of problems and system development opportunities in talking to the material control group than he is in the tool room. In such a case, his experience would tell him that capital equipment tooling, such as large punches, dies, and jigs, tends to be an inevitable, onetime expense which cannot be impacted as readily through system design as stocks of expendable inventory items.

A further need for experience and judgment centers around the importance of establishing rapport and cooperation with the user organization for the prospective system as early as possible. If the prospective system is to succeed, it will ultimately do so because its users have expended the will and effort to make it do so.

During the Preliminary System Study, where active user involvement has not yet begun, it is up to the systems analyst to work closely with the supervisors and managers with whom he deals to make them part of the project. He must lead them, through questioning and discussion skills, to identify the projected benefits for a new system as their own. He must initiate ideas and concepts for their consideration. He must provide opportunities so that key people in the user organization will make themselves a part of the projected system.

It is at this early stage that a basis must be built in the enthusiasm and the support without which the projected system cannot succeed.

WORKING FLOW

As Figure 4-1 indicates, the Preliminary System Study activity is highly documentation oriented as the project moves toward greater operating formality. Under the cumulative documentation concept, the documents generated in successive activities become, in effect, the developed system. Specified documents serve both to organize the work flow of system project activities and to communicate findings, recommendations, decisions, and policies between involved personnel and successive levels of activity.

In the case of the Preliminary System Study, even though the activity centers largely around the judgment of the individual systems analyst, a documented structure is vital to establishing responsibilities, guiding activities, and assuring the delivery of valid end products. In this respect, note that, even though the Preliminary System Study is a comparatively short activity, seven items of documentation are specified.

ORGANIZATION CHART

As the first task in the Preliminary System Study, the analyst should chart the organization of the group using the existing systems or procedures.

This organization chart will be drawn specifically to provide an operating guide—a kind of road map—which will help locate information sources for the rest of the activity.

Should the project involve a proposed system which is totally new, the analyst will have to develop a workable list of sources, either within or external to the sponsoring organization. In such a case, the analyst should bear in mind that his objective in this task is to compile a guide to information sources where applicable experience, and problems, exist and can be studied.

Where an organization chart is developed, the analyst should follow definite guidelines:

1. The chart must delineate organizational responsibility flow, including notations of functional, staff, and administrative relationships within the group under study.
2. Each department, group, or section included in the organization chart should be described in terms of its functions and responsibilities.
3. Organization chart documentation should include the names and titles of all key persons who might have to be contacted during the Preliminary System Study. That is, in addition to identifying positions and job titles within the organization chart, the names of key people should also be secured and included.

INTERVIEW SCHEDULES

In planning for the interviews which will make up the bulk of the Preliminary System Study activity, the systems analyst must be careful to allocate his time so that the overall effort is related realistically to the end-product results which will be expected of him.

Based on the structure and accompanying descriptions of the organization chart, the analyst must begin with a well-screened selection of the people to be interviewed. Obviously, interviews themselves must be scheduled carefully—partly because the interview subjects will be managers and supervisors who are apt to be working on busy schedules themselves and also because the Preliminary System Study activity will generally be performed within a specifically allocated time frame.

As a general rule, interviews within the Preliminary System Study activity can best be ordered beginning from the top of the organization and working down. In informational terms, this starts the information gathering with the general and adds specifics on an organized basis.

This approach is appropriate at this early point in the system project.

Later, during development activities such as System Requirements, the information-gathering approach will probably be reversed. When it comes to structuring actual procedures, the work is better handled beginning from the bottom and working up.

INTERVIEW DOCUMENTATION

Because of the tentative, probing nature of interviews during the Preliminary System Study, a relatively informal interview structure is generally best. Within the framework under discussion, systems analysts generally use forms incorporating a working guide—like the one shown in Figure 4-2.

During the Preliminary System Study, interview objectives are highly qualitative. Actual question content will tend to be elusive—even though the systems analyst knows exactly what type of information he is looking for. The problem, from an information-gathering standpoint, is largely that interviews will be conducted with varying types and levels of people who, themselves, have different interests and responsibilities. Therefore, a continually varying approach is necessary in the framing of questions to fit the backgrounds and qualifications of individual respondents.

Also significant during this activity is that a comparatively small number of respondents will be interviewed. Therefore, the quantitative processing and analysis advantages so important to activities of larger scope—and available routinely through the use of structured questionnaires—are not really necessary in this situation.

As Figure 4-2 shows, the Interview Summary form, through a checklist, specifies gathering of data on:

1. The function or responsibilities of the respondent
2. The objectives of the respondent as they relate to the present and proposed systems
3. The specific problems which the respondent can identify as requiring solutions
4. System plans which may currently be under consideration or development according to the knowledge of the respondent
5. The current uses for EDP services by the respondent and/or his organization
6. Information requirements which the respondent can identify as not being met by current system procedures
7. The addition of any general comments which may be pertinent to the Preliminary System Study activity

```
                                   INTERVIEW SUMMARY      PAGE___1___OF___1___
                                                         PROJECT NO. ___028___
         ORGANIZATION_ABC COMPANY_____             PREPARED BY__W.SMITH___
         APPLICATION TITLE LABOR DISTRIBUTION            DATE_____10-24_____

         Interviewee:  W.JOHNSON        Position:   MANAGER      Organization: MILLING DEPT.

                    A. FUNCTIONAL RESPONSIBILITIES      E. EDP USES

                    B. OBJECTIVES                       F. INFORMATION REQUIREMENTS

                    C. PROBLEMS                         G. GENERAL COMMENTS

                    D. SYSTEM PLANS


         A.  FUNCTIONAL RESPONSIBILITIES:

                 RESPONSIBLE   FOR ONE OF THE MANUFACTURING DEPARTMENTS.  THIS INCLUDES
                 DEPARTMENT BUDGETS, SCHEDULING, LABOR AND PRODUCTION REPORTING

         B.  OBJECTIVES:

                 TO KEEP THE DEPT. RUNNING SMOOTHLY WITHOUT AN OVERLOAD OF CLERICAL
                 TASKS.

         C.  PROBLEMS:

                 SPENDS TOO MUCH TIME ON THE PHONE TRYING TO GET INFORMATION FROM
                 ACCOUNTING.  ACCOUNTING CANNOT ALWAYS GET THE INFORMATION HE WANTS
                 WHEN HE NEEDS IT.

         D.  SYSTEM PLANS:

                 WOULD LIKE TO GET LABOR DISTRIBUTION INFORMATION COMPUTERIZED SO THAT
                 HE COULD GET VARIATIONS ON THE NORMAL REPORT.

         E.  EDP USES:

                 PRESENTLY GETS ONLY THE PAYROLL CHECKS FROM THE COMPUTER

         F.  INFORMATION REQUIREMENTS:

                 NEEDS TO BE ABLE TO INQUIRE ABOUT PAST MONTH'S INFORMATION
                 BY MAN AND BY TIME PERIOD

         G.  GENERAL COMMENTS:

                 ALSO NEEDS TO BE ABLE TO OBTAIN INFORMATION WHICH PERSONNEL
                 DEPT. KEEPS IN ITS FILES.
```

Figure 4-2

MANAGEMENT SUMMARY

Note that in Figure 4-1 the preparation of the Management Summary is parallel to the task of preparing the Systems Planning Work Plan. In actual practice, these tasks can be performed in parallel if the activity is supported with enough manpower to handle them this way. In general, however, some basic decisions must be reached for inclusion in the Management Summary before the full scope of the requirements can be determined for the Systems Planning Work Plan. Specifically, if the Management Summary will recommend the termination of the project, considerably less detail is required within the Systems Planning Work Plan.

The Management Summary should include:

1. Recommendations and/or findings of the person responsible for supervision of the Preliminary System Study. These should be brief and to the point. The EDP Systems Planning Steering Committee will be asked to make a straightforward continue/terminate decision. The person in charge of this activity should state his recommendation at the outset of the report. This reporting technique—beginning with recommendations—is analogous to accepted system study practices, which begin with output specifications and then trace back through the network of information and methodology needed to develop the indicated results. In reporting—particularly to executive-level management—it is best to begin with recommendations, conclusions, and/or findings.

   The remainder of the report supports these in a logical presentation sequence, making it possible for the manager to stop reading at any point where he feels he has seen enough to support his decision.

   In the actual preparation of reports, this first section is frequently written best if it is withheld until the last. That is, it is often effective to write all the supporting sections of a report first, then summarize these in an introductory statement which incorporates the item of greatest interest—the recommendations.

2. The Management Summary should describe, concisely, all problems identified during the Preliminary System Study.

   For the purposes of this discussion, a problem (or problem element) is an identifiable need which has a recognizable impact on the organization studied and which is not being met by existing systems or procedures. For each problem discussed, the analyst should provide descriptions in terms of environmental conditions, causes, effects, organizational units involved, and so on. The analyst should also describe ideas for the solution of each problem identified—if such possibilities have been uncovered during the study. The analyst should also describe the time considerations associated with the problem, such as frequency of occurrence, duration of the problem, the nature of distribution if it occurs randomly, and so on.

3. Information sources and requirements pertinent to problem solution should be identified as far as possible. These descriptions should in-

clude requirements for new, presently unavailable information, present information files, and descriptions of sources where additional files can be referenced. The information requirements section of the Management Summary should also indicate any known constraints or limitations which could apply to the extent, format, content, or availability of information.

4. The Management Summary should describe the prospective benefits for the proposed system, identifying conditions under which they are likely to be realized and situations which might inhibit their realization. As indicated in earlier discussions in this chapter, benefits identified and discussed should be of both an economic and nonfinancial nature. Insofar as possible, statements covering projected benefits should relate to overall plans and objectives of the general management of the company or governmental organization.

5. The Management Summary should include a comprehensive Statement of Objectives. This should identify specific goals, alternate methods for achieving the goals, and relationships of stated objectives to organizational operations in terms of time, costs, established policies, personnel considerations, technical requirements, business conditions, and the organization's environment.

6. An evaluation of system feasibility should be included. This should be related to previously stated objectives, alternatives, problems, constraints, environmental factors, and other pertinent conditions.

SYSTEMS PLANNING WORK PLAN

A copy of the Systems Planning Work Plan document developed for and used regularly on Touche Ross projects is illustrated in Figure 4-3.

In effect, this becomes a control document and guide if and when the project moves forward into its next activity, the System Planning Study.

The form itself is self-explanatory. Tasks associated with the System Planning Study are listed in the column at the left. Twelve of these have been identified and preprinted on the form. Space is provided for adding others which may have been recognized and specified by the analysts involved in the Preliminary System Study. For each task, columns are provided to designate responsible persons, estimate time required, and schedule performance. For scheduling purposes, this document uses standard Gantt chart techniques.

Note also that a column has been provided—through subdivision of hori-

ORGANIZATION _ABC COMPANY_   SYSTEMS PLANNING WORK PLAN   PAGE _1_ OF _1_

APPLICATION TITLE _LABOR DISTRIBUTION_   PROJECT NO. _028_

APPROVED BY_____   PREPARED BY _W. SMITH_

DATE _11-2_

	Resp.	Estimate DAYS	Actual	Weeks 11/8	11/15	11/22	11/29	12/6					
1. Present System Preliminary Requirements		3		3									
2. Present System Summary		2		2									
3. Proposed System Preliminary Requirements		6		2	4								
4. Proposed System Summary with Project Identification		2			2								
5. Manual System		2			2								
6. Preliminary Computer System Design		4				4							
7. Preliminary Program Specifications		3				3							
8. Computer Development Costs and Sched.		3					3						
9. Compute EDP Recurring Costs		2					2						
10. Economical Evaluation Summary		3						3					
11. Project Plan		3						3					
12. Administration		5		1	1	1	1	1					
TOTAL		38		8	9	8	6	7					

Figure 4-3

zontal spaces — for entry of actual task performance times as compared with the initial estimate.

REPORT TRANSMITTAL

The document shown in Figure 4-4 serves as a cover and transmittal sheet for the *Preliminary System Study Manual.*

Turning back to Figure 4-1, note that the flow chart calls for a review task for the completion of this document and the final compilation of the *Preliminary System Study Manual.* This review can be performed either at a single meeting or through a series of informal conferences between the systems analyst and the individuals whose review and approval are necessary. Note that specifically required approvals are designated for the systems manager and the person or persons requesting system consideration initially. Following these approvals, the manual should be duplicated, all the incorporated documentation bound together, index-tabbed, and distributed. Note also that spaces have been provided for alternate disposition decisions—authorized or unauthorized—by the EDP Systems Planning Steering Committee.

PRELIMINARY STUDY REPORT

PAGE ___/___ OF ___/___

PROJECT NO. ___028___

ORGANIZATION _ABC COMPANY_

PREPARED BY _W.SMITH_

APPLICATION TITLE _LABOR DISTRIBUTION_

DATE ___11-6___

TABLE OF CONTENTS

System Planning Manager Approval ___W.WHITE___   Date: ___11-6___

Requester(s) Acceptance(s) ___B.BROWN___   Date: ___11-7___

Date of System Planning Report Presentation ___11-9___

Authorized _____   Date: _____
  (Systems Committee Secretary)

Unauthorized _____   Date: _____
  (Systems Committee Secretary)

Distribution: System Planning Staff   X

Scheduling and Control

User Organization(s)

Accounting   X

Figure 4-4

STEERING COMMITTEE DECISION

Presentation of the *Preliminary System Study Manual* to the EDP Systems Planning Steering Committee marks the first continue/terminate checkpoint for the new project.

Insofar as is possible at this stage, the presentation to the committee should be interdisciplinary.   The system project leader will have to be on hand, of course.   The initiator of the request should also be at the meeting. If the initiator is not a system user, the user executive most closely associated with the project to date should be on hand.

If possible, the user should make the actual presentation.   However, at this point, familiarity with the proposed system and its consequences is important in determining roles in the presentation to the committee.

No matter who handles the actual presentation, the system project leader should assume a professionally impartial posture. His recommendations, of course, are positive and are included in the report considered by the committee. But, committee action will be based on an overview of the organization's total systems and project position. In the interests of professionalism, the system project leader should avoid any posture which would tend to pressure a committee decision.

Resource allocation in the system project field is always balanced delicately. The system project leader should be careful, in particular, not to exert pressures which could lead to work overloads and impact quality or work schedules.

If the committee's decision is to have the project proceed into its next activity, the System Planning Study, schedule and resource allocation commitments for this next step—as outlined in the Systems Planning Work Plan and modified to reflect priorities—must be determined and agreed upon by all parties. A summary of committee specifications, actions, and commitments should be prepared and incorporated into project documentation.

No matter which way the steering committee's decision goes, the important point to be made about the Preliminary System Study is that it presents management with a decision-pertinent overview of project implications on a minimum cost, nontechnical basis. For those projects which will be carried on to the next activity, this approach serves to establish the basis for working rapport, discipline, scope, specific mission, and management support.

CHAPTER FIVE

System Planning Study

ACTIVITY SIGNIFICANCE

The System Planning Study is the last activity during the Planning phase of the system project. Because of this, it is particularly critical from the standpoint of the role of the system project as a business venture. Following the System Planning Study, the EDP Systems Planning Steering Committee makes a commitment involving allocation of resources for system development.

The nature of this commitment is such that the project will go forward for as long as it is able to meet the goals agreed to at this juncture in the system development process. During the Development phase activities which follow, the project becomes more technical and the steering committee members become less conversant in and further removed from system development activities.

Because of this nature of the System Planning Study activity, coordination and working rapport between systems and user people must be at their closest. During this activity the system project team goes through full operational formation. For the first time, working representatives of the user department assume responsibilities side by side with systems analysts.

SYSTEM PROJECT TEAM—USER MEMBERSHIP

Beginning with this activity, the project stands or falls on the quality and capabilities of its user members. This, therefore, is a good place to comment on the type of person from the user organization who should be associated with the system project team.

Obviously, the leading user member of the team should be a person intimately familiar with the workings of the user organization. Therefore, he will probably come from the operational level. Further, he should be among the best, highest-qualified members of the user organization.

As a general rule of thumb, the system project leader is looking for the man the user department can least afford to assign. Conversely, people who can readily be spared for such assignments are probably not qualified to handle the work of the system project team or to assume the role of leadership within their own department which is necessary for the success of the new system. In general, the best qualified user representative to the system project team tends to be someone at the level of assistant manager within the user department.

PROJECT PRIORITY ASSIGNMENTS

The findings and documentation of the System Planning Study will form the basis for judgment and priority assignment of the project under consideration. The *System Planning Manual* documentation and recommendations form the basis of resource and schedule priorities assigned to the project by the steering committee. The documentation from this activity is considered by the committee in direct comparison with all the other system projects pending within the organization.

Based on Planning documentation, the committee assigns relative priorities and timetable positions to the specific project. In doing so, the committee reorders and, if necessary, reschedules other projects to make room for this one. Thus, the System Planning Study is critically important in determining whether and when the project moves ahead into Development. The return on investment and other benefits identified and specified during the System Planning Study become the basis for the committee's decisions and project's support.

Another significant aspect of this activity within the project as a whole is that a commitment is made during the System Planning Study on the technical feasibility of the system. That is, the user and technical members of the project team indicate that, on the basis of their study, they feel the system, as defined in the *System Planning Manual,* can be implemented from a technical standpoint. This includes a stipulation that all the equipment and software needed to bring the system into operation will be available under the schedules outlined.

Another significant position established during the Planning phase is that the user organization can absorb the impact of the new system. Any major new system will create an impact on the user department. To a large extent, this is unavoidable. The important thing, rather, is that management of the user department understand what is going to happen and accept both the consequences of change and the responsibility for implementation of the new techniques.

ACTIVITY SCOPE

A System Planning Study will vary widely in depth and breadth, depending on the nature of the individual project under consideration. That is, the levels to which a planning study will go will depend directly on the size and organizational implications of the system itself. For general, descriptive purposes, four different types of systems, each involving a different level of system planning depth, can be defined:

1. The lowest level of depth will be required in a project calling for a simple conversion from an existing manual system to EDP methods. To illustrate, if a company is converting its accounts receivable operations from a bookkeeping machine to a computer, the requirements of the system, both present and proposed, will have been established. Bookkeeping procedures are, of necessity, diagramed and documented. Forms and files are well delineated. This documentation, in turn, lends itself naturally to input for the design of EDP systems. The computer programs involved are relatively uncomplicated. Therefore, a System Planning Study in such an environment would be wasteful if it went to extreme depths of detailed job task analysis for individual employees, studies of office layout, and so on.

2. The next level of depth would involve a project in which two or more existing EDP systems were being incorporated into a broader, more integrated whole. This could be done to take advantage of technical capabilities of higher-capacity computers, to apply advanced data

base languages or operating system software, or to generate better or more timely management information. One type of program into which this level of activity would fit might be the incorporation of existing applications into an information processing EDP program. One example of this type of situation would include the incorporation of payroll, personnel records, and labor reporting applications into a single, broader-scale information system.

3. The project can involve redesign and/or reorganization of an integral business operation, taking in both manual and EDP procedures. The underlying identification for this type of project lies in the fact that it deals directly with line company operations rather than administrative or accounting support functions. To illustrate the difference, payroll processing would be an administrative job while attendance and job completion reporting by manufacturing personnel would constitute direct operational support.

A distinction is important because the depth of system studies must be much greater on projects directly involved with mainstream company operations. Where a system is of an administrative or an accounting nature, a System Planning Study would go to a level of file content and processing. Where line operations of a company are involved, information gathering for system planning must go to a far greater level of detail, taking in transaction routines and alternatives associated with the creation of source information. Studies at this level would go into considerably more detail on manual procedures than efforts connected with either of the two previously discussed levels.

As a further qualification, such projects are designed to improve line operations of a company, as distinct from simply automating them for the convenience or standardization of doing jobs by computer. Also implied is the possibility of basic changes in the organization, procedures, or both, for the line organization of the sponsoring company. These considerations, in themselves, make for added project scope and present requirements for added depth within a System Planning Study.

4. Still another level of investigation may be involved where the system under consideration is entirely new within the sponsoring organization. An example of this type of situation would occur in a project designed to establish a management information system encompassing information factors external to a company's operations. For example, objectives established for a management information system might

call for incorporation within a data base of information on industry-wide market trends, consumer statistics, land utilization forecasts, census figures, and so on. In such a case, both the information basis and processing routines involved could be totally strange to the organization for which the system is being developed. In such instances, a System Planning Study would have to go outside the organization. This would be necessary to identify and evaluate data base content and also to search for applicable system technique precedents. Literature would be searched for theoretical approaches to solving the problems at hand. Visits and studies might be arranged at facilities of other organizations which had developed systems similar to the one under consideration within the project at hand.

The same type of requirement would exist, of course, in situations where an organization was undertaking new activities. One example typical at this writing is the development and implementation of financial information systems for commercial banks. In effect, these are techniques being developed to enable bankers to evaluate activity costs and profitability in much the same way as manufacturing firms monitor product lines and customers.

Information-gathering requirements at this level also include situations where system precedents or the needed technology for a given project are not readily available. In such cases, study activities may include the building of mathematical models and computerized simulation of proposed systems and their environmental conditions.

All four types, or levels, of project described above relate directly to operational aspects of the sponsoring organization. This is in keeping with the overall scope intended for this book. The systems under discussion will all apply to operationally related information. No attempt will be made to describe system studies at an overall, or corporate, planning level. System projects involving proposed changes to the objectives, goals, or strategies of the business as a whole call for specialized, different types of technology—and different basic approaches—from those used in the design and development of operational systems.

However, the basic methodology under discussion in this book is, it is felt, generally applicable to the development of systems affecting an organization's operations. Even though four separate levels, or types, of system development requirements have been identified for operational systems, the same basic, project approach to system design and development can be applied in all four areas.

ACTIVITY WORK FLOW

Figure 5-1 is a flow diagram of the System Planning Study activity. Note that the task descriptions within this diagram imply the presence of an existing system. In fact, most system projects do involve existing procedures within an organization. Even where advanced information systems are being developed, they will almost always incorporate, at least partially,

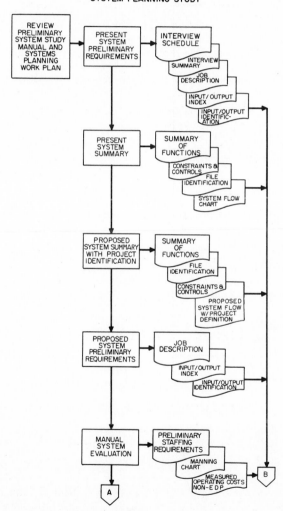

Figure 5-1a (Figure 5-1b follows)

SYSTEM PLANNING STUDY (CONTINUED)

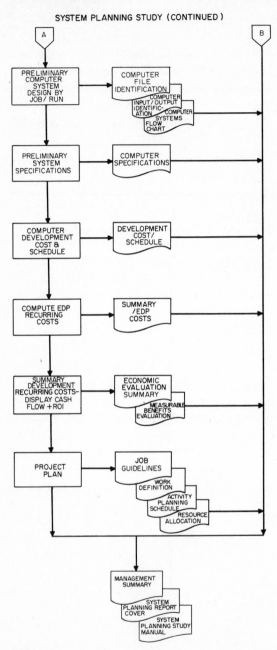

Figure 5-1b

some existing operations or procedures. At very least, present operations should be surveyed to determine how they will be impacted or altered by the proposed new system. In the area of computer-inclusive operational systems covered by this work, existing systems will have at least some relevance to those under development.

Highlights of the System Planning Study activity include:

- The activity begins with a review of the documentation generated by the previous activity: the *Preliminary System Study Manual* and the Systems Planning Work Plan. Naturally, any instructions or conditions established by the EDP Systems Planning Steering Committee in the course of reviewing and approving these documents will also be considered here.

- The present system is surveyed through interviews and the preparation of job description and information flow documents.

- The present system is summarized through formal documentation describing its functions, constraints and controls, file identification, and a flow chart diagraming the operation.

- The proposed system is documented at the same level as the present system. A project definition is also prepared.

- Preliminary functional requirements are established for the new system. The manual—or personnel subsystem—requirements of the new system are defined broadly in terms of staff and job requirements—and associated costs.

- The computer aspects of the new system are defined to a functional flow and file-processing level.

- Preliminary specifications are prepared for the computer system on which the new job will be processed.

- A development schedule together with development cost estimates are prepared for the computer portion of the new system.

- The recurring, or ongoing, costs of the EDP portion of the new system are estimated. Note the early stress, for management evaluation purposes, on a separation of development and recurring operational costs.

- A complete cost/benefit analysis is performed for the system under consideration. This goes to a broad cash flow and return on investment level.

Documentation which goes to the EDP Systems Planning Steering Committee at the conclusion of this activity includes the *System Planning Study Manual,* a cover report identifying contents of the manual and containing commitment approvals for the feasibility and benefit statements contained within the report, and a Management Summary reviewing the activity for the steering committee in nontechnical terms.

During the System Planning Study, the project's creeping commitment advances by an additional 5 percent of systems analysis time and expenditure. Within the bench-mark project involving 4 man-years of systems analysis, this activity would require approximately 10 man-weeks of effort by professional systems personnel. In addition, user members of the project team would devote approximately an equal amount of time to this activity.

ACTIVITY INITIATION

The task performance framework for this activity was established during the Preliminary System Study. Remember, one of the end-product documents of Preliminary System Study was a Systems Planning Work Plan like the one illustrated in Figure 4-3.

This established a schedule and work-requirement estimates for each of the tasks within the System Planning Study activity. Spaces were provided to indicate both the performance schedule and actual time expenditures as the system study is conducted.

The Systems Planning Work Plan, then, becomes the control document for completion of the current activity. Appropriate task performance entries are made as work is completed. During the initiation of the System Planning Study, the work plan serves as a guide for personnel assignment and task scheduling. In addition, the documentation within the *Preliminary System Study Manual* is duplicated and turned over to the systems and user people who will perform the individual tasks. Remember, the framework of the current and preceding activities is similar. This is by design. At this point in the project, studies cover the same general areas but go to succeeding levels of detail. Thus, persons assigned to specific tasks within the activity are given copies of the appropriate predecessor documents.

PRESENT SYSTEM PRELIMINARY REQUIREMENTS

The basic information-gathering technique during the System Planning Study activity remains interviews. At this point, however, user personnel take an active part in the interviewing. Depending on specific situations, users can conduct interviews on their own or they can work in interview teams with systems analysts. One common method is for the user members of the team to observe and participate in a few initial interviews along with systems analysts, then take over on their own as they gain a grasp of how interviews are conducted and what kind of information must be derived.

Documentation requirements in interview scheduling and interview summaries are pretty much the same as discussed in Chapter 4. The summarizing of interviews on forms like the one in Figure 4-2 is in narrative form with the interviewer following a general guide incorporated within the heading portions of the form.

An illustration of how succeeding activities within the system project move to deeper levels of detail can be seen in considering the three additional forms used within the task under discussion. These use the same interview summary form as an activity basis. But, from larger numbers of interviews which go to greater depth, project team members identify and describe the jobs within the present system, the documentary and data flow of the system, and the content of information files at each stage within the system.

Figure 5-2 shows a form used to prepare functional descriptions of jobs performed by interview subjects. As the form indicates, a separate document is prepared for each person interviewed. Spaces are provided to identify and describe each of the functions performed by this person. For each, an indication is entered on the percentage of the person's time required by the function, the number of hours per day, week, or month involved, some quantitative indication of work volume, and a narrative de-

Figure 5-2

scription of the function.   This isolation of functions within job descriptions is valuable because these work tasks are frequently reassigned within newly developed systems.

Figure 5-3 is a form used for identifying and describing all documents selected for relevance to the system under study.   Each document is identified by number and name.   Spaces are provided to indicate the volume of use for each document, its source, and distribution.

IMPORTANT WARNING: The extent and level of documentation in this and succeeding, similar activities represent a make-or-break point of economic feasibility for the system development project.   Too much detail can run costs out of line and, even worse, can trap designers in a series of unproductive blind alleys where they squander time and attention on details of little relevance.   In addition to wasting time, such practices also result almost invariably in schedule slippages.

As some measure of the importance of this type of selectivity, it can safely be assumed, on the basis of experience, that the "Rule of 80-20" for statistical relevance applies to system study activities at this level. In general, this establishes an 80-20 rule of applicability in almost any situation involving human interaction within large groups or broad environmental conditions.   In this case, experience has shown that at least 80 percent of the information flow of any given system will be captured by 20 percent of the documents generated and used within the system.

The real measure of systems analysis skill, then, lies in identifying and dealing with the relevant 20 percent of the documents encountered.

Specifically, it is not necessary to record and describe each document within the system on forms like those illustrated in Figures 5-3 and 5-4. Judgment should be applied.   Pertinence should be the yardstick.   Remember, most of the forms presently in use will have little current value, even within the existing system.   It is one of the objectives of system design to identify and leave out cost- and time-wasting operations and

	INPUT ☒ OUTPUT ☐	INDEX	PRESENT ☒ PROPOSED ☐			
				PAGE _/_ OF _/_		
				PROJECT NO. _0.28_		
ORGANIZATION _ABC COMPANY_				PREPARED BY _J JONES_		
APPLICATION TITLE _LABOR DISTRIBUTION_				DATE _11-13_		
Doc. No.	Document Name	Volume		Source	Distribution	
103	LABOR TRANSACTIONS	1500		TIMEKEEPERS	ACCOUNTING PAYROLL	
104	DEPARTMENT INQUIRIES	50		LINE DEPARTMENTS	—	

Figure 5-3

```
      ☒ INPUT                    ☒ PRESENT
                IDENTIFICATION
      ☐ OUTPUT                   ☐ PROPOSED

                                     PAGE____/____OF____/____
                                     PROJECT NO.___028_____
  ORGANIZATION  ABC COMPANY          PREPARED BY__J.JONES_____
  APPLICATION TITLE LABOR DISTRIBUTION   DATE____//-/3-_____
  ┌─────────────────────────────────────┬────────────────────────────────┐
  │ Document Name                        │ Document No.                   │
  │     LABOR TRANSACTIONS               │          /03                   │
  ├─────────────────────────────────────┼────────────────────────────────┤
  │          Content                     │          Source                │
  ├─────────────────────────────────────┼────────────────────────────────┤
  │ LABOR  HOURS  BY  INDIVIDUAL  TIME   │  PLANT  TIMEKEEPERS            │
  │ CARD                                 │                                │
  └─────────────────────────────────────┴────────────────────────────────┘
```

```
  ┌──────────────────────────────────────────────────────────────────────┐
  │ Use:                                                                   │
  │   TO PREPARE LABOR DISTRIBUTION REPORT AND PAYROLL                     │
  │                                                                        │
  ├─────────────────────────────────────┬────────────────────────────────┤
  │ Preparation                         │ Distribution                   │
  │ TIMEKEEPERS  SEND  PLANT            │ TIMEKEEPERS  TO  ACCOUNTING, THEN  TO │
  │ EMPLOYEE TIME CARDS  TO             │ PAYROLL                        │
  │ ACCOUNTING                          │                                │
  ├─────────────────────────────────────┼────────────────────────────────┤
  │ Frequency                           │ Volume                         │
  │    DAILY                            │    /500  TRANSACTIONS          │
  ├─────────────────────────────────────┼────────────────────────────────┤
  │                                     │                                │
  ├─────────────────────────────────────┼────────────────────────────────┤
  │                                     │                                │
  └─────────────────────────────────────┴────────────────────────────────┘
```

Figure 5-4

documentation requirements.   This rule of selectivity should be applied throughout a system project.   This need will be stressed throughout this book.

Documents used within the system are described in further detail through the use of a form like the one shown in Figure 5-4.   As a general rule, one of these forms is filled out for each document to be included in the survey. Space is provided for descriptions of content, identification of information sources, use of the document, preparation responsibility, distribution, frequency of issue, and transaction volume.   Within the cumulative documentation concept followed in this book, one of these forms is attached to each document selected during the System Planning Study.   The documents and associated systems analysis forms are then incorporated within the *System Planning Study Manual.*

All documents collected and described during this and succeeding study activities within the system project should be filled out with typical, live entries.   Where feasible, duplicates of actual documents are desirable.

WARNING: Documents without information entries are of comparatively little use in system design work.

JUDGMENT IN INFORMATION GATHERING

The presentation and discussion of forms which carry the main burden of system-descriptive information collection should not be interpreted to indicate that the entire job can be documented or controlled in this manner. On the contrary, the judgment and experience of the system project leader are vital in the gathering of information which cannot be quantified on forms like those shown in Figures 5-2 through 5-4. These nonformated requirements are of both a quantitative and qualitative nature.

Even though the forms illustrated in this chapter are quantitative in nature and call for volume figures as necessary, it should be stressed that there are large amounts of quantitative information relevant to any given system which must be identified and specified on the spot by the system project leader and members of the team.

These data, by nature, are measures of the performance of the present system. They are, therefore, necessary for the evaluation of proposed new systems, determination of benefits, return on investment factors, and so on. For example, depending on the individual system under investigation, the vital, nonformated quantitative information might include:

- The incidence rate and volume of stockouts in filling customer orders
- Percentage of customer orders serviced to completion
- Volumes of past-due accounts receivable
- Inventory turnover figures
- Employee turnover rates
- Manufacturing lead times
- Vendor lead times
- Insufficient cash flow or excessive cash balances

The list, obviously, could be virtually infinite. One critically important skill to be applied by the system project leader, therefore, lies in working with users to identify the necessary system measurement figures not covered by established forms and establishing mechanisms to be sure that the relevant information is collected.

Qualitative factors can be just as critical, possibly even more elusive to define. But it is important that they be identified and accounted for in the course of system studies. Critical information categories include:

- Employee morale and motivation
- Customer satisfaction

- Community relations
- Vendor relations
- Managerial efficiency and utilization of management time

Even these few illustrations indicate dramatically the difficulty of both finding and documenting these intangible types of data. But, the illustrations also indicate the relative importance of data to individual systems. As with other aspects of the project, it is the responsibility of the system project leader to work with user members of the project team, as well as with user executive and operational personnel, to find pertinent measures of system value and performance.

These nonformated information requirements—both quantitative and qualitative—serve also to highlight one of the major potential risks in a structured technique like the one under discussion. Specifically, the forms and procedures can be followed so rigorously that they hamper creativity. A form of occupational myopia can be bred by stolid adherence to the stated structure as a sole guide. It should be stressed that these are guideposts. But peripheral vision is still necessary in a field with horizons as broad as system design.

PRESENT SYSTEM SUMMARY

Once system requirements have been documented, they should be summarized in terms of functional significance. During this task, an interpretive translation of data takes place. In the course of interviewing, information is gathered chronologically as it relates to individual people and specific jobs. Now, it is important that common denominator functions be identified and isolated in terms of their relationship to system performance.

Figure 5-5 illustrates this point. It is a summary of functions performed. Note that it is closely similar to the job description form shown in Figure 5-2. The chief difference is that the column for the percentage of employee time devoted to the function is eliminated. Thus, this becomes a tool for the consolidation of duplicated functions and for the listing of functions in logical system sequence rather than according to job, section, group, or department. This form, when completed, pinpoints overall, functional time and effort expenditures within the system under study. It becomes a major tool for relating time expenditures to the value of functions. In turn, this becomes a road map pointing out areas for potential improvement.

There is also a major quantitative value in the data contained on such a form: By pinpointing where the effort is currently taking place, the system project leader knows where to put his major analytical effort. For this

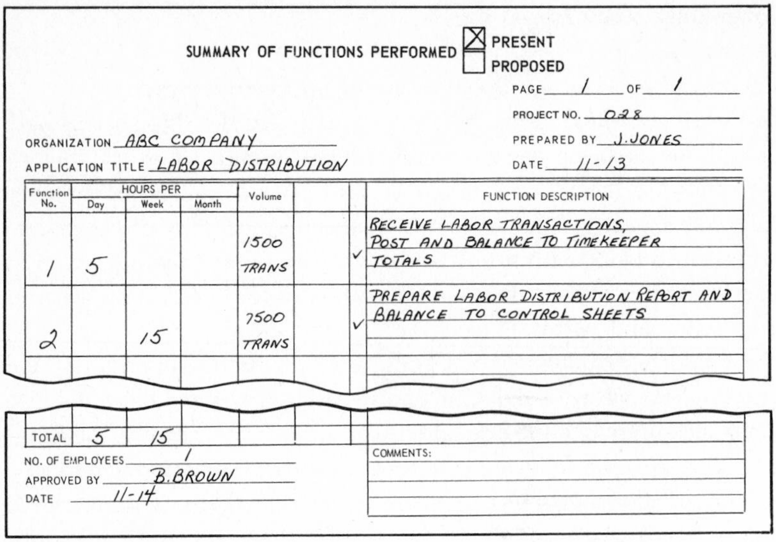

SUMMARY OF FUNCTIONS PERFORMED [X] PRESENT [ ] PROPOSED

PAGE 1 OF 1

PROJECT NO. 028

ORGANIZATION ABC COMPANY

PREPARED BY J. JONES

APPLICATION TITLE LABOR DISTRIBUTION

DATE 11-13

Function No.	Hours Per Day	Hours Per Week	Hours Per Month	Volume			FUNCTION DESCRIPTION
1	5			1500 TRANS		✓	RECEIVE LABOR TRANSACTIONS, POST AND BALANCE TO TIMEKEEPER TOTALS
2		15		7500 TRANS		✓	PREPARE LABOR DISTRIBUTION REPORT AND BALANCE TO CONTROL SHEETS
TOTAL	5	15					

NO. OF EMPLOYEES 1

APPROVED BY B. BROWN

DATE 11-14

COMMENTS:

Figure 5-5

reason, it is generally recommended that functions be listed on this form in descending order, according to the amount of time expended on each.

PRESENT SYSTEM—CONSTRAINTS AND CONTROLS

The review of interview-gathered information also leads to the preparation of separate forms, like the one shown in Figure 5-6, which are used to list constraints and controls applicable to the system under study.

For the purposes of this discussion, *constraints* are environmental or external limitations outside of the system itself. As the form indicates, these tend to be grouped in the areas of scheduling and timing, policy, and technical feasibility. Additional constraints might lie in laws, union contracts, vendor capabilities, trade practices, and so on.

Controls, within the present context, are limitations or safeguards applied within the system itself. Factors listed on the form include reconciliation, audit trails, and EDP internal controls. Others might include specified management summaries, examinations by governmental officials, and so on. As indicated by the design of Figure 5-6, this information is of a nature which is best suited for narrative description.

PRESENT SYSTEM—FILE DESCRIPTION

Working from the input/output documentation created during the previous task, project team personnel (either systems analysts or users, depending on the situation) identify and describe the system's files and their data elements—to the same level of relevance discussed earlier.   Figure 5-7 shows a form designed to guide this task.   As indicated, a separate form is used for each selected file.   Then, individual data elements within the file are listed and their sources given.   This is an important systems analysis step.   Modern systems are built around the processing of identifiable data elements.   Identification of files and their data elements, therefore, becomes a critical input to the system development effort.

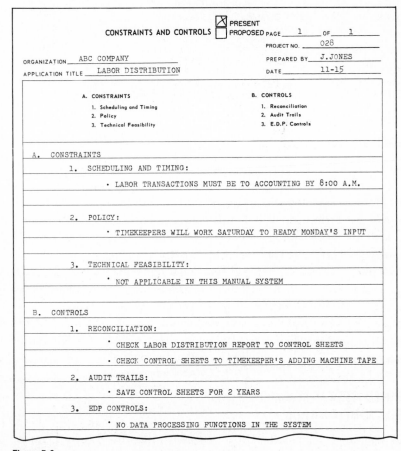

Figure 5-6

FILE IDENTIFICATION	☐ PRESENT ☒ PROPOSED	PAGE __/__ OF __/__

ORGANIZATION _ABC COMPANY_   PROJECT NO. _028_

APPLICATION TITLE _LABOR DISTRIBUTION_   PREPARED BY _J. JONES_

DATE _11-15_

File Name _LABOR/RATE MASTER_	Volume: _1500 EMPLOYEES_	Media _DISC._

ELEMENTS	SOURCE
JOB CLASSIFICATION CODE	PERSONNEL
JOB TITLE	PERSONNEL
JOB HOURLY PAY RATE	PAYROLL
JOB OVERTIME PAY RATE	PAYROLL
EMPLOYEE PLANT NUMBER	PERSONNEL
CLOCK NUMBER	PERSONNEL
EMPLOYEE NAME	PERSONNEL
EMPLOYEE DEPARTMENT NUMBER	PERSONNEL
EMPLOYEE JOB CODE	PERSONNEL
EMPLOYEE HOURS WORKED TO DATE	ACCOUNTING
EMPLOYEE PAY-TO-DATE	ACCOUNTING
EMPLOYEE SICK DAYS-TO-DATE	PERSONNEL

Figure 5-7

PRESENT SYSTEM—FLOW CHART

This task, as indicated in Figure 5-1, also calls for the preparation of a system flow chart representing the present system graphically. A general purpose form, completed with standard flow chart symbols, is used for this purpose. This form will not be illustrated here, since the same document is included elsewhere in this book (Figure 7-7).

At the level of detail called for in the System Planning Study, this flow chart should be drawn on a broad functional basis only. The interest at this point in the project lies in identifying and tracing information processing in a general, cycled sense. Fine points of processing detail, such as exception routines, error correction, and so on, are not necessary at this stage. Flow charting will be repeated, at increasing levels of depth, during several successive activities within the system project.

PROPOSED SYSTEM SUMMARY WITH PROJECT IDENTIFICATION

This is a highly creative task. Up to this point within the System Planning Study, emphasis has been on the evaluation and collection of existing information. Now, an original approach must be devised to improve upon the *status quo* to an extent which meets the stated objectives and projected benefits previously sighted for the new system.

As with any creative process, there can be no firm rules laid down for the performance of this particular task. Experience and imagination interact with environment to evolve a solution. The process actually begins with the evaluation of information collected and assembled in the study of existing systems and the associated examinations of literature and the work of others in parallel fields. As these functions are performed, the experienced systems analyst will begin to develop approaches, applicable techniques, and solutions in his own mind. Then, during this task, they are formalized.

As indicated in Figure 5-1, the forms used for this task are standard— identical with those already illustrated in Figures 5-5 through 5-7 (as well as a flow chart form). The degree of skill applied, however, is quite different. It is important that this point be stressed, even though it is, obviously, intangible.

During this task, formation begins for the entire future structure of the project. The size, scope, and nature of the problem have been delineated to a level sufficient for functional analysis and a presentation of new design concepts. The design techniques which emerge must, within this task, be shaped to the situation at hand.

Where possible, the new system will fall within the "chewable-bite" bounds stipulated for the project. However, in some cases, the logical solution may be beyond these bounds. If this proves to be the case, it is entirely feasible that two or more system projects may be spawned by the design concepts conceived and enunciated at this point.

In other words, this task involves the application of creativity at its highest level within the system project process. Therefore, it cannot, and should not, be tied down or encumbered. The general rules, constraints, and boundaries apply. The experienced systems analyst knows and respects these. But, he still should be given as much freedom as possible and encouraged to apply as much creativity as possible at this juncture.

The lack of controllability inherent in the creative process is, conversely, one of the basic reasons which led to the development of the methodology under discussion here. Creativity can be infinite. It can also be infinitely expensive. This is the underlying reason for the structure which incorporates scoped, scheduled activities in chewable bites. This is the reason for specifying that a series of four documents should emerge from the project identification effort. This stresses the point that end products are always expected, always fully defined, and reviewed at the appropriate management level.

PROPOSED SYSTEM
PRELIMINARY REQUIREMENTS

During this task, the project team describes the proposed system in the same general terms as was done for the present system in the task entitled Present System Preliminary Requirements. The descriptive forms used are the same as the last three described for the earlier task, as shown in Figures 5-2 through 5-4. (The interview schedule and summary forms, obviously, do not apply in the case of the proposed system. These forms are supplanted, in effect, by the project identification documentation generated during the last task.)

It should be stressed that documentation during this task is at a summary level only. Project team members identify outputs, primary input documents, files, and key data elements. No attempt is made to detail the system. Rather, the concentration is on the 20 percent of the data elements which will fill 80 percent of the information requirements. In addition to the three forms already cited as documentation for this task, a summary-level flow chart is also created.

MANUAL SYSTEM EVALUATION

This task begins a series of definitive cost estimates which mark a buildup toward the major continue/terminate decision at the close of the Planning phase of the project.

Specifically, this task and most of those which remain during this activity will accumulate and total costs for the development and implementation of the new system. These, obviously, will weigh heavily in the decision on whether the system moves ahead into development. And, if it does move ahead, the cost factors will figure in a determination of the priority assigned to this project.

The first step within this task is to develop a statement of Preliminary Staffing Requirements. The form used is shown in Figure 5-8. Note that the purpose of this summary is to identify the specific skills which will be needed in the development and operation of the new system. Also note that the form is designed to be time related. Spaces are provided for entry of job descriptions, salary levels, skill codes, and numbers of employees and costs for five operational periods. In other words, this form is a gross statement of staff needs through the remainder of the project.

Once the broad statement has been prepared according to job descriptions, personnel requirements are interpreted in terms of functions to be

PRELIMINARY STAFFING REQUIREMENTS	☐ PRESENT ☒ PROPOSED	PAGE _1_ OF _1_ PROJECT NO. _028_

ORGANIZATION _ABC COMPANY_
APPLICATION TITLE _LABOR DISTRIBUTION_

PREPARED BY _J.JONES_
DATE _11-17_

JOB DESCRIPTION	SALARY (Annual)	SKILL LEVEL	PROJECTION BY PERIOD – COST/NUMBER OF EMPLOYEES 1		2		3		4		5	
ACCOUNTING CLERK	$ 7,500	LEVEL 4	15,000	2	7,500	1	7,500	1	7,500	1	7,500	1
TIMEKEEPER	6,000	LEVEL 1	24,000	4	24,000	4	24,000	4	24,000	4	24,000	4
PAYROLL CLERK	7,000	LEVEL 2	14,000	2	14,000	2	14,000	2	14,000	2	14,000	2
SUB TOTAL	$ 20,500		53,000	8	45,500	7	45,500	7	45,500	7	45,000	7
FRINGE	2,100		5,600		4,900		4,900		4,900		4,900	
TOTAL	$ 22,600		58,600	8	50,400	7	50,400	7	50,400	7	50,400	7

Figure 5-8

performed by users on a Manning chart like the one shown in Figure 5-9. This form breaks down personnel needs according to project function, work volume, cost, and then staff requirements within the project function.

The final form executed in this task is shown in Figure 5-10. As indicated, this is a cost summary for the non-EDP portions of the system project. As will be seen, this becomes the first of the building blocks leading toward a preliminary cost estimate for the project and for continuous operation of the system.

These cost estimates also set the stage for later interaction during the project with the technical groups whose efforts will be needed. Documents to be generated during the remaining tasks in this activity will be transmitted to EDP operations, programming, and technical services personnel for concurrence that the estimates are realistic. In this way, the

MANNING CHART	☐ PRESENT ☒ PROPOSED	PAGE _1_ OF _1_ PROJECT NO. _028_

ORGANIZATION _ABC COMPANY_
APPLICATION TITLE _LABOR DISTRIBUTION_

PREPARED BY _J.JONES_
DATE _11-17_

Function	F/V	Skill Code	Base Volume	Prod. Rate	MANNING REQUIRED BY ACTIVITY LEVEL 1500 TRANS	2000 TRANS	2500 TRANS	3000 TRANS	3500 TRANS
RECEIVE LABOR TRANSACTION	V	4	1500 TRANS/DAY	500/HR	.39	.50	.64	.75	.87
PREPARE CONTROL SHEET	V	4	1500 TRANS/DAY	750/HR	.22	.25	.37	.50	.60
LABOR DISTRIBUTION REPORT	V	4	1500 TRANS/DAY	500/HR	.39	.50	.64	.75	.87
TOTAL					1.0	1.25	1.65	2.0	2.34

Figure 5-9

MEASURED OPERATING COSTS/NON-EDP				☐ PRESENT / ☒ PROPOSED		PAGE __1__ OF __1__ / PROJECT NO. _0-28_ / PREPARED BY _J·JONES_ / DATE __11-17__					

ORGANIZATION _ABC COMPANY_
APPLICATION TITLE _LABOR DISTRIBUTION_

Categories	Unit	Rate	Quantity/Dollar Costs by Period									
			1		2		3		4		5	
1. Personnel (w/fringes)	—	—	8	58,600	7	50,400	7	50,400	7	50,400	7	50,400
2. Equipment (non-EDP)	CALCULATOR	$200	1	200	—		—		—		—	
3. Operating Supplies	FORMS, PAPER AND OFFICE SUPPLIES	$250	1	250	1	250	1	250	1	250	1	250
4. Services												

TOTAL				59,050		50,650		50,650		50,650		50,650

Notes:

Figure 5-10

technical organizations will be "on board" and will have been given a chance to take exception to cost estimates which will be included in the *System Planning Study Manual.*

PRELIMINARY COMPUTER SYSTEM DESIGN BY JOB/RUN

With this task, the project team adds detail to the design of the new system by defining processing requirements for the EDP portion of the system. The forms used are the same as those already identified in Figures 5-4 and 5-7. In addition, a flow chart form is used.

The task begins with identification of file data elements and their sources on a form like the one shown in Figure 5-7. This information, in turn, is intrepreted and transposed from the documentation prepared during the Project Identification task for the proposed system.

Next, the key documents needed for the output from and input to the proposed system are described on a series of forms like the one shown in Figure 5-4. Since this form has been described previously in this chapter, no elaboration is needed here.

NOTE: This task is carried out at a job/run level. That is, a set of definitive documents is prepared for each job/run anticipated for the proposed new system.

PRELIMINARY SYSTEM SPECIFICATIONS

Using the documentation from the previous task, the systems analyst prepares a tally for the project as a whole.   On separate lines of a Computer Specifications form like the one shown in Figure 5-11, the systems analyst prepares a tally for the project as a whole.   On separate lines of a Computer Specifications form like the one shown in Figure 5-11, the analyst lists each run/module specified for the system and indicates the processing which will be necessary, the files which will be used, the data element and processing volumes, and computer time requirements.   It is clear that these specifications form a basis for determining the size, type, and capacity of the computer equipment which will be needed to implement the proposed project.

The Computer Specifications document also represents a communication vehicle between the project team and the EDP operations group.   In effect, transmission of this form describes the system for operations people in terms of processing requirements.   Further, it estimates the type of computer equipment and amount of processing time that will be required to run the new system.   By advising the operations people of prospective requirements this early in the system project, the team is establishing a rapport which will be important during later, more technical, activities.

During this task, EDP operations people become key members of the project team.   It is their job, specifically, to determine that the equipment and software support will be on hand, when needed, to implement the new system.   This may involve changes in equipment planning or installation if the system in the Development phase receives a commitment to proceed into Implementation.

COMPUTER DEVELOPMENT COSTS
AND SCHEDULE

This task is designed to let management know what it will cost to develop the new system and bring it up to operational status.   Where the previous task was oriented toward establishing cost estimates according to run/modules within the finished system, the purpose of this task is to determine what it will cost to get to that point.   The form shown in Figure 5-12 is designed as a working tool for the completion of this task.   Note that standard activities involved in system development are listed on the left.   Then, columns are provided for entry of skill codes, amount of effort needed, overall cost and distribution of the figures according to months over the project duration.

The form illustrated in Figure 5-12, the Development Cost/Schedule,

COMPUTER SPECIFICATIONS

APPLICATION TITLE LABOR DISTRIBUTION

PAGE 1 OF 1
PROJECT NO. 028
PREPARED BY J JONES
DATE 11-22

Run No.	Run Name	Processing Functions	Type	Comp.	File Name	File Media	No. of Records/Period 1	2	3	4	5	Est. Man Days Tech. Requirements	Programming	Hrs. of Computer Test Time	File Activity/Period 1	2	3	4	5	Estimating Basis (Indicate File(s) or processing reasons)	Frequency Interval Each	Total Computer Time Total	TOTAL ANNUAL
100	LABOR TRANS EDIT	EDIT DAILY LABOR TRANSACTIONS FOR VALIDITY	EDIT	B	LABOR TRANS / LABOR TRANS ED	CARDS / TAPE	1500	1500	1500	2000	2500	5	10	10	1500 TRANS	1500 TRANS	1500 TRANS	2000 TRANS	2500 TRANS	SIZE OF CARD DECK / MAX NUMBER OF ERRORS MADE	DAILY	.5 HR.	135 HRS.
101	LABOR MASTER UPDATE	ADD INFORMATION TO MASTER	UPDATE	C	LABOR/RATE MASTER	DISC	1500	1500	1500	2000	2500	10	20	25	1500 RECS	1500 RECS	1500 RECS	2000 RECS	2500 RECS	SIZE OF FILES	DAILY	1 HR.	270 HRS.
125	TELECOM	ANSWER CAT INQUIRIES OF LABOR RATE MASTER	ONLINE INQUIRY	D	LABOR/RATE MASTER	DISC	1500	1500	1600	2000	2500	25	30	50	300 RECS INCREASE	300 RECS INCREASE	300 RECS INCREASE	ADDITIONAL PROCESS	ADDITIONAL PROCESS	BASED ON CURRENT INQUIRY RATE	DAILY	1 HR.	270 HRS.
103	LABOR DISTRIBUTION REPORT PRINT	PRINT REPORT	PRINT	A	LABOR/RATE MASTER	DISC FORMS	1500	1500	1500	2000	2500	3	10	5	1500 RECS	1500 RECS	2000 RECS	2500 RECS		CURRENT REPORT SIZE	WEEKLY	2 HRS.	105 HRS.
										TOTAL		43	70	90							TOTAL		780 HRS.

Figure 5-11

92

ACTIVITY	Skill	Estimate Effort	Estimate Cost	JAN	FEB	MARCH	APRIL	MAY	JUNE	JULY	AUG
1. Project Organization and Planning		7 DAYS	$ 600	7 / 600							
2. System Requirements		10 DAYS	800		10 / 800						
3. System Specifications		15 DAYS	1200		5 / 400	10 / 800					
4. Technical Requirements		10 DAYS	800			10 / 800					
5. Implementation Planning		10 DAYS	1000			8 / 800	2 / 200				
6. Programming		70 DAYS	4000				25 / 1450	30 / 1800	15 / 750		
7. User Training		10 DAYS	800						5 / 400	5 / 400	
8. Systems Test		15 DAYS	1200							10 / 800	5 / 400
9. Conversion		15 DAYS	1200								15 / 1200
10. Administration		10 DAYS	1000	1 / 100	1 / 100	1 / 100	2 / 200	2 / 200	1 / 100	1 / 100	1 / 100
TOTAL		172 DAYS	$ 12,600	8 / 700	16 / 1300	29 / 2500	29 / 1850	32 / 2000	21 / 1250	16 / 1300	21 / 1700

ORGANIZATION ABC COMPANY
APPLICATION TITLE LABOR DISTRIBUTION
PAGE 1 OF 1
PROJECT NO. 028
PREPARED BY J. JONES
DATE 11-23

Figure 5-12

becomes a communication link between the project team and the organization's programming group. At this early stage in the project, this document advises the programming manager of both the planned schedule and estimated costs for project completion. The programming manager needs this information for his own planning and concurrence, since his group's contribution to the project will represent both a critical incident in project completion and a major cost. Thus, on an exception basis, if the programming manager does not state objections to the data incorporated in this form, concurrence is implied.

EDP RECURRING COSTS

The previous two tasks attacked specific areas of computer costs. The first was aimed at determining machine time and configuration requirements. After that, manpower development costs were estimated. Now, the project team looks at and estimates the recurring costs—those which will be encountered in running the new system on a continuing basis.

Note that the cost categories specified on the form in Figure 5-13 cover computer operations, data conversion, clerical costs, control, and maintenance. Spaces are provided to quantify and enter costs for each category.

SUMMARY-EDP COSTS   PAGE _1_ OF _1_

PROJECT NO. _028_

ORGANIZATION _ABC COMPANY_   PREPARED BY _J.JONES_

APPLICATION TITLE _LABOR DISTRIBUTION_   DATE _11-29_

Cost Category	Units	Rate	COST and QUANTITY by TIME PERIOD									
			Qty.	$	Qty.	$	Qty.	$	Qty.	$	Qty.	$
Computer Operation	OPERATOR	7,000	1/2	3,500	1/2	3,500	1/2	3,500	1/2	3,500	1/2	3,500
COMPUTER TIME	HOUR	20	780	15,600	780	15,600	780	15,600	780	15,600	780	15,600
TERMINALS	RENTAL/YR	1200	4	4,800	4	4,800	4	4,800	4	4,800	4	4,800
Key Punch or Data Conversion	OPERATOR	6,000	1	6,000	1	6,000	1	6,000	2	12,000	2	12,000
Clerical	CLERK	6,000	1/3	2,000	1/3	2,000	1/3	2,000	1/2	3,000	1/2	3,000
Control	CLERK	6,000	1/3	2,000	1/3	2,000	1/3	2,000	1/2	3,000	1/2	3,000
Maintenance	PROG.	9,000	1/3	3,000	1/3	3,000	1/3	3,000	1/3	3,000	1/3	3,000
Total				36,900		36,900		36,900		44,900		44,900

Figure 5-13

The form is flexible enough so that time periods can be adapted to the nature and mission of the new system. The time frames and costs used here should be generic to the system at hand — and comparable to the costs used in describing present systems, as appropriate.

The form illustrated in Figure 5-13 becomes a communication vehicle between the project team and the EDP operations manager. By forwarding a copy of this form at this comparatively early stage in the project, the team is, in effect, asking for concurrence that the estimates of system operating costs are realistic. Later in the project, during more technically oriented activities, the EDP operations manager will become a key figure in verifying the economics and feasibility of the projected system. By transmitting a copy of this form at this point, then, the project team keeps the operations manager advised and gives him a chance to state any objections or exceptions. If none are received, the project team can assume these estimates are on safe ground.

SUMMARY OF COSTS AND BENEFITS

This task summarizes the cash flows, returns on investment, and the measurable benefits anticipated from the proposed application. Benefits should be stated so that they correspond with those identified and forecast during the Preliminary System Study activity.

During the discussion of this activity in the last chapter, no formal documentation was recommended for the reporting of benefits. At this stage in the development of a system project, however, the authors have generally found it desirable to formalize the benefit statement to some extent. One form used during this task, shown in Figure 5-14, is an Economic Evaluation Summary. This, in effect, is a table summarizing the cost factors developed to date in the System Planning Study activity. Spaces are provided to total the cost elements of the present and proposed system and to subtract the totals to come up with net savings to the sponsoring organization. Return on investment and cash-flow factors are then calculated and listed. Note that spaces are provided for entry of both measurable and unmeasurable factors in making this economic evaluation.

To support the summary developed on the form shown in Figure 5-14, a work sheet like the one shown in Figure 5-15 is frequently used. This is

ECONOMIC EVALUATION SUMMARY

PAGE _/_ OF _/_
PROJECT NO. _O28_
ORGANIZATION _ABC COMPANY_   PREPARED BY _J JONES_
APPLICATION TITLE _LABOR DISTRIBUTION_   DATE _12-6_

Proposed System:	YEAR 1	YEAR 2	YEAR 3	YEAR 4	YEAR 5	
Development Costs	12,600	—	—	—	—	
Operating Costs- Non EDP	59,050	50,650	50,650	50,650	50,650	
EDP Recurring Costs	36,900	36,900	36,900	44,900	44,900	
Measurable Benefits	(10,200)	(9,200)	(9,200)	(9,200)	(9,200)	
Gross Cost (Benefit) Proposed System	98,350	78,350	78,350	86,350	86,350	
Present System:						
Operating Costs - Non EDP	80,000	85,000	90,000	95,000	105,000	
EDP Recurring Costs	—	—	—	—	—	
Total Present System	80,000	85,000	90,000	95,000	105,000	
Net Savings (Cost)	(18,350)	6,650	11,350	8,650	18,650	

Figure 5-14

MEASURABLE BENEFITS EVALUATION						

PAGE __/__ OF __/__
PROJECT NO. __028__
PREPARED BY __J.JONES__
DATE __12-6__

ORGANIZATION __ABC COMPANY__
APPLICATION TITLE __LABOR DISTRIBUTION__

BENEFIT DESCRIPTION	Cash Flow by Period					
	1	2	3	4	5	6
REDUCED FILING SPACE — 400 SQ.FT.	$ 1,200	1,200	1,200	1,200	1,200	1,200
SELL FILING CABINETS	1,000	—	—	—	—	—
REDUCED COST OF PREPARING INPUT FOR PAYROLL	8,000	8,000	8,000	8,000	8,000	8,000
TOTAL	10,200	9,200	9,200	9,200	9,200	9,200

Figure 5-15

a table for the listing and cash-flow projection of all the measurable benefits anticipated from the new system.

As those two forms indicate, the net result of this task is a complete economic evaluation of the proposed system—as compared with present methodology if applicable. Figures are stated both in terms of cash-flow improvement and in return on the investment required for system development.

PROJECT PLAN

A final, critically important documentation output of the Planning phase is a series of documents which make up the Project Plan. The forms involved are illustrated as follows:

Figure 5-16 — Job Guidelines

JOB GUIDELINES	

PAGE __/__ OF __/__
PROJECT NO. __028__
PREPARED BY __J.JONES__
DATE __12-8__

SUMMARY ☒
OBJECTIVES ☐
SCOPE ☐

ORGANIZATION __ABC COMPANY__
APPLICATION TITLE __LABOR DISTRIBUTION__

DESCRIPTION   __LABOR DISTRIBUTION SYSTEM__

THIS PROJECT WILL INCLUDE THE DESIGN AND IMPLEMENTATION OF A NEW LABOR DISTRIBUTION SYSTEM FOR THE ACCOUNTING DEPARTMENT. THE PROJECT WILL INCLUDE AN ANALYSIS OF THE REQUIREMENTS OF LINE DEPARTMENTS FOR LABOR DISTRIBUTION INFORMATION AND HOW BEST TO SATISFY THESE. ALSO, IMPROVED INTERFACE BETWEEN LABOR DISTRIBUTION AND EXISTING PAYROLL AND PERSONNEL SYSTEMS WILL BE STUDIED.

Figure 5-16

Figure 5-17 — Work Outline

Figure 5-18 — General Purpose Gantt Chart (for Activity Planning Schedules)

The function of these planning tools, together with the general description of their content and purpose, was incorporated in Chapter 1 as part of the general review of the project management concepts to be covered in this book. For the purposes of this discussion, the previous reference and the copies of the documents themselves contain all the detail necessary and relevant to this book.

The important consideration, within this discussion, is that project control documents should exist and project control techniques should be applied on an overview basis. In actual use, the Project Plan forms the interface between the system project leader and the company's systems manager. In other words, the Project Plan serves as the basis for monitoring and controlling individual projects within the larger context of an organiza-

---

WORK OUTLINE FORM

PAGE _1_ OF _1_
PROJECT NO. _028_
PREPARED BY _J JONES_
DATE _12-8_

ORGANIZATION _ABC COMPANY_
APPLICATION TITLE _LABOR DISTRIBUTION_

PROJECT LIST ☐
ACTIVITY LIST ☒
TASK LIST ☐

NO.	WORK DEFINITION	RESPONSI-BILITY	PERSONNEL TYPE	MAN DAYS REQUIRED	BUDGET	START DATE	TARGET DATE
01	PROJECT ORGANIZATION		—	7		1/20	2/1
02	SYSTEM REQUIREMENTS		—	10		2/1	2/22
03	SYSTEM SPECIFICATIONS		—	15		2/22	3/7
04	TECHNICAL REQUIREMENTS		—	10		3/7	4/1
05	IMPLEMENTATION PLANNING		—	10		4/1	4/8
06	PROGRAMMING		—	70		4/8	7/1
07	USER TRAINING		—	10		6/15	7/8
08	SYSTEMS TEST		—	15		7/8	8/8
09	CONVERSION		—	15		8/8	9/1
10	ADMINISTRATION		—	10		1/20	9/1
	TOTAL MAN DAYS			172			

☐ TASK LEVEL

Figure 5-17

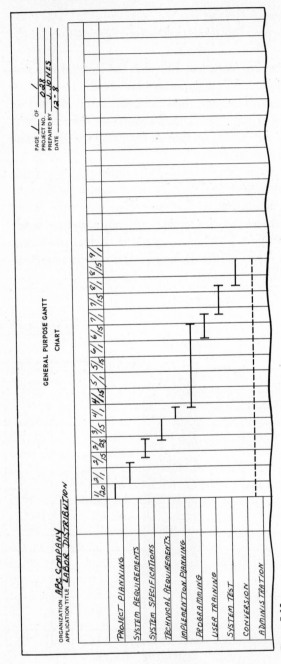

Figure 5-18

tion-wide, multiproject environment. Overall, multiple project control and its implications are discussed in a separate, companion work, *Managing the EDP Function.*

For the purposes of project Development and Implementation activities, however, it should be considered implicit that the Project Plan is initiated during the System Planning Study activity and carried forward throughout the remainder of any given project. Its role will be touched upon again in Chapter 9, in conjunction with the formalizing and documentation of an Implementation Plan for the individual project.

ACTIVITY REVIEW AND REPORT

The documentation created up to this point in the System Planning Study activity is incorporated into a *System Planning Study Manual.* This manual is generally covered by a report page like the one shown in Figure 5-19. In effect, this provides a checklist to be sure that all the documentation which was supposed to be prepared during this activity is in fact incorporated in the *System Planning Study Manual.* Note that this summary page also includes spaces for approvals by responsible operating managers and by the EDP Systems Planning Steering Committee.

In addition, the review and documentation task generates a Management Summary which will be used as the primary basis for the recommendation to and decision by the steering committee.

COMMITTEE DECISION

The fact that the System Planning Study activity marks the close of the Planning phase of a system project allows for a particularly critical decision and evaluation process in relation to the *System Planning Study Manual* on the part of the EDP Systems Planning Steering Committee.

This, of course, is the second time the committee will have reviewed the project. The first review came at the conclusion of the Preliminary System Study and was based on a first-level effort in defining present problems and future potential for the proposed system.

During the present activity, both the depth of information and the commitment to anticipated benefits on the part of users and systems people are substantially greater. Therefore, the committee will, naturally, place greater weight on this decision.

The importance of the committee decision at this point is also increased by the fact that this activity marks the end of the Planning phase for the

```
                    SYSTEM PLANNING STUDY REPORT

                                              PAGE  1  OF  1
                                              PROJECT NO.  O28
ORGANIZATION  ABC COMPANY                     PREPARED BY  J JONES
APPLICATION TITLE  LABOR DISTRIBUTION         DATE  12-8
```

SUMMARY OF STUDY	PAGES BY PROJECT NAME				
	1	2	3	4	5
1. Docket Cover Sheet	1				
2. Management Summary	2				
3. Economic Evaluation Summary	3				
4. Development Cost/Schedule	4				
5. Measured Operating Cost/Non - EDP - Proposed	5				
6. Summary EDP Costs - Proposed	6				
7. Measurable Benefit Evaluation	7				
8. Measured Operating Cost/Non-EDP - Present	8				
9. Summary - EDP Costs - Present	9				
10. Systems Flow Chart - Proposed - Manual	10-11				
11. Constraints and Controls - Proposed	12				
12. Preliminary Staffing Requirements - Proposed	13				
13. Manning Chart - Proposed	14				
14. Preliminary Staffing Requirements - Present	15				
15. Manning Chart - Present	16				

REPORT BODY

```
Systems Planning Manager Approval  W. WHITE          Date  1/3
Systems Development Manager Acceptance               Date
Operations Manager Acceptance  S JAMES               Date  1/3
User Acceptance  B. BROWN                            Date  1/3
Controller Div. Commentor                            Date
Marketing Div. Commentor                             Date
Auditing Div. Commentor                              Date

Authorized  A. THOMPSON, SYSTEMS MGR.               Date  1/4
            (Systems Committee Sec'y)

Unauthorized                                         Date
            (Systems Committee Sec'y)

DISTRIBUTION:  Systems Planning Staff  X    Systems Development
               Scheduling and Control       Marketing Division
               Controller's Division        Auditing
               User Organization(s)
               Accounting         X
```

Figure 5-19

project. If approval is granted, the major expense of system development will be authorized.

Further, in authorizing system development, the committee must weigh the value and importance of this proposed project against all others which are scheduled for development and/or implementation within the organization. In effect, then, this committee decision calls for a total review of the organization's system planning. If the project is approved, it will be given a priority value and placed accordingly in the work queue representing total system Development and Implementation activities within the organization.

This evaluation by the committee, obviously, takes into account both the intangibles and documented materials presented. For example, experienced committee members will weigh such factors as the extent of commitment and enthusiasm by user members of the project team (and by its own user member) because these elements bear directly on the probability of success which can be anticipated for the new system. This is the place where the quality, the pride, the attitudes, and the morale of the project team have a direct bearing on how the effort will fare.

PLANNING PHASE SUMMARY

The System Planning Study is also something of a division point in the types and levels of activities conducted by the project team. As the project moves forward into Development activities, efforts become far more detailed. Working levels are increasingly technical. Even the mixture of team members changes as EDP specialists come on board for the technical tasks during the Development phase.

From another aspect, steering committee approval at the close of the Planning phase generally marks a high point in the morale, the spirit, of the integrated, closeknit project team. The feeling which holds the group together as a working unit at this point should be protected and preserved as diligently as possible as the project moves forward into time-consuming, technical activities where interests tend to wane.

In summary, the completion of this activity represents an important bench mark and presents a new level of challenge for the system project leader and his team.

Development Phase

CHAPTER SIX

System Requirements

DEVELOPMENT PHASE OVERVIEW

The System Requirements activity marks the beginning of the Development phase of a system project. Because of the significance of the transition which takes place, this overview section will cover the material in this chapter and the six which follow. Note also that Figure 2-1, diagraming the system project cycle, has been repeated with the Development phase activities highlighted.

Although the differences are simple at first, the beginning of the Development phase of a system project definitely marks a transition in the type of effort required and in the depth of involvement by members of the system project team.

One immediate difference lies in the economics of this phase of the project. Some 65 percent of the time and money needed to develop a new system will be expended during the Development phase.

The tone, or emphasis, of efforts by the project team also shifts in the Development phase; the emphasis is on *doing* rather than on *planning,* as it has been up to this point in the project. This shift, in itself, is noticeable

THE SYSTEM DEVELOPMENT PROCESS

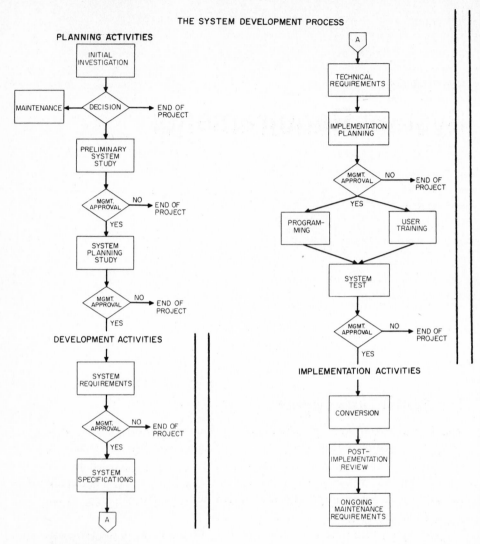

Figure 2-1 (*repeated*)

because of the extent of commitment inherent in Development activities. During the Planning phase, efforts and decisions were aimed at determining whether or not a new system was worthwhile. That decision is now behind. During the Development phase, each task brings the new system closer to a point of no return, or total commitment.

Another important difference is that Development activities are predominantly technical. The phase begins with the System Requirements activity, which calls for a great deal of interaction between user and EDP members of the project team.   But, even with this user-oriented emphasis, there is a definite change of purpose: The end result of System Requirements is a manual which presents specifications to the technical staff covering the system they are to develop.

SYSTEM REQUIREMENTS OBJECTIVES

During System Requirements, the project team interacts, thinks through, and documents the "what" of the system.   That is, the end product of this activity, the *System Requirements Manual,* is an explicit description of what the system is to be, what has to be done, and what is to be achieved.   To accomplish this objective, the System Requirements activity's highly interactive tasks are carried out at a level where they are meaningful to users and at which the documentation generated will be valid and useful as input to technical activities.   This documentation is vital as input to the remainder of the Development activities, which will be aimed at the "how" of the system and development of the methodology which will bring it to reality.

Among users, the System Requirements activity is critical because this is the point at which they begin to "buy" the new system.   The most common single cause of system failure comes from oversight or neglect in "selling" the system to its users.   Four separate user interaction requirements must be met:

1. Users must be *involved.*   Key people within the user group must feel that the system under development is theirs.
2. The entire user group must *identify* the new system with their operations and requirements, right from the beginning.   The earlier a system belongs to its users, the more likely it is to succeed.
3. The system must be *acceptable* within the user environment and to the user group.   This point has technical ramifications.   Frequently, it is possible to design a more advanced system than the one which is actually implemented.   But, it is sometimes necessary to sacrifice degrees of sophistication or "elegance" in favor of pragmatism.   The fact is that no system can be any more advanced than the will of its users to implement it.
4. *Commitment* is necessary on the part of the user group.   Before the major expenditure of technical development takes place, the user group must stipulate, unequivocably, that the system is wanted and that they will make it work.

User commitment also involves personnel and other resources within the department for which the system is being developed. Inevitably, system development becomes a staff type of function within the organization. Understandably, it tends to be given a lower priority than day-to-day line responsibilities. In this context, then, commitment implies that the user understands his own pressures and priorities and that he will, in fact, make the time and resources available to bring the new system to fulfillment.

The interactive nature of System Requirements is also important in that it provides the framework in which the systems people on a project team must come to understand the user environment and user problems. The systems people must become intimately familiar with the qualitative and quantitative aspects of user operations. They must understand the problem which the system is aimed at solving. They must determine, based on this acquired understanding, that the techniques they develop will, in fact, solve the problem which led to the system project in the first place. If the user does not get exactly the system he wants and needs, the project can, and probably will, fail. It is up to the systems analysts on the project team to solve the right problem with the right technology.

User involvement, identification, acceptance, and commitment must also be accompanied by an understanding that the user assumes the major responsibility at this point in the project. The System Requirements activity will go far enough in defining what the system will look like and what it will do so that the user must be willing to assume responsibility for saying that the results are what he wants and that the operational techniques and benefits are what he had in mind during the Planning phase.

Saying that this responsibility is a necessity is not to imply that it is easy for the user to understand or undertake such commitments. On the contrary, it is difficult for non-EDP people to visualize computerized systems or their operational implications. This difficulty, however, makes the assumption of responsibility all the more important. Somehow, the system project leader and his analysts must, in the interaction which takes place during System Requirements, make the full implications of the new system totally clear to the user group—to a point where the users make the system theirs and are willing to assume the risks associated with development and fulfillment.

Within the creeping-commitment concept, the new system takes more definitive forms and more information is developed during System Requirements to form the basis of another, more comprehensive, critical look at the project.   Specifically, costs and projected benefits can be defined more realistically with each passing activity.   At the conclusion of System Requirements, the requested steering committee commitment involves authorization for full technical development—the most expensive segment of the project.   Therefore, during this activity, the project team must keep the stakes in mind, must be aware that the increasing level of detail within their studies should support a more extensive commitment by their organization.

ACTIVITY STRUCTURE

In most cases, the System Requirements activity will mark a restart for the project.   Remember, at the close of the last chapter, it was indicated that the *System Planning Study Manual* served as a basis for establishing priorities and schedules for this project among all other system projects actively being pursued within the organization.   Typically, several months elapse between the completion of the System Planning Study and the priority rotation leading to the initiation of the System Requirements activity.

When the Development phase of the project is initiated, then, the membership on and composition of the system project team may be quite different from preceding activities.   The changes are less likely to be apparent on the user side.   Even if there are changes, user personnel on the system project team will still be involved on a day-to-day basis with the application area under study.

However, the systems analysts involved in the Planning phase of the project may well be off on other assignments by the time the Development phase is activated.   The system project leader himself may have been promoted or transferred.   Anyone familiar with the EDP field realizes that turnover is high in this business.   One of the reasons for cumulative documentation within the project structure under discussion here is that the disciplined information gathering makes for continuity both in management and in operation of project activities.

In picking up the responsibility for performance of the System Requirements activity, the task team will approach its work in two separate stages, or activity branches:

1. Requirements of the present system must be defined.
2. Requirements of the proposed system are determined.

Within this context, the word "requirements" is critical.   As used here, the word centers around the "what" of the situation under study.   The review of the present system determines what is being done.   The requirements for the new system are aimed at determining what the organization should be doing.

The two studies, covering the present system and the new one, are carried out separately. This is necessary because of the basic nature of how present and future systems should be reviewed. With a present system, a study is sequential. The analysts begin with source transactions and run through the system in a logical order. With a new system, however, the study effort begins with a careful definition of outputs, then traces back to input and processing requirements. Therefore, within this chapter, separate efforts and procedures will be described for studies of present and proposed systems.

PRESENT SYSTEM REQUIREMENTS

The most important starting point for a discussion of a study covering existing procedures is to stress that it should be done in the first place. Understandably, interest is keyed strongly toward the new system. The system project leader should clarify the importance of knowing where you are before you map out where you are going in any detail.

The road map, or exploration, analogy is a good one in discussing the importance of a requirements study of the present system. As a basis for development of a new system, analysts should be thoroughly familiar with the current environment and its problems. Even though this discussion will recommend a structured, orderly approach to determination of present system requirements, it should be stressed that the primary result sought is an understanding of the environment and its problems, on an interactive level, by analysts and users. The forms and documents described within this study, then, should be looked on as vehicles for gathering information which will lead to the necessary understanding. The documentation is not the most important end product in and of itself. Rather, it is intended as an educational foundation. The real end product is the comprehension level of the analyst in connection with the operations, the environment, and the problems of the business he is studying and which he will impact extensively.

The methodology under discussion in this chapter is offered as one way of achieving the necessary understanding. There are others. For example, IBM has a formalized technique known as SOP, for Study Organization Plan, which can be used as an alternative method for achieving the same general results.

PRESENT SYSTEM STUDY EMPHASIS

Because understanding and comprehension are the real end products of this task sequence, selectivity of attention and documentation becomes important. The project team should realize that, once the users and analysts establish a mutual understanding, the documentation has served its purpose. Therefore, many projects actually incorporate present system documentation into a manual separate from the *New System Requirements Manual.* Because of the transient nature of present system documentation, it is usually executed in rougher form and is not accorded the finalizing touches generally applied to documentation which will be carried forward as a basis for further development and implementation.

Also important is the exercise of selectivity in the direction of study efforts on the present system. Simply stated, it is not worth the time and effort which would be needed to study the present system in its entirety. Rather, the system project leader, through exercise of his experience and judgment, should give close direction to selection of areas of probable payoff. The present system is surveyed broadly to determine which areas of its operation are most subject to change within the new system. These are the operating areas which are studied in detail. In other words, in a review of currently used documents, the system project leader singles out those documents and supporting procedures which are most likely to be changed to the greatest extent. This is where study efforts are applied. Within these areas, then, the documentation and procedures are examined totally, in full detail.

To illustrate, if the project at hand involved development of a system for computerized production scheduling and inventory control, the present system survey would go into great detail on the decision rules applied in placing production orders or issuing purchase requisitions for buy-out items. These decision rules would be tested and recalculated in great depth.

However, within the same study, very little attention would be paid to the inventories of tools and dies. Processing techniques for the determination of such factors as die life or die repair requirements would not lend themselves readily to computerization in most manufacturing facilities. If the systems analyst determined that these characteristics of the present system were true to form, therefore, the study under his direction would concentrate on inventory and production scheduling and would virtually ignore the tool room.

Another typical example centers around studies for computerization of composition, scheduling, and billing for advertising in daily newspapers. Very quickly, the analyst would find that separate requirements and procedures are necessary for display and classified advertising. In familiarizing himself with the environment, the analyst would recognize readily that the great majority of display ads handled by the average daily newspaper are made up completely by the agencies which place them. There is little the new system can do to impact this segment of the business. Therefore, study of display-advertising procedures would concentrate on scheduling and billing, avoiding in-depth studies of typesetting or composition.

USING THE CUMULATIVE DOCUMENTATION PRINCIPLE

The other point to be stressed is that documentation duplication should be avoided during the System Requirements activity. Remember, the input to this activity is the *System Planning Study Manual,* which already takes in a good bit of the scope of the information requirements. However, as discussed in the last chapter, the depth of the System Planning Study documentation is at a comparatively shallow level, since analysts went only far enough to develop information which would support a decision to go ahead with system development.

In terms of policy, then, the system project leader should be sure that the interviews, document descriptions, job descriptions, data element descriptions, and flow charts generated during the previous activity are not repeated. Rather, these become starting points for studies which go to far greater depth in selected areas.

The carrying forward of documentation from one activity to the next also serves to reinforce a project's quality control. Reuse of previous documentation validates the accuracy of both the information gatherers and respondents who provided source information. A realization that documentation will be cumulative makes for responsibility in each segment of system study work.

PRESENT SYSTEM STUDY WORK FLOW

Figure 6-1 illustrates a typical functional flow for a study aimed at defining the requirements of a present system, if one exists within the using organization. Note that some of the initial forms are similar to those used in previous activities, and others are designed to take functional descriptions to added levels of detail.

DEFINE REQUIREMENTS OF PRESENT SYSTEM

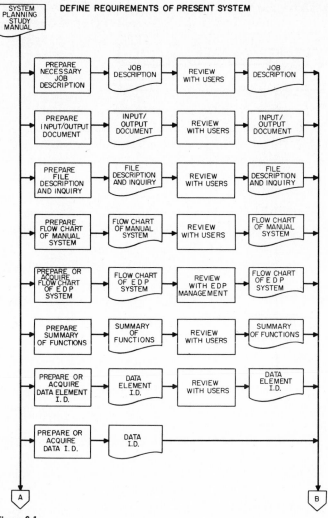

Figure 6-1a

JOB DESCRIPTIONS

For each area selected for study, the effort begins sequentially. Analysts prepare a job description form for the input position and for succeeding levels of personnel processing detail.

Figure 6-2 shows a form as it might have been executed in a typical situation at the level of detail required in the System Requirements activity. Note that transaction volumes are pinpointed for the job and that each function is broken out according to the percentage of time required

DEFINE REQUIREMENTS OF PRESENT SYSTEM (CONTINUED)

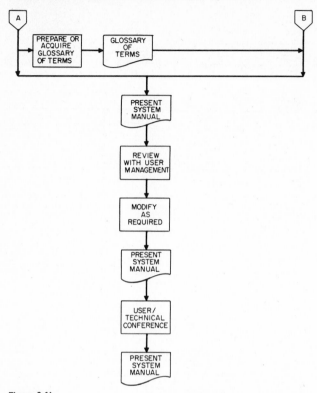

Figure 6-1b

for its performance.   Time allocation detail is also developed for the employee.

INPUT/OUTPUT DESCRIPTIONS

Within each job selected for study, relevant input and output documents are described on forms like the one shown in Figure 6-3.   Note that spaces are provided to indicate the manual processing applied to the document, its distribution, and transaction volumes.

FILE AND INQUIRY DESCRIPTIONS

Descriptions of the files and inquiry requirements within the jobs under study are completed on forms like the one shown in Figure 6-4.   This is a general purpose file description covering the size of the file, the inquiry rate, storage media, security, backup, retention, and arrangement of data elements within the file.

The same document can be used for describing either a manually maintained or a computer-based file. As a general rule, one of these forms will be developed to support each file covered within the study.

FUNCTIONAL FLOW CHARTS

After jobs, documents, and files have been described, manual routines within the present system are flow charted following techniques like the one shown in Figure 6-5. Flow charting techniques in this situation are designed to identify "the system cycle" of information as it flows through a single department or a series of departments. This system cycle has a logical beginning and end. It can generally be traced through input forms, files, processing functions, and outputs which have been identified during the previous tasks.

JOB DESCRIPTION

ORGANIZATION *ABC COMPANY*
APPLICATION TITLE *LABOR DISTRIBUTION*

PAGE *1* OF *1*
PROJECT NO. *028*
PREPARED BY *J. JONES*
DATE *2-3*

NAME: *JOHN DOE*   POSITION: *ACCOUNTING CLERK*

FUNC-TION NO.	% OF TIME	HOURS PER DAY	HOURS PER WK.	HOURS PER MO.	VOLUME	FUNCTION DESCRIPTION
1	25	2			1000 TRANS	RECEIVE LABOR TRANSACTIONS FROM TIMEKEEPERS, SORT TO EMPLOYEE SEQUENCE WITHIN DEPARTMENT
2	25	2			1000 TRANS	POST HOURS TO CONTROL SHEET BY EMPLOYEE
3	12½	1				FOOT CONTROL SHEET TO TOTALS PRODUCED BY TIMEKEEPER
4	–	—				FORWARD LABOR TRANSACTIONS TO PAYROLL
5	30		12			EXTEND REGULAR AND OVERTIME HOURS BY HOURLY RATE AND POST TO LABOR DISTRIBUTION REPORT BY EMPLOYEE AND DEPARTMENT
6	7½		3			BALANCE TOTALS OF LABOR DISTRIBUTION REPORT TO CONTROL SHEETS

TOT.	100	5	15		COMMENTS:

APPROVED BY *B. BROWN*
DATE *2/6*

Figure 6-2

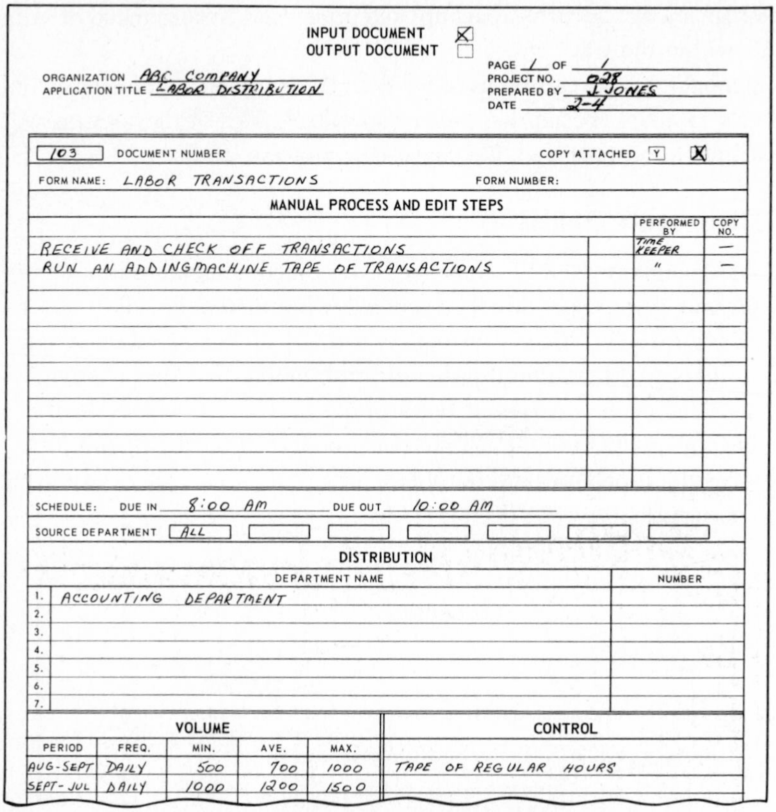

INPUT DOCUMENT ☒
OUTPUT DOCUMENT ☐

ORGANIZATION ABC COMPANY
APPLICATION TITLE LABOR DISTRIBUTION

PAGE 1 OF 1
PROJECT NO. 028
PREPARED BY J. JONES
DATE 2-4

103 DOCUMENT NUMBER	COPY ATTACHED Y ☒
FORM NAME: LABOR TRANSACTIONS	FORM NUMBER:

MANUAL PROCESS AND EDIT STEPS

		PERFORMED BY	COPY NO.
RECEIVE AND CHECK OFF TRANSACTIONS		TIME KEEPER	—
RUN AN ADDINGMACHINE TAPE OF TRANSACTIONS		"	—

SCHEDULE: DUE IN 8:00 AM DUE OUT 10:00 AM

SOURCE DEPARTMENT ALL

DISTRIBUTION

	DEPARTMENT NAME	NUMBER
1.	ACCOUNTING DEPARTMENT	
2.		
3.		
4.		
5.		
6.		
7.		

VOLUME					CONTROL
PERIOD	FREQ.	MIN.	AVE.	MAX.	
AUG-SEPT	DAILY	500	700	1000	TAPE OF REGULAR HOURS
SEPT-JUL	DAILY	1000	1200	1500	

Figure 6-3

Should EDP procedures be involved in the present system, they are flow charted through use of standard forms and symbols like the ones already described in earlier chapters. If appropriate, existing documentation used in EDP operations can simply be duplicated and incorporated within this study.

FUNCTIONAL SUMMARIES

At the same functional level as the flow chart of manual procedures, analysts should prepare a Summary of Functions Performed document like the one shown in Figure 6-6. This is a working summary of volumes and time requirements, on a functional basis, for the manual portions of the existing system.

This form is similar in design to the job description form used at the outset of this study. However, for the purposes of this document, job descriptions, volumes, and time requirements are summarized according to system function.

To complete the documentation cycle, the function numbers assigned in the execution of this form are annotated to the manual flow chart and the job description forms executed earlier. Check marks in the column to the left of the function description identify those manual functions which should be studied and considered for inclusion in the new system.

DATA ELEMENT IDENTIFICATION

The next task incorporates one of the basic reasons, and values, for studying the present system. Figure 6-7, which contains a Data Element ID form, illustrates how data captured in an existing manual system is formatted for inclusion in a computerized system. One of these forms is filled out for each data element which, in the opinion of the systems analysts, is a can-

---

FILE DESCRIPTION AND INQUIRY

ORGANIZATION _ABC COMPANY_
APPLICATION TITLE _LABOR DISTRIBUTION_

PAGE _1_ OF _1_
PROJECT NO. _028_
PREPARED BY _J. JONES_
DATE _2-5_

FO01	FILE NUMBER	FILE NAME: _EMPLOYEE RATE_	COPY ATTACHED Y ☒

UPDATE INTERVAL: _WEEKLY_	SECURITY: _FIRE PROOF SAFE_	
RECORDS IN FILE: _500_	BACKUP: _PERSONNEL DEPT. FILES_	
TRANSACTIONS: _500 - 1500/DAY_	RETENTION: _CONTINUOUS_	
MEDIA: _KARDEX_	SEQUENCE: _EMPLOYEE # WITHIN DEPT_	

ACCESS REQUIREMENTS

PURPOSE: _ANSWER QUESTIONS FROM DEPARTMENT HEADS CONCERNING RATES._

HOW FAST: _WHILE WAITING ON TELEPHONE_

HOW OFTEN: _4-5 TIMES/DAY_

BY WHOM: _DEPARTMENT HEADS_

WHEN: _EVERY DAY_

WHERE: _ALL PLANTS_

CONTROL AND UPDATE PROCEDURE

RATE CHANGE NOTICES AND NEW HIRES ARE RECEIVED WEEKLY FROM THE PERSONNEL DEPARTMENT. NEW RATES ARE POSTED TO THE FILE. THERE IS NO REGULARLY SCHEDULED CONTROL PROCEDURE FOR THIS FILE.

Figure 6-4

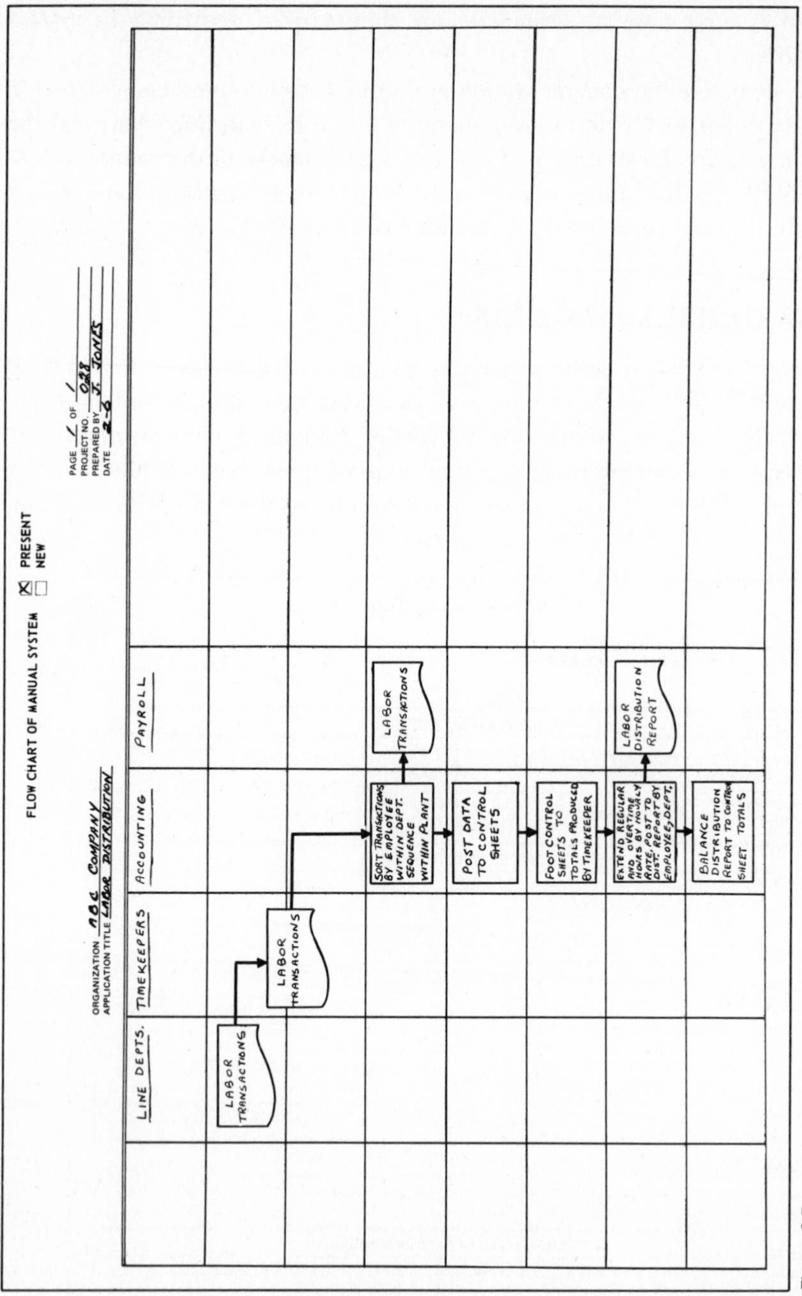
FLOW CHART OF MANUAL SYSTEM
PRESENT
NEW
ORGANIZATION ABC COMPANY
APPLICATION TITLE LABOR DISTRIBUTION
PAGE 1 OF 1
PROJECT NO. 028
PREPARED BY J. JONES
DATE
LINE DEPTS.
TIMEKEEPERS
ACCOUNTING
PAYROLL
LABOR TRANSACTIONS
LABOR TRANSACTIONS
SORT TRANSACTIONS BY EMPLOYEE WITHIN DEPT. SEQUENCE WITHIN PLANT
LABOR TRANSACTIONS
POST DATA TO CONTROL SHEETS
FOOT CONTROL SHEETS TO TOTALS PRODUCED BY TIMEKEEPER
EXTEND REGULAR AND OVERTIME HOURS BY HOURLY RATE, POST TO DIST. REPORT BY EMPLOYEE & DEPT.
LABOR DISTRIBUTION REPORT
BALANCE DISTRIBUTION REPORT TO CONTROL SHEET TOTALS

Figure 6-5

didate for carrying forward to and inclusion in the data base of the new system.

As is evident from the content of the form in Figure 6-7, each element is given an identification, a formal name (identified in terms of size and the file with which it is associated), and, in general, described in full for machine-processing purposes. In addition, a full descriptive definition for the data element identified on this form is entered in provided spaces.

With all this descriptive information included on a single document, the Data Element ID form becomes a tool for agreement on system building blocks between user and analyst members of the project team. Each data element is identified, named, and defined. It thus becomes unique, accorded a special meaning, within the system and the systems organization involved. Note that the form is designed for ease of machine input transcription. This is for usability within systems which incorporate automated data dictionaries.

As a next step in file organization for the system under development, data elements are organized according to logical processing groups, or sets,

SUMMARY OF FUNCTIONS PERFORMED

PAGE 1 OF 1
PROJECT NO. 028
PREPARED BY J. JONES
DATE 2-8

ORGANIZATION ABC COMPANY
APPLICATION TITLE LABOR DISTRIBUTION

FUNCTION NO.	HOURS PER DAY	WEEK	MONTH	VOLUME			FUNCTION DESCRIPTION
1	2			1000 TRANS.		✓	SORT LABOR TRANSACTIONS
2	2			1000 TRANS.		✓	POST TO CONTROL SHEET
3	1					✓	BALANCE CONTROL SHEET
5		12				✓	PREPARE REPORT
6		3				✓	BALANCE REPORT
TOTAL	5	15					

COMMENTS:

NO. OF EMPLOYEES 1
APPROVED BY B.BROWN
DATE 2/9

Figure 6-6

DATA
ELEMENT ID

PAGE _1_ OF _1_
PROJECT NO. _028_
PREPARED BY _J. JONES_
DATE _2-10_

ORGANIZATION _ABC COMPANY_
APPLICATION TITLE _LABOR DISTRIBUTION_

ELEMENT IDENTIFICATION
L D O T R A T E

ELEMENT NAME
O V E R T I M E - R A T E

UNDERLYING POLICY DATA ID
L D W A G E T B L 1

MIN SIZE | MAX SIZE
0 0 3 | 0 0 4

UNDERLYING POLICY DOCUMENT NAME
UNION CONTRACT AND WAGE RATES

ELEMENT GENERAL EDIT PICTURE
9 9 V 9 9

ELEMENT DOCUMENT PICTURE
Z Z 9 9

1st ASSOCIATED ELEMENT ID
L D R E G R A T

2nd ASSOCIATED ELEMENT ID
L D S H F T R T

3rd ASSOCIATED ELEMENT ID
L D L A B C L S

4th ASSOCIATED ELEMENT ID

ELEMENT DEFINITION

THIS ELEMENT DEFINES THE WAGE
RATE FOR HOURS WORKED IN
EXCESS OF 8 MONDAY THROUGH
FRIDAY AND ALL HOURS ON
SATURDAY SUNDAY AND HOLIDAYS.

THE VALUE OF OVERTIME-RATE
WILL FALL BETWEEN 4 35 AND
8.50 PER HOUR AND WILL BE
TREATED ALWAYS AS POSITIVE
AND NUMERIC

CHANGES WILL OCCUR ANNUALLY
AS THE CONTRACT IS
RE-NEGOTIATED.

Figure 6-7

through use of a form like the one shown in Figure 6-8. Clearly, this is designed to identify, name, and describe processing and updating procedures; to describe inquiry conditions; and to define length, volume, and content of data element groups, or sets. Again, this form is designed for compatibility with automated data libraries.

It should be stressed that, if an existing system already uses EDP techniques, either the Data Element ID or Data ID forms, or suitable equivalents, may exist already. If so, they can simply be duplicated and incorporated in the documentation for this study.

GLOSSARY OF SYSTEM TERMS

Another step toward the assembly of the data base for the new system is taken with the preparation of a glossary of terms, which are recorded as they are identified on a form like the one shown in Figure 6-9. As indicated in the illustration, this form is used to enter names and descriptions for identified data elements. It functions, basically, as a communications tool and working guide during system development.

With a cumulative log of data names like the one shown in Figure 6-9, there is a safeguard against duplication or conflict in terminology. Further, the maintenance of a record of this type serves to assure that all members of the project team are aware of and have agreed to the content of the data dictionary to be associated with the new system.

PRESENT SYSTEM MANUAL

As indicated in the flow chart in Figure 6-1, the cumulative documentation on the existing system is incorporated into an initial draft of a *Present System Manual.* This, in turn, is reviewed with user management. Modifications are made as necessary.

After this initial review and revision, the *Present System Manual* is ready

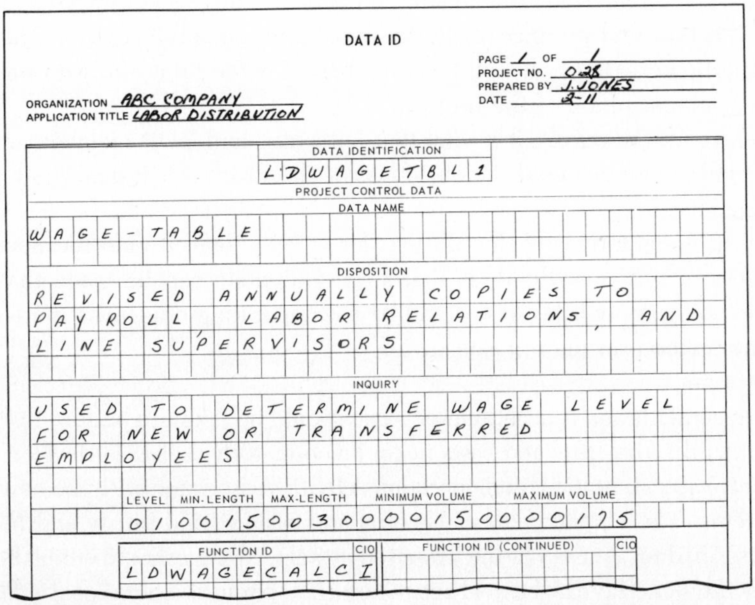

Figure 6-8

GLOSSARY OF TERMS

PAGE _/_ OF _/_
PROJECT NO. _0-28_
PREPARED BY _J. JONES_
DATE _2-13_

ORGANIZATION _ABC COMPANY_
APPLICATION TITLE _LABOR DISTRIBUTION_

TERM	MEANING
CLOCK NO.	NUMBER ASSIGNED TO AN EMPLOYEE FOR REPORTING OF HOURS WORKED
DEPT No.	OPERATING GROUPS WITHIN COMPANY
REGULAR HRS.	HOURS WORKED <8 MONDAY — FRIDAY
OVERTIME HRS.	HOURS WORKED >8 MONDAY —FRIDAY AND ALL HOURS ON SAT. SUN. AND HOLIDAYS.
SHIFT BONUS	PREMIUM FOR WORKING 4-12 SHIFT OR 12-8 SHIFT

Figure 6-9

for a final study review, at a User/Technical Conference. This is an over-all examination of the documentation generated to be sure that, in fact, agreement and full comprehension have been achieved as far as the existing system is concerned. This agreement is important because the *Present System Manual* approved at this conference becomes the basis for the study of the proposed system which follows.

PROPOSED SYSTEM STUDY OBJECTIVES

Defining and documenting the requirements of the proposed new system is the important end product of the System Requirements activity. The documentation created here will form the basis for the total effort during the Development phase of the project.

Therefore, at the outset, it is vital that both user and EDP members of the project team understand the objectives of the Proposed System Study. These include:

- The documentation created during this study should define the new system in sufficient depth so that a determination can be made that user problems will be solved and/or user operating objectives met — either or both to the full satisfaction of the user members of the project team.
- As documentation is accumulated, care should be taken to be sure that it quantifies benefits and costs in conjunction with projected development, implementation, and operation activities associated with the new system. These statements of benefits and costs should satisfy and be subscribed to by users of the proposed system. Users should stipulate that the benefits can be realized when the system is operational and

that the projected costs are realistic within the operational environment of the system under development.

- This study must determine, formulate, and select any new decision rules or processing techniques needed within the proposed system. It should be borne in mind that a new system under development today will almost surely cover greater scope and have greater implications for the mainstream of the business than anything it replaces. Special care should be taken to be sure that policies and operating conditions in business areas which have not previously been automated are provided for. If new techniques are involved, particularly if on-line processing is being considered, functional and operational impacts should be studied with care.

- Particularly where new techniques or new areas of the business are involved, the Proposed System Study should be broad enough to consider alternative approaches, performance criteria, costs, and user service levels. To cite just one example, if on-line processing is being considered, costs should be estimated and the consequences of slower, far less expensive, batch techniques should be weighed in terms of environmental requirements.

- Organizational implications of the new system should be considered and accounted for. This element was brought up during the System Planning Study. It should be reconsidered here. If realization of the full benefits of a proposed system calls for reorganizing or restructuring the user organization, the consequences should be faced and recommendations should be tailored to the realities of the situation.

FINALIZING SYSTEM REQUIREMENTS

Implicit in the objectives and the definition tasks associated with the Proposed System Study should be a determination to finalize—freeze—System Requirements as a result of this activity. Obviously, any system development project must have enough flexibility to alter direction or activities to incorporate the unforeseen. But, it should be emphasized that such changes, once the system has been designed and technical development begun, are accomplished only at extremely great expense. Therefore, at every stage during the Proposed System Study, the users should be asked to examine solutions and procedures and to agree to them on a "last chance" basis.

In point of fact, many proposed changes which are introduced late in the system development process are not incorporated in the initial version of the operational system. Rather, constraints, schedules, budgets, time avail-abilities, and other practicalities lead to an approach under which system maintenance requests are prepared and documented even before the system is initially implemented. Then, modifications are added as priorities permit, after the initial version of the system is functioning routinely.

PROPOSED SYSTEM STUDY PRINCIPLES

The study of the proposed system remains highly interactive. Users must be closely involved because their evaluations and acceptances constitute the chief measure of success against which the new system will be measured.

As indicated previously, the Proposed System Study is output-oriented. The study begins with a definition of outputs and acceptance of their format and content by users. From that point, the system study can go back and define the inputs and processing necessary to achieve the output.

However, it must be borne in mind that output acceptability is the chief concern. After that, availability of input data and support files must be studied. These considerations, in turn, are followed by examination of the technical requirements of the system.

While the Proposed System Study is described within this work as a separate entity from the study of the present system and from succeeding activities, it should be realized that divisions of efforts are not actually that clear-cut. People do not divide their time or attention with the same definitive sharpness as must be done in describing these activities for the purposes of a book.

In the real world, a systems analyst working on a study of a present system realizes that he will be defining requirements of the proposed system as his next working assignment. In his mind, he is cataloging logical associations between present and proposed systems which will be carried forward. The astute analyst even begins executing some of the documentation for the Proposed System Study while he is working on the present system, setting these forms aside for use at the appropriate time.

The same, in general, applies across activity boundaries. The analyst knows that when System Requirements have been specified, he will have to move on to a greater technical depth during the System Specifications and Technical Requirements activities. These future challenges are in his mind if he is experienced at what he is doing. Therefore, although textual descriptions must, necessarily, be black and white in their description of functional operations, it is important, in reviewing the project management process as discussed here, that this perspective be kept in mind.

Again, the approach to be discussed in connection with the Proposed System Study is mechanistic, highly structured, and formatted. These techniques are offered as one method for doing the job. The discussion will be in terms of activity requirements. However, alternate methods exist and are equally acceptable as long as the functional requirements of the development process are accounted for. To illustrate, another approach to defining proposed systems is represented by a technique developed by NCR known as ADS, for Accurately Defined Systems. This approach, too, is output-oriented. Its emphasis is on graphic documentation.

PROPOSED SYSTEM STUDY WORK PLAN

As indicated in Figure 6-10, the Proposed System Study begins with a review of pertinent documents in the *System Planning Study Manual* and the *Present System Manual.* The same warning repeated earlier holds true: Care should be taken not to duplicate previous work, but to pick up where existing documentation leaves off.

OUTPUT DESIGN

The really critical task, and documentary result, of the Proposed System Study is the design of outputs or reports which initiate this effort. Maximum flexibility should be provided at this point. Analysts should avoid, if possible and appropriate, becoming "locked in" with conventional printer layout sheets or other highly structured documents.

Because these conventional report layout forms do tend to inhibit creative thinking and imaginative evaluation, the authors recommend more of a free-form document, like the one shown in Figure 6-11. This, as can be seen, has lightly printed guidelines. By design, these do not inhibit thinking or formatting to a given output technique. The same form, therefore, is equally applicable for laying out cathode-ray-tube displays, terminal inquiry formats, line printer reports, or even data base elements which are not printed formally but just represented for potential reference or reporting.

This is by way of stressing that, at this point in the system development process, the emphasis should be on communicating and understanding information requirements between users and systems analysts. Structure is unimportant. Content and comprehension are everything.

Note that the entries on the illustration on Figure 6-11 include identification for and relative positioning of data elements. At this point, users

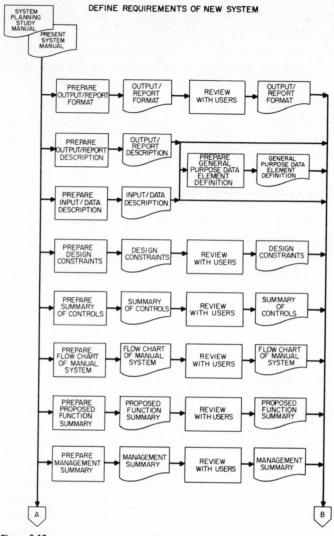

Figure 6-10a

and systems analysts interact to determine and describe the full content necessary in system output. In a subsequent task, this document can be referenced back against the data dictionary which has already been started for the new system. Data elements which have not already been cataloged can be incorporated in the provisions for the data base.

It is important to stress the interaction between users and systems analysts necessary to output specification. Several separate work sessions may be needed to settle on content and layout for a system output.

The user's job performance requirements provide the criteria for design and evaluation of outputs. In a typical interactive situation, a user can begin by telling the systems analyst the kind of information he needs to make the decisions for which he is responsible. The analyst, either during the work session or separately, can sketch an output layout. The user and analyst review this. Several iterations of critique and revision may be necessary to arrive at an acceptable product. The important thing to realize is that these efforts are essential. The entire design of the new system will be based upon the requirements incorporated in this document.

The unstructured form of the document used in Figure 6-11 also serves to emphasize a basic characteristic of this task: It is nontechnical. The form

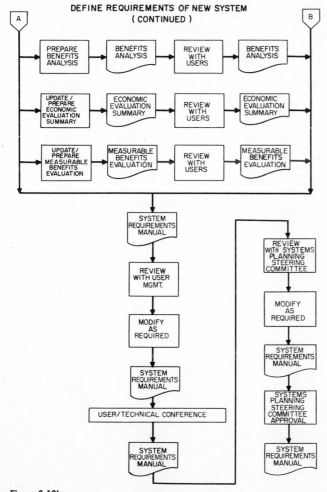

Figure 6-10b

OUTPUT/REPORT FORMAT

ORGANIZATION __ABC COMPANY__
APPLICATION TITLE __LABOR DISTRIBUTION__

PAGE _1_ OF _1_
PROJECT NO. _0235_
PREPARED BY _L. JONES_
DATE _2-14_

SEQUENCE DATA ELEMENT
DEPARTMENT
CLOCK NO.

LABOR DISTRIBUTION REPORT

DEPARTMENT	CLOCK NO.	REGULAR HOURS	OVERTIME HOURS	SHIFT BONUS HOURS	REGULAR DOLLARS	OVERTIME DOLLARS	TOTAL DOLLARS
GENERAL LEDGER DEPT. NUMBER	NUMBER ASSIGNED TO EACH EMPLOYEE	HOURS WORKED DURING 1 DAY =<8; OR 1 WK =<40	HOURS WORKED DURING 1 DAY >8; OR 1 WK >40	HOURS WORKED BETWEEN 5PM AND 7AM	REGULAR HOURS X HOURLY RATE	OVERTIME HOURS X 150% OF HOURLY RATE	SUM OF REGULAR $ + OVERTIME $ + SHIFT $
TOTAL BY CLOCK NO.		(SUM THIS COL.)	(SUM THIS COL.)	(SUM THIS COL.)	(SUM THIS COL.)	(SUM THIS COL.)	(SUM THIS COL.)
TOTAL BY DEPT.		"	"	"	"	"	"
TOTAL AT END OF REPT.		"	"	"	"	"	"

RATE DATA PRINT OUT

DEPARTMENT.	CLOCK NO.	HOURLY RATE
(SEE ABOVE)	(SEE ABOVE)	RATE OF PAY FIXED PER EMPLOYEE

Figure 6-11

illustrated is chiefly a vehicle by which the user stipulates what he expects to receive from the system.

In working with the user at this point, the systems analyst should not let himself get bogged down by future technical considerations or requirements. He should not introduce these into his discussions with the user. This is not the place to worry about the technical aspects of how the computer will produce these data or print this report. In particular, it is much too early for the analyst to let himself become concerned with how the report under discussion can be combined with or generated as a by-product of other processing which will be incorporated within the proposed system.

It should also be understood that a number of output or report layouts like the one shown in Figure 6-11 may be required in the design of a single system. An overall system effort may begin with the creation of literally dozens of output layouts like the one shown here. Each, of course, will be followed up with appropriate, supporting documentation.

OUTPUT SPECIFICATIONS

For each output stipulated for the proposed system, the analyst, with user concurrence, should prepare a preliminary technical description sufficient to carry the development effort into the next activity. A document like the one shown in Figure 6-12 has the information which will be used, during the next activity, for specifying System Requirements at a further technical depth.

INPUT REQUIREMENTS

Once output requirements have been determined and documented, the next task in the Proposed System Study is to identify any new input data which will be required to arrive at the specified output. An important distinction is to be made here. Data already accounted for in an existing system or elsewhere within already-prepared documentation need not be redefined at this point. Rather, the systems analyst, with user concurrence, specifies input data requirements at a technical level compatible with his specification of output data descriptions. This can be done on a form like the one shown in Figure 6-13.

This form also illustrates another important characteristic of the task level at this point: The systems analyst does not design forms within this activity. Rather, he specifies data content for elements not already accounted for in previous documentation.

OUTPUT/REPORT DESCRIPTION

ORGANIZATION *ABC COMPANY*
APPLICATION TITLE *LABOR DISTRIBUTION*

PAGE *1* OF *1*
PROJECT NO. *0-28*
PREPARED BY *J. JONES*
DATE *2-14*

| *101* DOCUMENT NUMBER | | | | COPY ATTACHED Y ☒ |

NAME: *LABOR DISTRIBUTION REPORT*   FORM NUMBER:

DISTRIBUTION DEPARTMENT NAME	DEPT. NO.
1. *EACH LINE DEPARTMENT*	—
2. *ACCOUNTING*	*2100*
3.	
4.	
5.	
6.	
7.	

SEQUENCE DATA ELEMENT	SUM ON	
DEPARTMENT	×	MAJOR
CLOCK NO.	×	
		↓
		MINOR

FREQUENCY

DAILY ☐   MONTHLY ☐   DEMAND INQUIRY ☐   WEEKLY ☒   OTHER ☐

PER PAGE PRINT LINE

	VOLUME		
	MIN.	AVE.	MAX.
HEADER LINES	*3*	*3*	*3*
DETAIL LINES	*10*	*20*	*25*
SUMMARY LINES	*10*	*20*	*20*
LINE TOTAL	*23*	*43*	*48*
SPACE	*5*	*5*	*5*
SKIP	*38*	*18*	*13*
TOTAL LINES ACCOUNTED FOR	*66*	*66*	*66*
TOTAL LINES AVAILABLE ON			
A *14 x 11* SIZE PAPER *66*	NO. OF PAGES *85*	*126*	*166*

OUTPUT OTHER THAN PRINTED DOCUMENT

MEDIA:	CARD	MAG. TAPE	PAP. TAPE	OTHER			
VOLUME OF RECORDS:							

COMMENTS

BURST AND BIND FORMS BEFORE DISTRIBUTION

USE STOCK PAPER

Figure 6-12

DATA ELEMENT CATALOGING

Once the output and input data elements have been defined, they should be, in effect, cataloged for compatibility with the system's data dictionary. This is done, through straightforward entries, on a document like the one shown in Figure 6-14.

SYSTEM CONSTRAINTS

After output and input data elements have been defined and cataloged— and before definition of processing requirements begins—system constraints should be identified and stated. This is done in narrative form.

As indicated in Figure 6-15, the constraints applied to the design of a new system fall into three general categories:

1. Scheduling and timing
2. Policy
3. Technical feasibility

At this level, the statement of constraints serves largely to establish communication and understanding between systems analysts and users. Constraints will be further identified and defined in greater technical depth during succeeding activities. At this point, however, it is important that

Figure 6-13

GENERAL PURPOSE DATA ELEMENT DEFINITION

ORGANIZATION *ABC COMPANY*
APPLICATION TITLE *LABOR DISTRIBUTION*

PAGE *1* OF *1*
PROJECT NO. *0.28*
PREPARED BY *J JONES*
DATE *2-16*

SUPPORT OF DOCUMENT NUMBER [*103*]   NAME *LABOR TRANSACTIONS*

DATA ELEMENT	FILE/SUB. NO.	ELE. NO.	SIZE	A/N	PICTURE	VOLUME %/FREQ.	SOURCE *
1. DEPARTMENT NO.	001	001	4	N	9999	20	NA
2. CLOCK NO.	001	002	6	N	999999	100	NA
3. REGULAR HOURS	001	003	3	N	599V9	100	NA
4. OVERTIME HOURS	001	004	3	N	599V9	50	NA
5. SHIFT BONUS HOURS	001	005	3	N	599V9	10	NA
NA - NOT APPLICABLE TO THIS DOCUMENT							

Figure 6-14

both user and systems analyst establish a basis of understanding for any operating requirements or difficulties which can be identified as early as possible within the system development process.

For example, if a system under development will call for the scheduling of a second shift in an organization's computer operations department, this is the point in the system project where implications should be considered from both a cost and feasibility standpoint. As another example, in the area of scheduling and timing, it could develop that stipulated input cannot be created in time to meet output schedules without putting impossible operational or cost burdens on the input section.

Similarly, legal or company policy situations which affect the proposed system should all be noted at this point.

Technical feasibility constraints to be listed are apt to involve either processing capacities or questions concerning the applicability of new hardware or software to the system under development. As was discussed in Chapter 5, members of the EDP operations group serve as key members of the project team in determining whether the system will run on installed equipment or whether new hardware or software are needed. If additional equipment or software is required, this group must coordinate delivery and implementation schedules closely with project requirements.

For any functional constraints identified in conjunction with the proposed system, the accountability factors within the environment of the proposed system must be taken into consideration during this relatively early design stage through the definition of controls which will be built into the proposed system. Every functional EDP system will be subject to some sort of verification and/or audit.

In this respect, controllers, auditors, inspectors, examiners, or reviewers by any other title should be considered as affected users of the proposed system. They should be dealt with interactively by the primary users and systems analysts. Their needs should be defined and recorded, as has been done in the form illustrated in Figure 6-16.

By incorporating these control requirements into system design at this point, they become a basic part of the procedures. They are dealt with much more efficiently than if they were to be handled later on an exception or maintenance basis. A system cannot go into full-scale operation without acceptable controls. Therefore, if provision is not made at this point, a major expense can be incurred later.

DESIGN CONSTRAINTS

PAGE _1_ OF _1_
PROJECT NO. _028_
PREPARED BY _J JONES_
DATE _2-18_

ORGANIZATION _ABC COMPANY_
APPLICATION TITLE _LABOR DISTRIBUTION_

A. SCHEDULE/TIMING B. POLICY C. TECHNICAL FEASIBILITY	DOCUMENT NUMBER
A. SCHEDULE/TIMING:	
1. LABOR DISTRIBUTION REPORT MUST BE PREPARED AND DISTRIBUTED BY 8:00 AM EACH MONDAY	
2. THE ON-LINE INQUIRY SYSTEM WILL BE OPERATIONAL BETWEEN 10:00 AM AND 3:30 P.M. MONDAY THRU FRIDAY	
B. POLICY:	
1. TIMEKEEPER WILL WORK EACH SATURDAY FOR 4 HOURS TO PREPARE THE INPUT	
2. DATA PROCESSING WILL WORK FROM 12:00 P.M. (MIDNIGHT) SUNDAY TO 8:00 A.M. THE UNION MAY REQUIRE THAT THE TIMEKEEPER BE PAID 8 HOURS PLUS OVERTIME FOR SATURDAY.	
C. TECHNICAL FEASIBILITY: THE EXISTING COMPUTER WILL REQUIRE EXPANSION TO HANDLE THE ON-LINE INQUIRY CAPABILITY. THE HARDWARE ADDITIONS ARE:	
1. 20 MILLION BYTES OF RANDOM ACCESS STORAGE	
2. 4 CRT'S WITH NECESSARY CONTROL UNITS AND LINE ADAPTERS	
3. 16,000 ADDITION CORE POSITIONS.	

APPROVED BY _W SMITH_
DATE _2-19_

Figure 6-15

```
                        SUMMARY OF CONTROLS
                                        PAGE  1  OF    1
                                        PROJECT NO.   028
                                        PREPARED BY   J. JONES
  ORGANIZATION  ABC COMPANY             DATE        2-18
  APPLICATION TITLE  LABOR DISTRIBUTION
```

DESCRIPTION OF CONTROL	DOCUMENT AND ADDED FUNCTION REFERENCE
INPUT CONTROL :	
TIMEKEEPERS RUN ADDING MACHINE	103
TAPE OF REGULAR LABOR HOURS	
BY DEPARTMENT	
OUTPUT CONTROL :	
DATA PROCESSING CONTROL SECTION	101
BALANCES TAPE OF LABOR	
TRANSACTIONS TO LABOR	
DISTRIBUTION REPORT	

APPROVED BY W. SMITH
DATE   2-19

Figure 6-16

PROPOSED SYSTEM FLOW CHART— MANUAL PROCEDURES

The next task specified in Figure 6-10 calls for development of a flow chart on the manual procedures to be incorporated within the new system. Note in the example illustrated in Figure 6-17 that this flow chart is similar to a corresponding representation developed during the study of the present system. Where the new system will replace existing procedures, a direct comparison between the two flow charts is intended. In practice, the user reviews these closely. Through them, he identifies the manual functions which may be added, deleted, or modified in the course of implementing the new system and bringing it into operation.

Where new manual functions will be needed to implement a proposed system, they are summarized and quantified on a form like the one illustrated in Figure 6-18. Note this is similar to the functional summary used in describing the manual portions of the present system. Within this context, the form is used to single out, describe, and indicate volume and working time requirements for new manual functions which do not currently exist or which will be substantially modified within the proposed system.

This task also brings forward and incorporates, on the same form, the functions within a present system which will be incorporated without change in the new one. In this way, it summarizes, by function, the complete manual processing and work time requirements for the proposed system. This

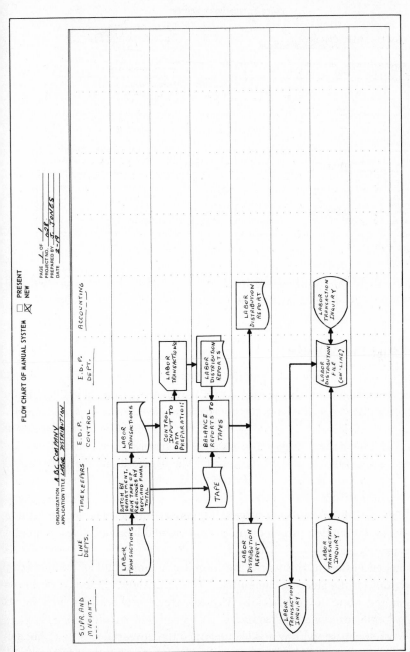

Figure 6-17

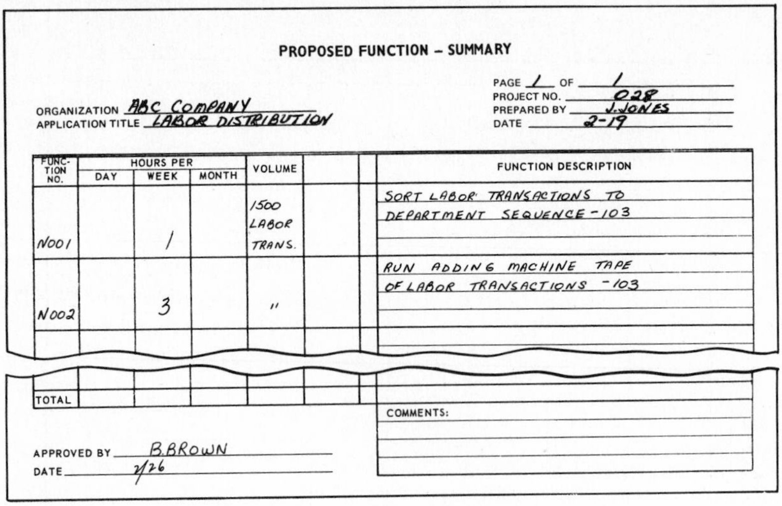

```
PROPOSED FUNCTION – SUMMARY
```

				PAGE _1_ OF _1_			
ORGANIZATION _ABC COMPANY_				PROJECT NO. _028_			
APPLICATION TITLE _LABOR DISTRIBUTION_				PREPARED BY _J. JONES_			
				DATE _2-19_			

FUNC-TION NO.	HOURS PER			VOLUME			FUNCTION DESCRIPTION
	DAY	WEEK	MONTH				
N001		1		1500 LABOR TRANS.			SORT LABOR TRANSACTIONS TO DEPARTMENT SEQUENCE - 103
N002		3		"			RUN ADDING MACHINE TAPE OF LABOR TRANSACTIONS - 103

TOTAL		COMMENTS:
APPROVED BY _B. BROWN_		
DATE _2/26_		

Figure 6-18

information, too, can be used for direct comparison between present and proposed systems as benefits and costs are quantified and evaluated.

MANAGEMENT SUMMARY

On the basis of study tasks and documentation generated to date, the project team begins, at this point, to pull together a Management Summary which will serve as the basis for steering committee review of this activity. Under the methodology which provides the basis for this book, a series of four documents are prepared in parallel. Actually, they may not be executed in the order shown. But, since the Management Summary illustrated in Figure 6-19 is the overview document supported by the others, it should be examined first.

Note that this calls for narrative statements covering a general description of the system under development, the anticipated benefits, a description of the processing which will take place, and a description of outputs. As discussed earlier in this work, the format is unimportant in summarizing activities for the steering committee. The form shown here is used for its discipline value, largely because it incorporates a checklist which serves as a guide for project personnel.

Work sheets supporting and leading up to the preparation of the Management Summary include the Benefits Analysis form shown in Figure 6-20. This is designed specifically to incorporate a yardstick within basic system documentation so that results of the system project can be measured realistically following Implementation—or at any time in the future.

One of the major difficulties encountered, historically, by EDP departments is a determination of their value and contributions to the sponsoring organization. After a system is implemented and operational, it becomes a part of the organization's way of life. Benefits and values tend to be assumed once they are routine.

Yet, as indicated earlier in this work, it is important that a continuing yardstick be applied to system development projects so that management can evaluate both established results and proposed system projects.

Further, if benefits are not identified early in a project—and individuals

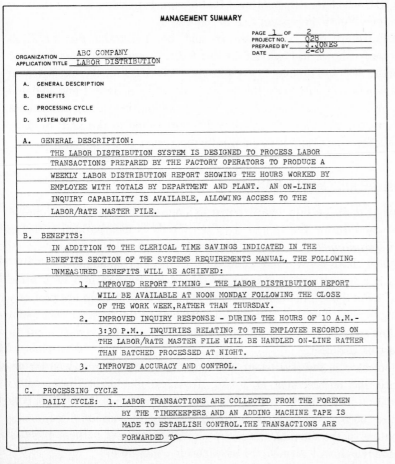

Figure 6-19a

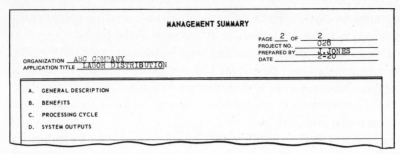

Figure 6-19b

do not undertake the responsibility to realize them—they may, in fact, never happen. The approved work sheet in Figure 6-20, then, provides a sort of IOU which management says that it expects to redeem from the user group once it gets the system that is requested.

The Economic Evaluation Summary and the Measurable Benefits Evaluation forms shown in Figures 6-21 and 6-22, respectively, were initiated during the System Planning Study activity. As a basis for the management report which will culminate this activity, they are reviewed and updated as appropriate. As indicated, they serve as supporting documentation for the Management Summary which will be presented to the EDP Systems Planning Steering Committee along with the *System Requirements Manual.*

SYSTEM REQUIREMENTS MANUAL

As indicated in the flow chart shown in Figure 6-10, the documentation accumulated during the Proposed System Study is incorporated within a *System Requirements Manual.* The first draft of this manual, as indicated in the flow chart, is reviewed, in detail, with the user manager.

This is a formal conference which should be entered into with some gravity, even though the members of the system project team are probably working in close personal harmony at this stage of the project. The point should be stressed that approval of the manual is an act of commitment on the part of the user.

As indicated in the flow chart, the modified manual is reviewed for acceptance and endorsement at a User/Technical Conference prior to its presentation to the EDP Systems Planning Steering Committee. This conference is both a review and a planning session. In addition to endorsing the content of the manual, the group also plans for and outlines the presentation which will be made to the steering committee.

At this particular juncture in the project, the User/Technical Conference holds particular significance.   Through the approach of probing increasingly deeper in successive activities, the project team has reached a point where, at the conclusion of the System Requirements activity, the group has developed a specific, definitive picture of what the new system will look like.   At this point, the team should be able to pinpoint costs, benefits, and other operating implications with greater precision than at any point previously in the project.   This increased depth of evaluation and commitment should be reflected in both the *System Requirements Manual* and the presentation to the steering committee.

BENEFITS

PAGE _/_ OF _/_
PROJECT NO. _Q-28_
ORGANIZATION _ABC COMPANY_
PREPARED BY _J. JONES_
APPLICATION TITLE _LABOR DISTRIBUTION_
DATE _2-21_

DESCRIPTION OF BENEFIT
   HOW BENEFIT WILL BE ACHIEVED
   WHEN BENEFIT WILL BE ACHIEVED
   VALUE OF BENEFIT
   METHOD OF CALCULATION
   RESPONSIBILITY FOR ACHIEVING BENEFIT

BENEFIT #1 : REDUCTION OF CLERICAL TIME :
          · REQUIRED TO PRODUCE WEEKLY LABOR DISTRIBUTION REPORT
          · REQUIRED TO ANSWER INQUIRIES
HOW — THROUGH PREPARATION OF REPORT ON COMPUTER
HOW — THROUGH ON-LINE INQUIRY TO DATA FILE

WHEN — ONE MONTH FROM THE DATE THE REPORT PREPARATION IS
       PLACED ON THE COMPUTER

VALUE — $7,020/YR.

METHOD OF CALCULATION: 40 HRS./WK × $3.00/HR. × 52 WEEKS
                 5 HRS/WK × $2.00/HR. × 52 WEEKS

RESPONSIBILITY FOR ACHIEVING BENEFIT : PLANT CONTROLLER

BENEFIT #2 : IMPROVED ACCESS TO INFORMATION FOR MANAGEMENT (UNMEASURABLE)

Figure 6-20

ECONOMIC EVALUATION SUMMARY

PAGE ___/___ OF ___/___
PROJECT NO. __028__

ORGANIZATION _ABC COMPANY_

APPLICATION TITLE _LABOR DISTRIBUTION_

PREPARED BY _J. JONES_

DATE _2-21_

Proposed System:	YEAR 1	YEAR 2	YEAR 3	YEAR 4	YEAR 5	
Development Costs	12,600	—	—	—	—	
Operating Costs- Non EDP	59,050	50,650	50,650	50,650	50,650	
EDP Recurring Costs	36,900	36,900	36,900	44,900	44,900	
Measurable Benefits	(10,200)	(9,200)	(9,200)	(9,200)	(9,200)	
Gross Cost (Benefit) Proposed System	98,350	78,350	78,350	86,350	86,350	
Present System:						
Operating Costs - Non EDP	80,000	85,000	90,000	95,000	105,000	
EDP Recurring Costs						
Total Present System	80,000	85,000	90,000	95,000	105,000	
Net Savings (Cost)	(18,350)	6,650	11,350	8,650	18,650	

Figure 6-21

A preliminary presentation to the steering committee, conducted by the user member of the committee if feasible, results in possible modification and updating of the *System Requirements Manual.* After modification, the manual comes before the committee again for final review and for a major continue/terminate decision.

Approval at this point authorizes the project team to go ahead with a comprehensive, expensive series of technical steps prior to another formal review. On approval of the *System Requirements Manual,* the project

MEASURABLE BENEFITS EVALUATION

PAGE ___/___ OF ___/___
PROJECT NO. __028__

ORGANIZATION _ABC COMPANY_

APPLICATION TITLE _LABOR DISTRIBUTION_

PREPARED BY _J. JONES_

DATE _2-21_

BENEFIT DESCRIPTION	Cash Flow by Period					
	1	2	3	4	5	6
REDUCED FILING SPACE - 400 SQ. FT.	$ 1,200	1,200	1,200	1,200	1,200	1,200
SELL FILING CABINETS	1,000	—	—	—	—	—
REDUCED COST OF PREPARING INPUT FOR PAYROLL	8,000	8,000	8,000	8,000	8,000	8,000
TOTAL	$ 10,200	9,200	9,200	9,200	9,200	9,200

Figure 6-22

moves forward into the System Specifications activity. This marks a continuing transition into increasing technical and complexity depths for the project.

CHAPTER SEVEN

System Specifications

ACTIVITY SCOPE

System Specifications is a transitional activity. Its objective is to begin with the *System Requirements Manual* developed by an interdisciplinary team made up largely of user personnel during the System Requirements activity and to add the technical dimensions necessary for full system development.

System Specifications, therefore, is an activity carried on entirely by technical personnel, chiefly systems analysts, closely supported by technical services, operations, and programming people. The activity gets its name from the specifications which will be developed. These will provide an initial, technical level of description of user requirements. Ultimately, the *System Specifications Manual* created during this activity will serve as the basis for further, more detailed preparation of programming specifications, hardware configuration planning, hardware specifications, communications network specifications, implementation planning, implementation scheduling, and so on.

More specifically, at this point, the activity is designed to establish the kind and size of computer which will be needed, operating system, executive program, application programs, and actual processing times which will be required when the system is operational.

In particular, personnel assigned to this activity will try to identify and quantify any technical constraints which might impact the system under development. For example, such factors as the times needed to capture and process data will be compared with data availabilities specified in the *System Requirements Manual.* Should any potential schedule bottlenecks appear, they will be pinpointed and dealt with during this activity.

As another example, if the new system is to run on an existing computer installation, operations personnel would be asked to evaluate processing time availabilities in light of requirements for the new system. Again, should any constraints appear, required adjustments will have to be identified during this activity.

ACTIVITY WORK FLOW

Figure 7-1 is a flow chart diagraming the tasks and documents associated with the System Specifications activity. As this illustration indicates, activity work patterns begin with a review of the *System Requirements Manual.*

- The first three tasks during the System Specifications activity—output layouts, input data layouts, and data flow diagrams—are conducted by senior systems analysts working in close coordination with qualified user members of the project team. The object of this coordination is to establish validity for the technical interpretation placed on user requirement specifications incorporated in the *System Requirements Manual.*
- After user concurrence has been established for the portions of the system where interaction between EDP and user groups will be involved, the systems analysts go on to perform two further tasks—master file design and definition of computer process and run/module functions.
- After the initial five design tasks have been performed, the systems analysts meet with EDP operations, technical services, and programming people for a full review during a Technical Feasibility Conference.
- Following the Technical Feasibility Conference, the emphasis turns to establishing implementation controls. On the basis of conference findings, the design documents are modified as required and con-

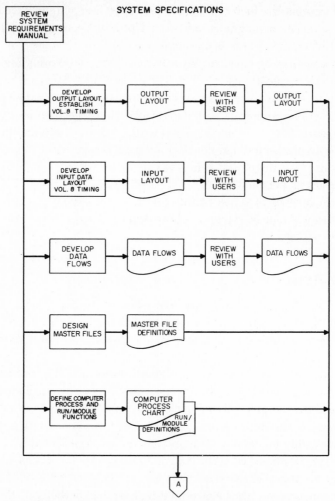

Figure 7-1a

straints are identified and defined. Then, in two succeeding tasks, operational controls and backup procedures are defined and documented. At this point, document generation for the activity has been completed, unless revision requirements are uncovered during the User/Technical Conference which follows.

- As indicated in Figure 7-1, the end product of the System Specifications activity is a manual which becomes input to the more technical activity which follows, Technical Requirements.

To put these work requirements in perspective, System Specifications is a relatively short activity, primarily interpretive in nature. The short duration is due largely to the fact that most of the work is done by experienced professionals who are setting up work specifications for each other. In a project which will involve 4 man-years of total system development activity, System Specifications assignments would consume between 6 and 8 man-weeks.

SENSITIVITY REQUIREMENTS

As indicated, in its basic nature the System Specifications activity is both interactive and transitional.   Therefore, attention must be focused on main-

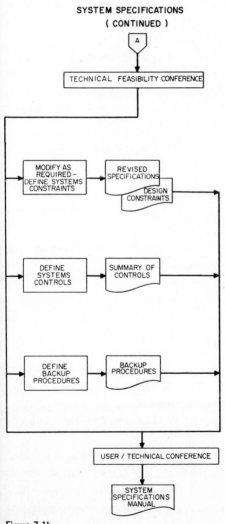

Figure 7-1b

tenance of the rapport and coordinating relationships between the EDP and user groups which should have reached a high point in cooperative effort during the preceding, System Requirements activity. The outputs and constraints within the System Specifications activity area are, to be sure, primarily technical. But, it should also be kept in mind that this is, typically, a point in the project where users can begin to feel that they are losing touch or being left out. Such conditions should simply not be allowed to develop.

Conversely, conscious attention to interaction between EDP and user people at this point can help keep interest in the project stimulated. A continuing consciousness is necessary because a system project is a long, drawn-out endeavor. Enthusiasm is always high at the outset. It is at this point in the process, however, that discouragement, disinterest, or loss of interest are apt to set in among users and/or management. Personnel involved in the System Specifications activity should take special steps to be sure that this does not happen. Implications and techniques for establishing user involvement and rapport are discussed in greater depth in Chapter 11.

OUTPUT/REPORT LAYOUT

Because of the transitional nature of the System Specifications activity, the user-oriented working approach of beginning with output design is still retained at this point. That is, System Specifications procedures begin with output design—to a more technical level than was done in support of user conferences during the System Requirements activity. Figure 7-2, for example, illustrates the type of Output/Report Layout created during the System Specifications activity. Note that the body of the form itself contains standard entries under which headings are spelled out according to print position. "X" symbols are used to indicate alphanumeric print positions, and "9" symbols are used to indicate computed outputs.

It should also be mentioned that the title of this form, Output/Report Layout, is general purpose in nature. That is, the same principles apply whether the design is for a report to be generated on an on-line printer, a transaction document, a cathode-ray-tube display, a typewriter terminal, or any other output device.

Obviously, in situations where system output is neither printed nor displayed, a layout presentation appropriate to the application will be developed. For example, if the output were to be a punched or magnetic tape to operate a numerically controlled machine tool, the designers could use

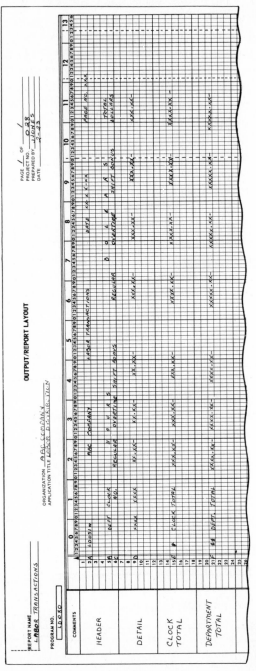

Figure 7-2

a data layout form like the one which will be discussed in conjunction with input record diagraming.

In other words, this technique applies in any EDP system design situation, from the simplest to the most sophisticated, even though the application example used in Figure 7-2 is, for illustration purposes, a relatively simple printout report for a labor distribution application.

Note that a program number has been assigned. In general, this will follow the specific application throughout the project. As a rule, the numbering systems used within the procedures described here are detailed to a run/module level. In the case of the report diagramed in Figure 7-2, for example, the number would apply to this specific run.

Note also that sections and lines of the report have been identified in the left margin. The alphabetic designations for report print lines will be picked up as the basis of more detailed technical design tasks during the next, Technical Requirements, activity. The descriptions in the "comments" column at the far left are the mnemonic titles given to output lines for identification throughout the system design process.

INPUT LAYOUT

Input layout during the System Specifications activity is aimed at representing data in the image format which will be presented to the computer. Typically, design is done with the aid of a data input layout form like the one shown in Figure 7-3. Note that this particular form is modular in design. Each line contains spaces for eighty data characters, making the

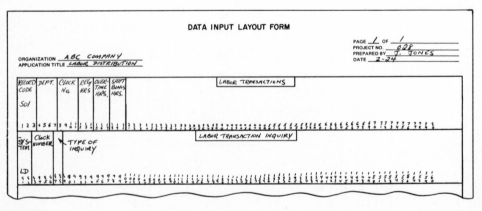

Figure 7-3

form usable either for multiple card input situations or record formats involving on-line terminals, direct tape, or disc entries.

Input design, with a form of this type, is a relatively simple matter of transposing data elements from source documents into the sequence and data element length to be presented to the computer. Note that this is done simply by ruling off character/numeral positions on the layout form and identifying each data element with the name previously assigned in the data glossary during the System Requirements activity. This data glossary, it should be stressed, will become the basic nomenclature guide throughout the remainder of the system project.

DATA FLOW DIAGRAMS

Once input and output specifications have been developed and agreed to in coordination with users, graphic diagrams of processing steps are developed on forms like the one shown in Figure 7-4.

In simplest terms, these flow diagrams are communication tools. They help users and technical people understand each other in describing and specifying what is happening within a system. Between technical people, such diagrams, understandably, become more detailed. But they serve the same function—making sure that all bases have been touched between the initiation point, or input, and the delivery of final system results.

Rules governing preparation of flow diagrams are straightforward: Standard flow chart symbols are used. Individual departments or areas where system functions take place are identified in separate columns. This format of diagram, as distinct from conventional system flow charts, is designed to highlight departmental or functional interfacing within a total system. The usefulness of this diagraming technique applies chiefly at the functional level, as indicated in the accompanying illustration.

It should also be pointed out that the technique is equally effective in charting manual subsystems, as the accompanying illustration does, or in diagraming distribution, use, modification, reentry, reprocessing, and so on for computer-produced documentation.

During the System Specifications activity, the actual value of the data flow diagram as a communication tool rests with the fact that both users and technical people have graphic presentations of just what is happening to the information flow of the system. During more detailed technical activities, the same form can be used to outline data flow for either the present or proposed systems.

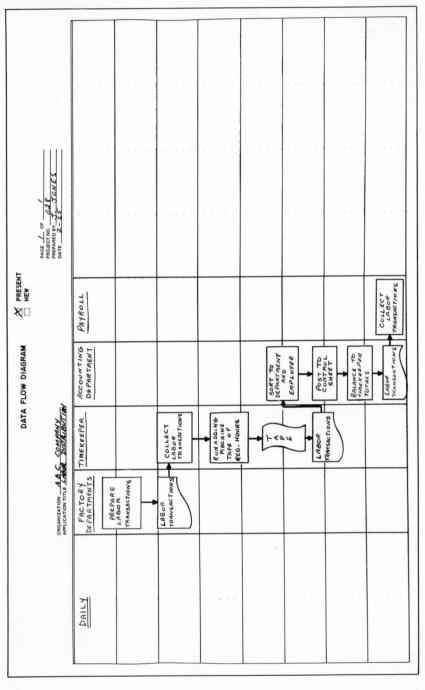

Figure 7-4

MASTER FILE DESIGN

During the System Specifications activity, data files are defined to the master-file level. Although file definition procedures are uniform throughout system development, it is important to understand that the level of detail at this point remains within user comprehension but is still meaningful enough to serve as a basis for further technical design by EDP people. Figures 7-5 and 7-6 show the types of working forms used in this task. Figure 7-5, obviously, is the first page of the document set used in file definition. Figure 7-6 is used where file size requires additional space.

Note that the heading areas provided in Figure 7-5 call for a number of processing-relevant entries. For example, data entry boxes are provided beside entry lines for designation of the user, the system description, and the file name. These will ultimately be used in setting up live system files. Further, spaces are provided for entry of identifications of up to seven separate programs which use this file. Also designated are storage media, file label, record length, the number of records per block, block length, and the number of records in the total file.

The "Sequence Data Element" portion of this form is used for listing, in

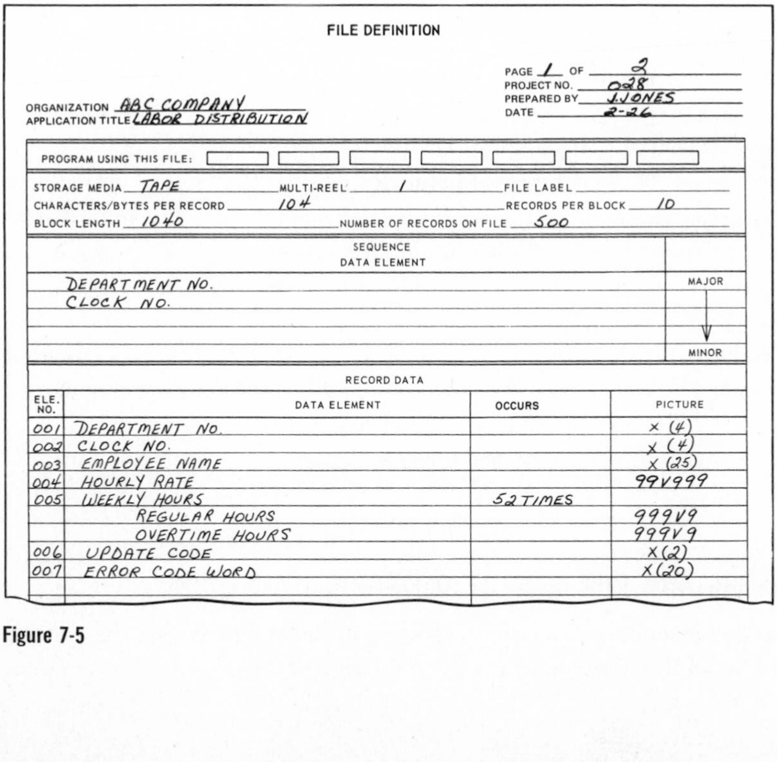

Figure 7-5

| FILE DEFINITION | PAGE _2_ OF ___3___ |
| PROJECT NO. ___O28___ |
| PREPARED BY ___J JONES___ |
| DATE ___2-26___ |

ORGANIZATION _ABC COMPANY_
APPLICATION TITLE _LABOR DISTRIBUTION_

RECORD DATA			
ELE. NO.	DATA ELEMENT	OCCURS	PICTURE
	THIS FORM WOULD BE USED IN		
	THE EVENT THAT ADDITIONAL DATA		
	ELEMENTS MUST BE DESCRIBED. FOR		
	PURPOSES OF THIS EXAMPLE THIS SHEET IS		
	NOT REQUIRED.		

Figure 7-6

order of prioritization, the significant data elements which control the ordering of the file.

The body of the form is used to define file content for identification within data element catalogs used by program compilers such as COBOL and to identify all data elements within a file for processing and programming purposes. Each element is numbered sequentially and described with its data glossary term.

In the column following the data element description, the analyst enters, as appropriate, the occurrence frequency of data elements which will be repeated within the file record. In the illustration in Figure 7-5, for example, the entry of the number 52 in the "occurs" column would tell the programmer to provide space to accommodate weekly hours worked for every week in the year for the employee.

A final descriptive requirement in file definition is the picture, or delineation, of the data element as the computer will see it. Again, standard symbolism is used. An "X" indicates an alphanumeric field. A "9" indicates a computed field. A "V" implies a decimal position. The numerals in parentheses indicate data element width in terms of total alphanumeric characters of input. Note that this width figure is not provided for computed data elements. This is because the compiler for each different make of computer handles this requirement for computed data elements. In different cases, a computed numeral might occupy a full-byte position or may be "packed" two to the byte.

PROCESSING AND RUN/MODULE DEFINITION

During the System Specifications activity, computer processing flow charts are developed to a file/report level. As indicated in Figure 7-7, the detail

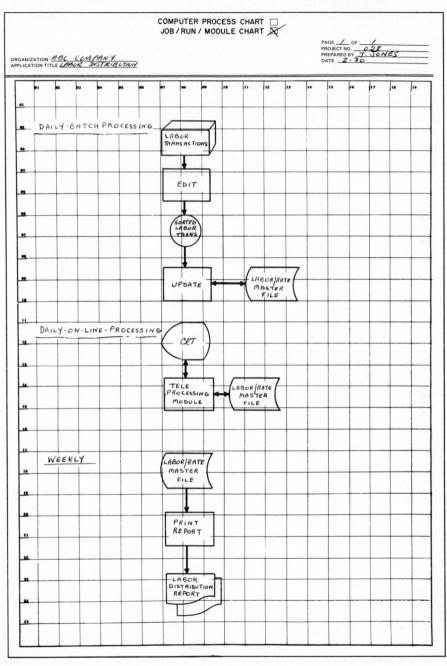

COMPUTER PROCESS CHART ☐
JOB / RUN / MODULE CHART ☒

PAGE _1_ OF _1_
PROJECT NO. _028_
PREPARED BY _J. JONES_
DATE _2-30_

ORGANIZATION _ABC COMPANY_
APPLICATION TITLE _LABOR DISTRIBUTION_

DAILY-BATCH PROCESSING

LABOR TRANSACTIONS

EDIT

SORTED LABOR TRANS

UPDATE — LABOR/RATE MASTER FILE

DAILY-ON-LINE-PROCESSING

CRT

TELE PROCESSING MODULE — LABOR/RATE MASTER FILE

WEEKLY

LABOR/RATE MASTER FILE

PRINT REPORT

LABOR DISTRIBUTION REPORT

Figure 7-7

is kept simple enough to keep the document valid as a communication tool in user interaction situations.

Note, however, that volume factors, such as file sizes, run lengths, run frequencies, and so on, are incorporated in this documentation.

The form illustrated in Figure 7-7 is general purpose in nature. It can be used either for processing charts or for run/module diagraming.

Also associated with the processing definition task during the System Specifications activity is the preparation of a form incorporating the Run/Module Function Design, illustrated in Figure 7-8. One of these forms is executed for each function specified on a computer process chart. This

Figure 7-8

form serves chiefly as a vehicle for communicating work specifications between members of the technical group. As a rule, it is not presented in discussions with users. Elements of this form provide areas for describing the operation functionally, for identifying input files, for describing functions within each processing step, and for describing outputs from each function. Note that columns are provided on the form for cross reference entries with other pertinent technical documentation identifying inputs, processing, decision tables, output definition forms, and so on.

TABLE DEFINITION FORMS

As a further step in processing definition, systems analysts prepare processing definition documentation associated with the functions listed on the form in Figure 7-8 on an as-needed basis. To illustrate, the entry of the number "DT 1" alongside the "update labor/rate file" description indicates that a decision table document, shown in Figure 7-9, has been prepared to describe this function.

As the printed form indicates, other symbols for supporting function descriptions are available as part of the system:

TF = table form
MPF = multipurpose form
PS = printer support sheet

The use of these three forms will be described in Chapter 8.

To illustrate the process under discussion, the decision table in Figure 7-9 provides spaces for indication of conditions, actions, and rules for application.

Greater depth of explanation on design and technique for decision tables is beyond the scope of this chapter. Though further discussion on this subject will be incorporated in the next chapter, a full-dress review of decision tables will provide enough material for a book in itself. A complete technical discussion of this subject, therefore, is beyond the scope of this work.

TECHNICAL FEASIBILITY CONFERENCE

This is primarily a work session among EDP professionals. The documentation developed up to this point in the System Specifications activity is reviewed in detail and "wrung out" in an effort to identify errors, problems, or previously undiscovered constraints.

DECISION TABLE NO. __1__

PAGE _1_ OF _1_
PROJECT NO. __ORR__
PREPARED BY __J.JONES__
DATE __3-2__

ORGANIZATION _ABC COMPANY_
APPLICATION TITLE _LABOR DISTRIBUTION_

TABLE NAME: _LABOR COST COMPUTATION_

LINE	CONDITION/ACTION	RULE → 1	2	3	4	5	6	7	8	9
1	END OF FILE	Y	N							
2	IS REGULAR HOURS PUNCHED	Y	–		N					
3	IS OVERTIME HOURS PUNCHED	Y	–	N	–	Y	–	N		
4	IS SHIFT BONUS HOURS PUNCHED	Y	N	Y	N	Y	N	Y	N	
10	REGULAR DOLLARS = REGULAR HOURS * (HOURLY +.005)	X	X	X	X					
11	OVERTIME DOLLARS = OVERTIME HOURS * 150 % (HRS.+.005)	X	X							
12	SHIFT DOLLARS = SHIFT BONUS HOURS * $.10	X		X						
13	ERROR; NO SHIFT OR OVERTIME WITHOUT REGULAR					X	X	X		
14	NEXT RECORD	X	X	X	X	X	X	X	X	
	GO TO – – F (FUNCTION); R (RULE, SAME TABLE); T (TABLE)	T2	R1	R1	R1	R1	R1	R1	R1	

NOTES: THE ERROR MESSAGE AT LINE 13 SHOULD BE DISPLAYED IN THE "DOLLARS" AREA OF THE REPORT, TO THE RIGHT OF A DISPLAY OF THE 501 RECORD

Figure 7-9

This conference is something of a technical summit meeting. All groups who will contribute to the technical aspects of system development are represented. All participate. Each group states its problems, constraints, or acceptance of specifications to the level incorporated within this activity. In a technical sense, this is a planning session. For example:

- Programming personnel participating in this conference contribute initial estimates of their time and schedule requirements for the preparation of technical specifications, as well as the writing and testing of programs. These estimates are on the level of individual, identified program modules.
- The operations people involved in this session will reaffirm their earlier commitment, that the proposed system will, in fact, run on installed equipment or indicate whether newly specified equipment will handle the job and can be accommodated in available facilities.
- Technical services personnel reaffirm their earlier commitment that existing software support will handle the new system, whether new software will be needed or whether operating systems or software will have to be modified.

As part of this joint task, the economic and operational forecast for the proposed system is reviewed and revised as necessary. The figures which are accumulated at this session are, in turn, compared closely with those developed during the System Requirements activity—which served as authorization for initiation of the technical development of the system by the EDP Systems Planning Steering Committee. One of the reasons for a cost review at this point is that the succeeding task during the System Specifications activity will include identification and documentation of system constraints. Since the economics of any project are potentially a major source of constraint, it is important that the Technical Feasibility Conference cover the entire spectrum of functional system conditions.

Should constraints beyond the boundaries of steering committee approval emerge, the activity is halted at this point until they can be reviewed with the systems manager, the user group, and, if necessary, the steering committee.

Allowing that this in-depth technical review indicates feasibility for continuance, the activity proceeds to its next task.

CONSTRAINT DEFINITION

In the task which follows the Technical Feasibility Conference, modifications and constraints identified during the conference are defined and documented. These constraints, it should be stressed, represent a next level from those discussed and outlined in Chapter 6. As part of the earlier activity, general operating constraints, such as work schedules of user groups, were identified and documented. At this level, system modifications and constraints fall into such areas as available processing time, input volumes, and the time needed to capture data, and so on.

Forms used for reporting constraints during this activity are similar to those described in the last chapter. If modifications are indicated, the already-prepared forms are either corrected or redrafted. The importance of documenting all applicable constraints during this task cannot be overemphasized. Even though the documents are of a qualitative, descriptive nature, it is important that they be executed just as diligently as forms which call for checking off of alternatives or entry of specific data elements.

CONTROL DEFINITION

The relationship of the control definition task within this activity as compared with the fulfillment of the same responsibility during the System Requirements activity is approximately the same as was indicated above in relation to system constraints.

The same form is used for listing controls as was done in the earlier activity. Once again, the purpose of the task is to carry controls to a level of detail commensurate with the activity as a whole. For example, where controls in the System Requirements activity dealt with end-product documents, during this activity the task would delve down to establishing subtotals, end-of-page totals, file control totals, working control totals covering file reference, and so on.

BACKUP PROCEDURE DEFINITION

Although this task is generally associated with on-line systems, the requirements for backup should be considered in connection with the development of any EDP system. For example, even where a system utilizes batch-processing techniques, provision should be made for identifying and arranging to use an alternate computer where operating or maintenance bottlenecks are encountered.

Another aspect of this task could involve planning for protection against loss of files through accident or disaster. Some schemes will call for the remote storage of interim files. In other cases, tapes or discs from one day will be saved to the next as backup in the event of damage to storage media.

With on-line systems, of course, there must be off-line subsystems which are activated when communication is interrupted between user and computer. Backup procedure planning in the case of an on-line system should also include specifications for situations where the system will switch to alternate processors. For example, with on-line savings-account systems used by banks, it is common to have two processors installed at the central facility. Typically, one of these is providing on-line service while the other is doing off-line batch work. In the event of on-line system failure, mechanical or system-activated switches are frequently provided to bring the alternate processor into the on-line loop.

USER/TECHNICAL CONFERENCE

This is a final activity review. Based on constraints, controls, or other factors introduced following the Technical Feasibility Conference, another overall examination is applied to the projected costs, benefits, operating feasibility factors, schedules, and other elements of the system under development.

If all conditions still remain within the bounds approved by the EDP

Systems Planning Steering Committee, the systems manager can authorize continuation of the project into the next activity.

If information uncovered during this activity indicates any deviation from the previously accepted commitment in terms of benefits, operations, constraints, costs, or other specifications, the steering committee should be advised and a review by the committee should be arranged.

SYSTEM SPECIFICATIONS MANUAL

This manual is a compilation of all documentation generated during the activity. If the activity has been accomplished according to plan, the manual is passed along as the basis for the Technical Requirements activity.

CHAPTER EIGHT

Technical Requirements

ACTIVITY SCOPE

During this activity, system development is carried to a level of detail which will serve as the working basis for programming and operational implementation. The documentation generated will be complete enough so that the programming group will have all the functional design specifications needed to proceed with actual coding. Further, this documentation will be designed with a modularity which will permit both tight scheduling and working control during the actual writing of programs.

To make this level of documentation feasible, all the decisions must be made during this activity which will control the run/module breakdown of the application programs and the work units to be used in assigning them for coding.

Under the creeping-commitment approach, Technical Requirements is an activity of medium-range expense which gets the project ready for the massive outlays which will be involved in program preparation. Actual working time and duration of the Technical Requirements activity will, of course, vary with the size and scope of the individual system project. As a general rule of thumb, about 5 percent of the total effort will be expended during this activity. In the base-reference project used within this work, involving 4 man-years of systems analysis time, Technical Requirements would call for about 10 man-weeks.

This activity is also in an intermediate area functionally. The previous activity, System Specifications, started with a user interface and was designed to interpret user requirements for technical people. Now technical people take this documentation, as represented in the *System Specifications Manual,* and interpret it in still greater technical depth for those highly specialized people who will be closely involved in the technical aspects of the project.

ACTIVITY RESPONSIBILITY

The Technical Requirements activity is carried out entirely by EDP professionals. Actual task assignments during this activity will depend on the individual backgrounds, likes, dislikes, work schedules, and time availabilities of the people assigned to the effort.

Assignments within this activity will depend initially on the background and skills of the system project leader himself. Actual performance of Technical Requirements tasks is best handled by a person with several years of programming experience. The system project leader may have this qualification. On the other hand, he may have been a system designer initially. Or, as another possibility, he may have been a programmer during the second generation era and a third generation systems man. In other words, he may be a former programmer who is not technically current. If the system project leader has not maintained his programming proficiency, direct supervision of Technical Requirements tasks is probably best assigned to someone who has.

From another viewpoint, the jobs to be performed during Technical Requirements lend themselves well to the provision of advancement opportunities for promising senior programmers. The tasks associated with this activity can provide logical steps upward in the career path of a person who started as a programmer. Wherever possible, experience has shown it best to use this activity to provide advancement and achievement opportunities for promising programmers. Also, the continuing shortage of qualified people makes advancement-from-within potential attractive.

No matter who is assigned to job performance during this activity, however, it should be stressed that there is no shift of responsibility. The system project leader must be totally cognizant. The responsibility for this activity is his entirely—even if he does none of the actual work.

During this activity, the system project leader will determine whether or not to specify programming logic as part of Technical Requirements documentation. As a general rule, particularly with business applications, programming logic decisions are left to the programming group. However, where special requirements exist in this area, as they would if a complex algorithm were necessary as part of a production line scheduling system, this can be developed and specified during the Technical Requirements activity.

Administration of this activity is rendered practical through the cumulative documentation approach referred to earlier. The system project leader should satisfy himself that all the necessary forms and reports are being executed fully and on time. He should review them on a scheduled basis with all project personnel involved in this activity. He must be able to report to EDP management on the status and quality of work progress on a regular basis—generally at weekly review meetings.

WORK DEFINITION

At this point in system development, functional diagraming is done at three separate levels of computer processing detail:

- *Job.* This is an overall, separately identifiable application from a user standpoint.
- *Run.* A run is a subdivision of the job for processing convenience and efficiency.
- *Module.* A module is the basic unit of computer processing. Groups of modules are incorporated within runs, which, in turn, make up jobs.

An understanding of these levels of documentation and specification is necessary to a discussion of the Technical Requirements activity work flow, which is diagramed in Figure 8-1. During this discussion, it will be noted that the documentation generated utilizes essentially the same design, report, and specification forms introduced in the last chapter. For this activity, alternate heading designations are checked to indicate the use to which the form is being put. And, of course, the level of detail applied by project personnel is at greater depth.

ACTIVITY WORK FLOW

In brief, the task sequence during the Technical Requirements activity is as follows:

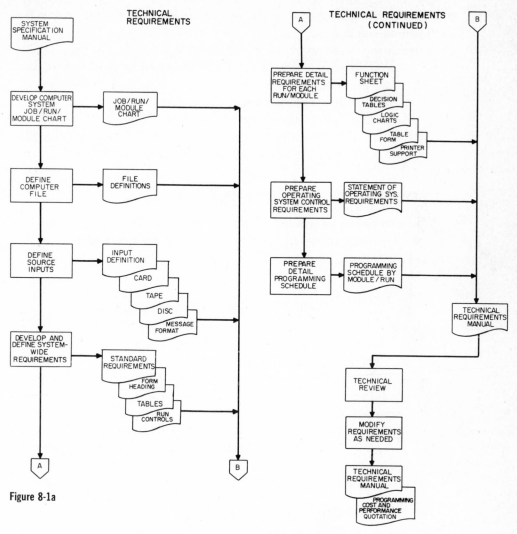

Figure 8-1a

Figure 8-1b

- A series of job/run/module flow charts is developed. These break down computer programs and processing as they will be executed in the operational system.
- Within the framework established by the flow charts, computer files are defined in technical terms. These definitions diagram all files as they will be presented to and output from each module, run, or job.
- Inputs are defined in technical detail.

- Job, run, and module specifications are defined in terms of operating and output requirements.
- All the necessary detail requirements for program coding—function sheets, decision tables, logic charts, table forms, printer support sheets—are prepared for each module, run, and job.
- Operating system requirements are defined.
- A programming schedule is developed.
- All documentation is incorporated in a *Technical Requirements Manual*, which is reviewed, modified as necessary, and finalized.

DEVELOPING JOB/RUN/MODULE CHARTS

Figure 8-2 shows a typical flow chart at the job/run level. The diagram in the illustration covers the processing of daily labor transactions. Three runs are involved in this job:

1. Transactions are sorted for processing.
2. Files are updated.
3. Errors are identified and merged into a file which will be used, in a separate run, to report them for user correction.

In carrying out this task, the experience of a senior programmer highly familiar with the equipment to be used is necessary to establish effective scope for jobs and runs. In the case illustrated, there are fairly standard systems to fall back on for guidance in breaking down the job into processing components. However, in more advanced applications, the experience of the designer assigned to this specific task could become a make-or-break factor. Selection of the right man and documentation of his efforts are critical, particularly at this stage in system development.

DEFINING COMPUTER FILES

During the System Specifications activity, master files were defined and their content and specifications were agreed to by users. It was indicated in the discussion of this subject in the last chapter that the master-file definition would serve as input to the design and documentation of working file requirements in support of program execution.

Within Technical Requirements, then, detailed definitions are developed for each file which will be needed within the system. These include transient and working files as well as those which will be stored on magnetic media for run or job interfacing.

Within this specific task, file definition begins with the examination and

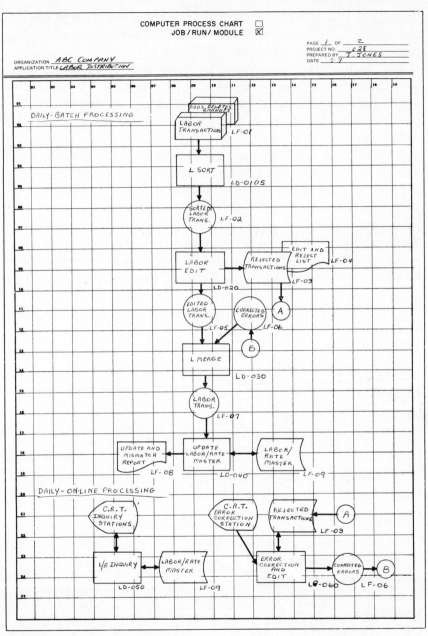

COMPUTER PROCESS CHART ☐
JOB / RUN / MODULE ☒

PAGE _1_ OF _2_
PROJECT NO. _c28_
PREPARED BY _T. JONES_
DATE _5.7_

ORGANIZATION _ABC COMPANY_
APPLICATION TITLE _LABOR DISTRIBUTION_

Figure 8-2

validation of the master-file layout incorporated in the *System Specifications Manual*. Each data element is examined to verify its integrity of the specified size and characteristics.

Then, in developing files for jobs, runs, and modules, data elements are added as they are needed to support system operations. For example, the master file for a job running in a multiprogramming environment would need data elements for record counts, hash totals for control and balancing, and so on.

Documentation of file definition at this level is illustrated in Figure 8-3, which covers the error file generated during the daily labor distribution job. Note that each data element is numbered and defined in terms of a picture recognizable to the compiler and operating system under which the program will run. Note also that sequencing keys are specified above the description section of the form in the order of relevance.

In the last chapter, a second file definition form, used for overflow where necessary, was illustrated. It is not relevant that this form be repeated

---

FILE DEFINITION

ORGANIZATION _ABC COMPANY_
APPLICATION TITLE _LABOR DISTRIBUTION_
FILE NAME _LABOR/RATE MASTER_

PAGE _1_ OF _1_
PROJECT NO. _028_
PREPARED BY _J. JONES_
DATE _9-10_

PROGRAM USING THIS FILE: _LD-040_ _LD-050_ _LD-070_ [   ] [   ] [   ]

STORAGE MEDIA_____DISC_____MULTI-REEL ____—____FILE LABEL _STANDART_
CHARACTERS/BYTES PER RECORD ___110_____RECORDS PER BLOCK ___1___
BLOCK LENGTH _____110_____NUMBER OF RECORDS ON FILE ____3000____

SEQUENCE DATA ELEMENT	
PLANT NO.	MAJOR
DEPT NO.	
CLOCK NO.	MINOR

RECORD DATA

ELE. NO.	DATA ELEMENT	OCCURS	PICTURE
001	PLANT NO.		9(3)
002	DEPT NO.		9(4)
003	CLOCK NO.		9(6)
008	JOB CLASSIFICATION CODE		X(3)
009	JOB TITLE		X(15)
010	EMPLOYEE NAME		X(20)
011	JOB HOURLY PAY RATE		9(2)V9(3)
012	JOB OVERTIME PAY RATE		9(2)V9(3)
013	REGULAR HOURS MONTH-TO-DATE		9(3)V9(1)
014	OVERTIME HOURS "		9(3)V9(1)
015	REGULAR HOURS YEAR-TO-DATE		9(4)V9(1)
016	OVERTIME HOURS "		9(4)V9(1)
017	EMPLOYEE SICK DAYS MONTH-TO-DATE		9(2)V9(1)
018	EMPLOYEE SICK DAYS YEAR-TO-DATE		9(3)V9(1)
019	EMPLOYEE PAY YEAR-TO-DATE		9(5)V9(2)
020	FILLER		X(19)

Figure 8-3

within the context of this chapter. However, it should be remembered that provision must be made for full description of all data elements within every file.

It should also be noted that the data element descriptions used in Figure 8-3 are compatible with data catalog, or dictionary, requirements for the system under which the program was to be run. In this case, the job was designed for programming in COBOL. Under the data definition division of a COBOL program, the programmer could simply use the catalog numbers assigned on this form to call up each data-file definition required by the module or run he is writing.

DEFINING SOURCE INPUTS

The relationship of input definition to file content in Technical Requirements is the same as discussed during the last chapter for System Specifications (see Figures 7-5 and 7-6). That is, all input data elements which will go to make up a working, transient, or master file must be specified on an input form. The same general purpose form is used. As indicated in Figure 8-1, this form can diagram input from punched cards, magnetic tapes, punched tapes, disc files, or messages received from on-line terminals.

DEFINING SYSTEM-WIDE PROGRAM REQUIREMENTS

This task is designed to identify and code standard specifications which will be used throughout the programs for the system under development. These specifications serve two important functions:
1. Specification writing time is saved within individual programming tasks because standard specifications need not be repeated from module to module or module to run.
2. The opportunity for errors in describing reports or documents to be generated by a system is eliminated, since all basic descriptions are written once and carried uniformly throughout the programming and operational portion of the system.

To illustrate, a set of specifications for a labor distribution system like the one under discussion would include:
1. Headings for all reports other than printed forms should include the program number, date, company name, and name of report. These heading specifications would be designated on a standard report layout form like the ones illustrated previously in this book, as was

layout form like the ones illustrated previously in this book. This form is incorporated within the *Technical Requirements Manual* as a basic specification to be used in programming. The programmer then picks up these heading designations on each report programmed within the given module. Documentation, in this sense, establishes control and responsibilities for programming accuracy.

2. A data table would be set up for system reference in converting department numbers to names. This could be listed on any convenient form or sheet available to the system designer.

3. File control records would be defined on file definition forms. These would be positioned at the end of the file being processed—as a trailer on a magnetic tape file, for example. Data elements within these control records would include record counts, hash totals, security reference information, and so on.

Although no forms have been illustrated in conjunction with this discussion, it is important to stress that these are formal documentation requirements. These program specifications must be part of the *Technical Requirements Manual* which serves as the basis for the Programming activity.

RUN/MODULE REQUIREMENTS SPECIFICATIONS

During this task, the designer establishes the framework for programming the system under development. The techniques used and documentation generated have a direct correspondence, at the specification level, with the actual procedures of program coding. The obvious advantage of this planning step prior to programming is that senior people can do the design work. This is largely because the comparatively small time requirements for program planning, as separated from program writing, make it both feasible and economical to put an organization's best programming talent onto this job. In turn, the investment in planning makes it possible to use programmers with varying levels of skill and experience in actual coding.

Further, by specifying the job in total technical overview, firm schedules can be established, managed, and controlled during the Programming activity. This can be one of the greatest cost-effective advantages within the overall system-development project. Programming is the activity where costs most commonly get out of line in system development. Dividing responsibility and separating planning from implementation under the creeping-commitment concept make for both working effectiveness and implementable management control.

The full detail of this programming control methodology is beyond the scope of this work.   However, some of the key forms and their applications are relevant within the context of this discussion of system project management.   Only these selected forms will be discussed and illustrated here.

As will be noted, a whole family of special purpose specification forms has been created for specification of programming requirements.   These forms have been tailored to the state of the art in application programming at the time of this writing.   Using these tools, specifications begin with the isolation and description of the macro or library functions provided by computer manufacturers or software firms.   After the potential for these program building blocks has been identified and covered, the designer proceeds to describe the overall objectives and requirements of the program.   The remaining forms then specify detail areas relevant to program writing.

MERGE MACRO SPECIFICATION

If the program specified on the job/run/module chart calls for a merge, the designer begins by filling out a form like the one shown in Figure 8-4.   As indicated, this provides spaces for three separate types of specification:

1. Input files to be processed in the merge operation are named and identified.
2. The record conditions which will cause merging to take place and the action to be performed are entered in the control section of the form.
3. The output file to result from the merge is described.

SORT SPECIFICATION

As indicated in Figure 8-5, the form used to specify this program macro parameterizes sort routines at virtually an input-ready level.   Input and output files are described, and sort keys (including data element descriptions and positions within their files) are identified.   If the program designer wishes to utilize special coding in conjunction with the sort macro, space is provided to specify what is to be done.   Also, special options to be used with the sort routine are described at the bottom of the form.

PRINT/REPORT SPECIFICATION

The form illustrated in Figure 8-6 can be used in two ways:

1. To specify file content to be processed under a print image function for system output

FILE SPLIT ☐
FILE MERGE ☒

PAGE *1* OF *1*
PROJECT NO. *028*
PREPARED BY *J. JONES*
DATE *3-11*

ORGANIZATION *ABC COMPANY*
APPLICATION TITLE *LABOR DISTRIBUTION*
PROGRAM NAME *LMERGE*   PROGRAM NO. *LD-030*

INPUT FILE DATA

	FILE NAME	NUMBER	MEDIA
01	CORRECTED ERRORS	LF-06	TAPE
02	EDITED LABOR TRANSACTIONS	LF-05	TAPE
03			
04			
05			
06			
07			
08			

CONTROL

	CONDITION	ACTION
01	COMPARE BOTH FILES	
02	ON PLANT, DEPARTMENT, AND	
03	CLOCK NO.	MOVE LOWEST RECORD TO
04		OUTPUT FILE
05		
06		
07		
08		
09		
10		
11		
12		

OUTPUT FILES

	FILE NAME	NUMBER	MEDIA
01	LABOR TRANSACTIONS	LF-07	TAPE

Figure 8-4

2. As a support specification for report printing in cases where the print-out is to be produced as a by-product of a major program and where printed information is processed selectively from a file of a scope larger than needed specifically for the print function

The application shown in Figure 8-6 calls for a print image output operation. In this case, the designer simply identifies the file and the sequence of data elements within it.

In cases where printout is to be selective, data elements to be included are detailed in section 4 of the form.

RUN/MODULE FUNCTION SPECIFICATION

The form shown in Figure 8-7 is the same basic document as was illustrated in the last chapter, when it was used in its run/module design capacity.

At this level of technical detail, the same form is used to specify the functions to be performed within the modules which make up a program run.

In terms of preprogramming documentation, this form serves as a cover sheet within the *Technical Requirements Manual* to guide program writing. It is equivalent to the initial parameter sheet which a programmer normally prepares in initiating code writing.

Note that the description portion of this form has only a few lines for entries. This has been done purposely. The idea behind this design feature was to keep this description short to avoid the temptation to cover

---

SORT PROGRAM PARAMETER FORM

PAGE _1_ OF _1_
PROJECT NO. _038_
PREPARED BY _J. Jones_
DATE _3-12_

ORGANIZATION _ABC COMPANY_
APPLICATION TITLE _LABOR DISTRIBUTION_
PROGRAM NAME _L SORT_   PROGRAM NO. _LD-010S_

PROGRAM BEFORE SORT:	PROGRAM AFTER SORT:
NO._____ NAME _____	NO. _LD-020_ NAME _EDIT_

INPUT FILE DATA

FILE NO. _LF-01_ NAME _LABOR TRANSACTIONS_ MEDIA _CARD_ MULTI REEL _NO_

CHARACTERS/BYTES PER RECORD ____80____ RECORDS PER BLOCK _____

BLOCK LENGTH _____ ESTIMATED NUMBER OF RECORDS ON FILE ___1500___

OUTPUT FILE DATA

SAME AS INPUT? ☐ YES ☒ NO   IF NO, COMPLETE THIS SECTION

FILE NO. _LF-02_ NAME _SORTED LABOR TRANS._ MEDIA _TAPE_ MULTI REEL _NO_

CHARACTERS/BYTES PER RECORD ____50____ RECORDS PER BLOCK ___10___

BLOCK LENGTH ___500___ ESTIMATED NUMBER OF RECORDS ON FILE ___1500___

SEQUENCE PARAMETERS

		DATA ELEMENT	PICTURE	RECORD POSITION		COMMENT
MAJOR	01	PLANT NUMBER	9(3)	FROM: 1	TO: 3	
	02	DEPARTMENT NO.	9(4)	FROM: 4	TO: 7	
	03	CLOCK NO.	9(6)	FROM: 8	TO: 13	
	04			FROM:	TO:	
TO	05			FROM:	TO:	
	06			FROM:	TO:	
	07			FROM:	TO:	
	08			FROM:	TO:	
	09			FROM:	TO:	
MINOR	10			FROM:	TO:	

OWN CODING OPTION   USED? ☐ YES ☒ NO

PRESORT/PHASE I

EXIT POINT NO. _____ SEE PROGRAM FUNCTION SHEET NO. _____

EXIT POINT NO. _____ SEE PROGRAM FUNCTION SHEET NO. _____

MERGE/PHASE IV

EXIT POINT NO. _____ SEE PROGRAM FUNCTION SHEET NO. _____

OTHER SORT OPTIONS USED – EXPLAIN _____

(USE REVERSE SIDE IF NECESSARY)

Figure 8-5

```
                        PRINT REPORT PROGRAM SHEET  ☒   PAGE __1__ OF ____1____
                            PRINTER SUPPORT SHEET  ☐   PROJECT NO. ___028___
                                                       PREPARED BY __J JONES__
                                                       DATE ____3-14____
   ORGANIZATION ABC COMPANY
   APPLICATION TITLE  LABOR DISTRIBUTION
   PROGRAM NAME PRINT LABOR DISTRIBUTION   PROGRAM NO. LD-080
```

REPORT NAME: LABOR DISTRIBUTION REPORT

I. INPUT FILE DATA

FILE NO. _LF-10_ NAME _LABOR DIST. REPORT_ MEDIA _TAPE_ MULTI REEL _No_

CHARACTERS/BYTES PER RECORD _____100_____ RECORDS PER BLOCK ____5____

BLOCK LENGTH __500__ ESTIMATED NUMBER OF RECORDS ON FILE _____7500_____

II. IF PRINT IMAGE FILE IS USED, COMPLETE THIS SECTION

FILE GENERATED BY PROGRAM: NO. _LD-070_ NAME _WRITE LABOR_

III. FILE SEQUENCE

		DATA ELEMENT	PICTURE	COMMENT
MAJOR	01	PLANT NO.	9(3)	
	02	DEPARTMENT NO.	9(4)	
	03	CLOCK NO.	9(6)	
TO	04			

Figure 8-6

program logic descriptions in narrative format. Experience has shown that this limited amount of space tends to restrict use of the description area for its intended purpose—a general statement on what the run is to accomplish in terms of file processing.

The remaining sections of this form are fairly self-explanatory: They describe the input files, the functions to be performed, and the output files to be created.

DECISION TABLE SPECIFICATION

During Technical Requirements, decision tables are developed to a run/module level. This calls for greater detail than was applied in the development of decision tables discussed in the last chapter.

Decision-table formats commonly used for this task are shown in Figure 8-8. These, as experienced system designers will note, represent only one commonly used technique for decision table specification. Again, a full-dress discussion of decision tables is beyond the realm of this work.

The decision principle applied in Figure 8-8 calls for data elements or decision functions to be considered sequentially, as listed on the form from top to bottom. Within each of these logical operations, decision rules are tested as listed on the form from left to right.

Thus, in the example, the first question posed is whether the data elements for department and clock number from the input file match the same data elements for the record input from the master file. If the answer is yes, the program proceeds to execute a series of functions, in this case those listed as numbers 1 and 4. Should the answer to the first logic condition be no, the decision table instructs the programmer to proceed with the next test. The process is repeated until all logical decisions and actions have been executed.

FILE CONTROL SPECIFICATION

The entries on the general, multipurpose form illustrated in Figure 8-9 show one commonly used method for specifying for the programmer the run

RUN/MODULE FUNCTION DESIGN ☐	PAGE _1_ OF _1_
RUN/MODULE FUNCTION SPECIFICATION ☒	PROJECT NO. _098_
	PREPARED BY _J.JONES_
ORGANIZATION _ABC COMPANY_	DATE _3-15_

APPLICATION TITLE _LABOR DISTRIBUTION_
PROGRAM NAME _UPDATE L/R_   PROGRAM NO. _LD-040_

DESCRIPTION: _THIS PROGRAM WILL UPDATE THE LABOR/RATE FILE AND PRINT THE LABOR UPDATE AND MISMATCH REPORT_

INPUT FILES

NO.	FILE NAME	NO.	MEDIA
1.	LABOR TRANSACTIONS	LF-07	TAPE
2.	LABOR/RATE	LF-09	DISC
3.			
4.			
5.			
6.			

FUNCTIONS

NO.	FUNCTION DESCRIPTION	SUPPORT SHEETS*
1	COMPUTE RECORD COUNTS FOR INPUT AND OUTPUT FILES	MPF 1
2	UPDATE THE LABOR/RATE FILE	DT4TF16
3	PRINT UPDATE AND MISMATCH REPORT	PS1
4	PRINT ALL RECORD COUNTS AT EOJ - SEE STD. LAYOUT	

*USE THE FOLLOWING PREFIXES IN NUMBERING SUPPORT SHEETS:
DT = Decision Table   TF = Table Form   MPF = Multi-Purpose Form   PS = Printer Support Sheet

OUTPUT FILES

NO.	FILE NAME	NO.	MEDIA
1.	LABOR/RATE	LF-09	DISC
2.	LABOR UPDATE AND MISMATCH REPORT	LF-08	PRINTER
3.			
4.			
5.			
6.			

Figure 8-7

DECISION TABLE [*4*]
NO.

PAGE _*1*_ OF _*1*_
PROJECT NO. _*028*_
PREPARED BY _*J. JONES*_
DATE _*3-16*_

ORGANIZATION *ABC COMPANY*
APPLICATION TITLE *LABOR DISTRIBUTION*
PROGRAM NAME *UPDATE L/R*   PROGRAM NO. *LD -040*

TABLE NAME: *UPDATE THE LABOR/RATE FILE*

LINE	CONDITION/ACTION RULE →	1	2	3	4	5	6						
A	"DEPART" + "CLOCK NO." (LI) = "DEPART" + "CLOCK NO." (L9)	Y	N				
B	"DEPART" + "CLOCK NO." (LI) < "DEPART" + "CLOCK NO." (L9)		Y	N			
C	"DEPART" + "CLOCK NO." (LI) > "DEPART" + "CLOCK NO." (L9)			Y	N		
D	END OF FILE					Y	N
1.	PERFORM THE FOLLOWING ADDS	X					
	"OVERTIME HOURS" (LI) + "OVERTIME HOURS" (L9)						
	"SHIFT BONUS HOURS" (LI) + "SHIFT BONUS HOURS" (L9)						
2.	ERROR DO NOT PROCESS PRINT INPUT			X			
	RECORD (LI) ON CONSOLE WITH COMMENT						
3.	GET NEXT RECORD FROM (L9)		X				
4.	GET NEXT RECORD FROM (LI)	X		X			
5.	PROGRAM BUG - HALT				X		
6.	GO TO - - F (FUNCTION); R (RULE, SAME TABLE); T (TABLE)	RS	RS	RS		T2	RI

NOTES: (LF-05) = TRANSACTION FILE
(LF-09) = LABOR/RATE FILE

Figure 8-8

controls to be applied to the job diagramed in Figure 8-2. In the column at the left, the designer has listed the transaction codes which will instruct the programmer to add the identified fields into the counters specified and described on the right. The nomenclature used here is individualized according to custom or job terminology established between the system designer and the programmer.

TABLE SPECIFICATION

The form illustrated in Figure 8-10 is a general purpose matrix designed for use in specification of actions to be taken within a program on recognition of specified conditions. On this form, the conditions are listed vertically in the column on the left. The actions to be taken are listed across the top. Placement of correspondence marks in the matrix positions instructs the programmer to code functional instructions based on recognition of stipulated numbers or codes within the transaction file.

As described in connection with the application illustrated, the role of the general purpose matrix form appears highly similar to that which could be assigned to a conventional decision table. However, note that the matrix format is used where multiple correspondence is likely to take place between identifying codes and functions to be performed. For example, the code number 650 calls for application of four separate functions within the module under description or within the modules of a single run. Where such requirements exist, it is easier to specify them on a matrix table than through the iterative techniques required in conventional decision tables. The programming which results is the same in either case. However, in some situations, the matrix approach simplifies the job of the system designer.

PRINTER SUPPORT SPECIFICATION

Note that Figure 8-11 uses the same basic form as Figure 8-6. In Figure 8-6, the document was used to specify print image file data elements. In Figure 8-11, the form is being used to describe, in precise, technical references pertinent to program writing, the output report to be produced in the run under description.

The form in Figure 8-11, in turn, is used in conjunction with the one

MULTI-PURPOSE FORM		

PAGE _1_ OF _1_
PROJECT NO. _038_
PREPARED BY _J. JONES_
DATE _3-17_

ORGANIZATION _ABC COMPANY_
APPLICATION TITLE _LABOR DISTRIBUTION_
PROGRAM NAME _UPDATE L/R_   PROGRAM NO. _LD-040_

USE THE FOLLOWING AS A GUIDE FOR I/O COUNTS	
TRANSACTION CODE	COUNTER-USE NAME FOR PRINT-OUT
FILE LF-01 (IN):	
621-630	REGULAR DIRECT LABOR
631-640	SPECIAL DIRECT LABOR
641-643	FILE MAINTENANCE
FILE LF-09 (IN):	
ALL RECORDS	INPUT FROM L/R FILE
FILE LF-09 (OUT):	
ALL RECORDS	OUTPUT TO L/R FILE

Figure 8-9

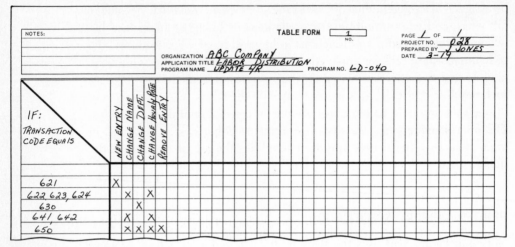

Figure 8-10

shown in Figure 8-12, a printer control sheet which identifies all data elements in a report and specifies processing of this data within the printer. This is the form used, for example, to specify assignment and functioning of counters which will support the printing output operation.

The data conveyed in the forms shown in Figures 8-11 and 8-12, along with the report layout form, give the programmer all the information he needs to prepare the coding which will generate the specified output.

OPERATING SYSTEM CONTROL SPECIFICATIONS

As part of the Technical Requirements activity, the system designer must be sure to specify all the entries or instructions which the programmer must make to interface the application under development with the operating system or executive programs which will be used to control their execution. In effect, the designer is assembling the job streams necessary for effective processing of the system under development.

This phase of program specification preparation is highly hardware-oriented and hardware/software dependent. Obviously, the make of computer to be used and the system software which has been selected to reside within that computer are the controlling elements in specification of job control instructions. Therefore, this book will not go into detail in describing this specific task because it would be necessary to narrow the scope of the discussion in favor of one particular make or model of computer.

However, systems management people should be aware, at this point, that job control specifications must be prepared. These should be done in accordance with instructions contained in appropriate manuals provided by manufacturers or software houses. Forms used should be either those provided by the manufacturer or software house or documents which conform to the standards set in the appropriate manuals.

PROGRAMMING SCHEDULE PREPARATION

This is the time within a system project to make definitive commitments on the scheduling of people, resources, and time frames for program writing. The requirements for scheduling and commitment at this point are basic—whether the actual programming will be done in-house or by subcontractors.

PRINT REPORT PROGRAM SHEET ☐
PRINTER SUPPORT SHEET ☒

PAGE 1 OF 2
PROJECT NO. 028
PREPARED BY J. JONES
DATE 3-30

ORGANIZATION ABC COMPANY
APPLICATION TITLE LABOR DISTRIBUTION
PROGRAM NAME UPDATE L/R PROGRAM NO. LD-040

REPORT NAME: UPDATE AND MISMATCH REPORT

I. INPUT FILE DATA

FILE NO. ______ NAME ______ MEDIA ______ MULTI REEL ______

CHARACTERS/BYTES PER RECORD ______ RECORDS PER BLOCK ______

BLOCK LENGTH ______ ESTIMATED NUMBER OF RECORDS ON FILE ______

II. IF PRINT IMAGE FILE IS USED, COMPLETE THIS SECTION

FILE GENERATED BY PROGRAM: NO. ______ NAME ______

III. FILE SEQUENCE

		DATA ELEMENT	PICTURE	COMMENT
MAJOR	01			
	02			
	03			
TO	04			
	05			
	06			
MINOR	07			

IV. LINE CONTROL

		CONDITION	PRINT LINE	SPACING	SEE PRINT CONTROL ITEMS
DETAIL(S)	01	STANDARD HEADING - HDF			THRU
	02	HEADER 1	A	1	1 THRU 1
	03	HEADER 2	B	2	2 THRU 2
	04	EACH TRANSACTION - FROM L1	C	1	3 THRU 11
	05	CLOCK NUMBER CHANGE	D	1	12 THRU 19
	06	DEPARTMENT NUMBER CHANGE	E	1	20 THRU 27
TO	07				THRU

Figure 8-11

PROGRAM NAME _UPDATE L/R FILE_   NO. _LD-040_

PRINT CONTROL SHEET

ITEM	DATA ELEMENT	ELE. NO.	PICTURE	COMMENT
01	HEADER – SEE LAYOUT			
02	HEADER – SEE LAYOUT			
03	"DEPART"	1	X(4)	NOTE: FIELDS 1 THRU 9 ARE PRINTED
04	"CLOCK NO"	2	X(4)	FROM THE TRANS. RECORD FILE (L1)
05	"REGULAR HOURS"	3	Z(2).Z(2)-	ADD TO COUNTER FOR CLOCK TOTAL
06	"OVERTIME HOURS"	4	Z(2).Z(2)-	" " " " " "
07	"SHIFT BONUS HOURS"	5	Z(2).Z(2)-	" " " " " "
08	"REGULAR DOLLARS"	6	Z(3).Z(2)-	" " " " " "
09	"OVERTIME DOLLARS"	7	Z(3).Z(2)-	" " " " " "
10	"SHIFT BONUS DOLLARS"	8	Z(3).Z(2)-	" " " " " "
11	"TOTAL DOLLARS"	9	Z(3).Z(2)-	" " " " " "
12	CLOCK TOTAL COUNTERS ARE PRINTED FIELDS 10 THRU 16			
13	REGULAR HOURS	10	Z(2).Z(2)-	ADD TO COUNTER FOR CHECK TOTAL
14	OVERTIME HOURS	11	Z(2).Z(2)-	" " " " " "
15	SHIFT BONUS HOURS	12	Z(2).Z(2)-	" " " " " "
16	REGULAR DOLLARS	13	Z(3).Z(2)-	" " " " " "
17	OVERTIME DOLLARS	14	Z(3).Z(2)-	" " " " " "
18	SHIFT BONUS DOLLARS	15	Z(3).Z(2)-	" " " " " "
19	TOTAL DOLLARS	16	Z(3).Z(2)-	" " " " " "
20	DEPARTMENT TOTAL COUNTERS ARE PRINTED FIELDS 17 THRU 23			
21	REGULAR HOURS	17	Z(2),Z(3).Z(2)	
22	OVERTIME HOURS	18	Z(2),Z(3).Z(2)	
23	SHIFT BONUS HOURS	19	Z(2),Z(3).Z(2)	
24	REGULAR DOLLARS	20	Z(2),Z(3).Z(2)	
25	OVERTIME DOLLARS	21	Z(2),Z(3).Z(2)	
26	SHIFT BONUS DOLLARS	22	Z(2),Z(3).Z(2)	
27	TOTAL DOLLARS	23	Z(2),Z(3).Z(2)	
8				
9				
0				

Figure 8-12

In either case, it is desirable to handle programming schedules on a module/run basis. As a general rule, the authors plan for programming in work increments which do not exceed ten days of programming time each. In this way, losses or unproductive efforts are minimized if oversights or unforeseen problems enter the picture.

A full-dress discussion of programming schedules is beyond the scope of this book. As indicated earlier, the subject itself is too large to be covered briefly in an overall review of system project management techniques. However, discussion of techniques for modularizing and controlling program writing will be brought up in somewhat greater depth in Chapter 10.

TECHNICAL REQUIREMENTS MANUAL

The documentation accumulated in the course of the Technical Requirements activity is incorporated, in logical program writing sequence, into a *Technical Requirements Manual.* Since this is a technical activity entirely, no Management Summary is necessary. The cumulative documentation, properly indexed and reproduced in necessary quantities, becomes the manual.

As indicated in Figure 8-1, this manual is reviewed technically after it has been assembled. This review is performed by the system project leader, a representative of the programming group, the designer responsible for preparation of the Technical Requirements documentation, and technical services personnel.

As the flow chart in Figure 8-1 indicates, the manual is modified as necessary to conform to review critiques and specifications. The final version of the manual then goes forward to serve as the basis for Programming.

PROGRAMMING COST AND PERFORMANCE QUOTATION

A final document produced during the Technical Requirements activity, as illustrated in Figure 8-13, is the Programming Cost and Performance Quotation. As indicated, this is a summary which commits the technical personnel who have performed this activity to schedules and budgets for the completion of the Programming activity. In effect, this form indicates that, on the basis of detailed specifications, the system project leader and those people who have carried out this activity on his behalf have established time and cost requirements as indicated in this document.

These figures, of course, are validated against earlier estimates before work moves along to the next activity in the project. Should any major discrepancies develop, the situation can be called to the attention of management. However, if estimates are within bounds, the Programming Cost and Performance Quotation serves as authorization for the next activity,

Implementation Planning.   At the close of Implementation Planning, this becomes part of the documentation reviewed by the EDP Systems Planning Steering Committee, which makes a continue/terminate decision at that point.   Since there is little likelihood that members of the steering committee will have any interest in the *Technical Requirements Manual*, the quotation form becomes, in effect, the Management Summary report of the Technical Requirements activity.

PROGRAMMING COST AND PERFORMANCE QUOTATION

☒ NEW PROJECT   ☐ MAJOR SYSTEM MODIFICATION

PAGE _1_ OF _1_
PROJECT NO. _028_
ORGANIZATION _ABC COMPANY_   PREPARED BY _R. BATES_
APPLICATION TITLE _LABOR DISTRIBUTION_   DATE _3-27_

DESCRIPTION OF REQUEST: _LABOR DISTRIBUTION SYSTEM_

COST ESTIMATE:

	DEVELOPMENTAL					RECURRING	
	Man Days	Man $	Test Time Hours	Test Time $	Total $	Hours Per Month	$ Per Month
PROGRAMMING	70	4,000	90	1,800	5,800		
SYSTEMS TEST	15	1,200	20	400	1,220		
TOTAL	85	5,200	110	2,200	7,020		

$ - Dollars

DEVELOPMENT SCHEDULE: Work to be completed within proposed development schedule ☒ Yes ☐ No

	Start Date	End Date
PROGRAMMING	4/1	6/15
SYSTEM TEST	7/15	8/5

Figure 8-13

CHAPTER NINE

Implementation Planning

ACTIVITY OBJECTIVES

In the evolution of the project management process under discussion in this book, the Implementation Planning activity was the last to take formal shape. The tasks incorporated within this activity were, in earlier versions, handled elsewhere within the Development phase.

Based on experience, however, several good reasons emerged for formalizing a separate Implementation Planning activity at this stage in the system project:

1. It is extremely valuable to pause at this point, review the status of the system project, and prepare a detailed plan for the accomplishment of the remainder of the activities which lie ahead. This study and planning effort, experience has shown, pays off. Ideally, there should be no surprises ahead during the remainder of the Development and Implementation phases of the project. The term "surprises" is used here in reference to unforeseen critical incidents, equipment inadequacies, or procedural failures which should have been provided for during Planning activities—but which were overlooked. Such occurrences are no stranger to experienced systems people. Many systems

fail or are returned to the drawing boards because of such unforeseen problems. Experience has shown that specific concentration on planning for the remainder of the project at this juncture catches and solves the majority of this type of potential problem.

2. During this activity, the system project team establishes criteria for the scope, performance, and acceptance standards to be applied during the System Test and Conversion activities.

3. The overall Project Plan, initiated during the System Planning Study activity (covered in Chapter 5) is reviewed and updated at this point. This review has a direct bearing on overall project control.

ACTIVITY CHARACTERISTICS

During this activity, the system project team is brought back up to full strength, reorganized as necessary, and oriented for completion of the project activities which lie ahead. This characteristic of the activity bears emphasis because the project itself is in a transitional state at this point. The activities which preceded Implementation Planning were largely technical in nature. The full project team may actually not have worked together for a few months. Now, a requirement presents itself for intense involvement on the part of both users and systems people. Following Implementation Planning, the users will implement their training requirements while the technical personnel will move forward into program preparation. Therefore, it becomes critically important that user relationships and enthusiasm be reestablished.

It is also important that these organizational steps be taken at this point in the project because the team is in a better position to finalize plans and commitments at this stage in Development. Simply stated, the group is a lot smarter than it was at the completion of the Planning phase. During the first three activities in the Development phase, many questions have come up, and many points have been resolved. Constraints and rules which did not exist at the conclusion of the Planning phase have been developed. More is known about the people who will use the system. There is a better insight about what will be expected of the system.

This is true particularly if the new system's operations have been simulated on computers. This experience actually serves to preview the conditions under which the new system will function. It can bring to light unforeseen requirements or problems which, in turn, may result in major changes in the specifications or operating and performance characteristics of the system itself.

Further, at this point, the system project leader may be working under new decision rules. The system may be subject to newly developed governmental regulations or other environmental constraints. Equipment deliveries will be firmly committed. Software will have been investigated, and, very possibly, compromises will have been reached on capabilities to be provided by operating system or executive programs.

In the face of all these developments, user executives and user members of the project team must reevaluate their own position. It is important that the user commitment to the system be defined even more rigidly and established more solidly at this point than at any previous juncture in the project. As discussed in the chapters on System Specifications and Technical Requirements, a continuing interaction has been taking place between key user personnel and systems analysts who were carrying the project to definitive technical depths. Some of the explanations and agreements which evolved during the technical activities may not have been understood in their full implications. At any rate, it is important, during this pause for project orientation, that full consideration be given and full understanding achieved on how the system will impact the user environment and how users will interact with the new, computerized procedures.

A normal tendency at this point is for users to express a preference that further commitment on their part be put off until they can see and handle live output being generated by the new system. Such postponements must be avoided! It should be considered mandatory that users review system implications in depth at this point and that they commit themselves to implementing the system and realizing the stipulated benefits before the project moves ahead into the next, expensive activities of Programming and User Training.

The importance of user concurrence at this point is underscored by the fact that design alterations or operational changes become increasingly expensive with each new activity. This is particularly true at this juncture. After programs are written and the user group trained, changes become increasingly expensive.

The system project leader, therefore, should be sure that user executives and project team members are continually aware of the increasing consequences of their involvement and commitment. The Implementation Planning activity offers an opportunity to underscore the importance of this situation and fulfill the commitment requirement.

CONVERSION PLANNING

Planning for the Conversion activity, during which the tested system will "go live," is a critically important part of Implementation Planning. This should be stressed early in the chapter, even though the activity sequence to be reviewed will take up User Training and Programming before the mechanisms for Conversion are considered. Actually, this requirement represents one of the important reasons for the isolation of Implementation Planning as a separate activity.

The basic approach to system conversion must be established well in advance of actual cutover. User Training and clerical procedures will vary greatly with the Conversion approach selected. Therefore, it is important that the basic decisions on Conversion methodology be made at the outset of the Implementation Planning activity.

In particular, two vital elements of the Conversion plan must be established at this point:

1. Will parallel processing be used? If the answer is affirmative, the techniques to be applied must be outlined early in the Implementation Planning activity.
2. Conversion sequences and system cutover stages must be established.

PARALLEL PROCESSING

The first step in determining whether parallel processing will be used in Conversion is to establish whether or not this approach is feasible. In some cases, parallel processing simply will not work. For example, parallel processing between clerical and computerized procedures is generally not practical in a production control system. Entirely different procedures and methodologies are employed in manual and computerized production control systems. Entirely new functional criteria and decision rules are applied when a production control system is computerized. For instance, new inventory quantities and methods of calculating both stock levels and reorder quantities are established. Parallel processing cannot be practiced in such a case because there is no basis for comparison.

On the other hand, with accounting applications, such as payroll, parallel processing is generally considered mandatory. In such cases, parallel processing is also highly workable because there are accounting balances which establish absolute standards.

In determining whether or not to use parallel processing during Conversion, the degree of risk between alternative methods should be identified and evaluated. For example, if a complete audit trail and working totals are incorporated within the new system, it may be decided that there is not enough to be gained through parallel processing to make it worthwhile.

In other cases, factors external to the system under development or its immediate environment may introduce risk criteria which make parallel processing mandatory even though it is not economical. For example, the end product of a ticket reservation system—whether it be for an airline, a railroad, a theater, or a sports stadium—is the seat for which the customer holds a reservation. With such systems, some service interruption must be assumed during Conversion. Therefore, even though it may be necessary to devise and implement separate clerical procedures to parallel the computerized system, this may have to be done to maintain the level of service specified by the sponsoring organization.

Another important facet of parallel processing which must be considered is the determination of which totals will be considered as the constant. That is, where parallel processing takes place, a balance must be established between the old and new systems. It can make a big difference which total is considered the constant. For example, if the manual system is to balance the computer totals, employees handling the old system will be more responsible for accuracy than if the computer totals will be expected to match those developed under the manual procedures. The nature of the individual organization and the customs within the industry must be considered carefully in making this determination. However, where parallel processing is to be used, this determination should be made as early as feasible.

CONVERSION SEQUENCE

The job of bringing a new data processing system into operation has been likened to putting a refinery on line. Valves are opened one at a time to bring the facility up to full production—smoothly and with minimum risk.

Where feasible, the same approach is recommended for a data processing system. It becomes important, however, to determine which segments of a system are to be converted, in what order. The overall work load of the organization should be studied in terms of its normal functions or files. For example, conversions can be scheduled according to accounting cycles, branches, plants, product lines, or other logical breakdowns.

As a general rule of thumb, the best approach is to convert those segments of the job first which will offer the least trouble. In other words, the sequence would be set up to start with the simplest products, the smallest cycles, the best managed departments, and so on. The total effect of this aspect of Conversion planning should be to start the new vehicle from a standstill and bring it up to full speed in a smooth acceleration. To do this, concentration should be on the system itself and its requirements—

insofar as is possible. That is, requirements of the operational departments or external environment within which the system exists should be kept at minimum impact during Conversion if this can be done.

As a final element in setting up the Conversion sequence, the Implementation Planning activity should establish what the system will look like at the time it is to be considered operational. This factor, too, will vary with systems. In some cases, a system will not be considered operational until all cycles or departments are being processed normally under the new system. In other cases, the final elements of Conversion can be handled routinely after the system has been firmly initiated. For example, if a manufacturing system is operational for about one-quarter of a company's product lines, the others can usually be added routinely at the convenience of production management.

ACTIVITY SCOPE

The Implementation Planning activity is comparatively short. In the typical project involving 4 man-years of effort, this would occupy about 10 manweeks of time on the part of the project team. About 5 percent of the expenses of the project are encountered here.

At the conclusion of Implementation Planning, the EDP Systems Planning Steering Committee reviews progress to date. In particular, the committee looks at any deviations from plans approved at the conclusion of the System Planning Study. If forecasts and commitments are still within the schedule and economic parameters established prior to the last committee review, the project proceeds routinely. If deviations have been identified, a new continue/terminate decision is necessary.

ACTIVITY WORK FLOW

The work flow for the Implementation Planning activity is diagramed in Figure 9-1.

The task sequence within Implementation Planning begins with a thorough review of the current status and documentation of the project. Then it moves on to a sequence of preparations for the System Test and Conversion activities. In brief, the sequence is as follows:

- The project team is reassembled. A thorough review is conducted of the Project Plan, the *System Requirements Manual,* the *System Specifications Manual,* and the *Technical Requirements Manual.* Programming and EDP operations people also participate in this review.

- If necessary, plans, estimates, and schedules are modified and agreed to during this review. One end product of this review is a currently updated Project Plan.
- A checklist which will serve as a guide for the User Training activity is developed. This includes assignment of both task responsibilities and schedule dates.
- A plan for implementation of the User Training activity is developed.
- The group then prepares a System Test Checklist, which will serve as a guide to the System Test activities.
- A Computer Test Plan is developed.
- A Conversion Checklist for guidance in the Conversion activity is prepared.
- A Conversion Plan is drawn.
- A detailed plan is developed for the acquisition of file data which will be required by the new system.
- A definitive Manpower and Equipment Plan is developed.
- The Implementation Plan, incorporating documentation accumulated during this activity, is reviewed with user management and modified as necessary.
- A User/Technical Conference is held for a further review and modification, as necessary, of the Implementation Plan.
- The completed Implementation Plan, including a Management Summary, is presented to the EDP Systems Planning Steering Committee.

ACTIVITY INITIATION REVIEW

The chief purpose of the Initiation Review within the Implementation Planning activity is to establish the consensus needed between systems and user people for successful implementation of the new system. This is the point at which the team is assembled and the project retuned. The implications of this function were discussed earlier in this chapter. No further review is needed here, except to point out that, as indicated in Figure 9-1, the end product of this review task is an updated, agreed upon Project Plan.

As necessary, separate sessions are held to modify the Project Plan and programming estimates and schedules. This reviewing and reorientation effort could take a good portion of the time devoted to this activity. The important thing is that there must be full agreement on current status and future objectives before the activity moves on to tasks directly related to preparation for the User Training, System Test, and Conversion activities.

ACTIVITY PLANNING IMPLICATIONS

During the Activity Planning task, attention is focused on preparations for the three critical activities which will follow—User Training, System Test, and Conversion.

The nature of advance planning for future activities—and the philosophy for activity planning in general—are worthy of a passing note at this point.

As the reader has undoubtedly observed by this time, it is basic to the methodology under discussion here that each separate activity begins with a review during which detailed plans are established for completion of the immediate tasks at hand.

Advance planning for future activities is incorporated within the project structure to meet specific requirements. This is the underlying purpose of the Implementation Planning activity. This look-ahead emphasis is built into a project at points where major commitments of manpower, facilities, and resources must be made in advance because of the critical nature of given activities. When this is done, advance planning is conducted on a broad, general basis only. Specific, detailed plans will still be drawn at the initiation of the individual activities involved.

To illustrate, Programming schedules were established during the Technical Requirements activity because of the need to allocate heavily loaded resources. The planning and scheduling undertaken for the System Test and Conversion activities during Implementation Planning are similar in nature and intent. That is, planning is done on a broad, rather than a detailed, basis.

USER TRAINING CHECKLIST

The first of the planning tasks of the Implementation Planning activity calls for preparation of a User Training Checklist like the one shown in Figure 9-2. This form incorporates a complete list of potential requirements during the User Training activity. Included are provisions for preparation of all needed job outlines, training materials, and other documents which will be needed to complete the User Training activity. At this point, commitments are made in terms of responsibilities and schedule dates for all tasks appearing on the list which are relevant to the User Training activity as it will be carried out within the system under development.

This checklist, in effect, applies a discipline which calls for the commitment of the people, the facilities, and the time which will be needed to go ahead with User Training.

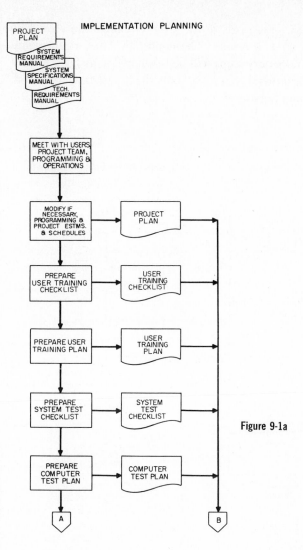

IMPLEMENTATION PLANNING

Figure 9-1a

USER TRAINING PLAN

The User Training Plan, as illustrated in Figure 9-3, is a sequential, narrative description of the steps which will be followed within the User Training activity. As a guide to be sure that all activity requirements are incorporated within the plan, a subject checklist is incorporated in the heading of the form.

This is a good place to restate the policy that planning for future activities should not go into detail. Elements of the User Training Plan should be described in minimum, general terms. The important thing, at this point, is to make sure that all necessary steps will be taken and to assign responsibilities and describe performances for the individuals and tasks involved. Aside from these minimum, general ground rules, the form in Figure 9-3 speaks for itself.

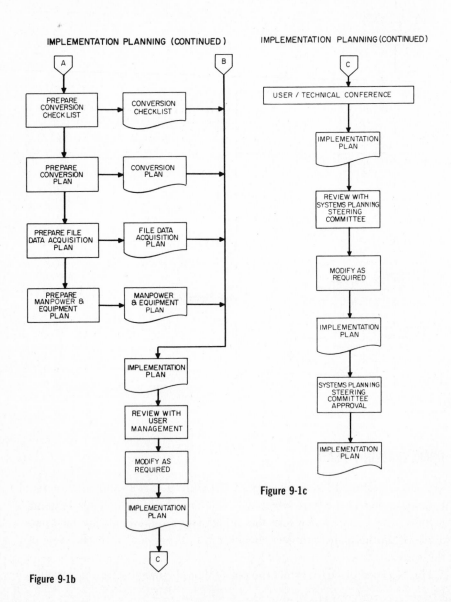

Figure 9-1b

Figure 9-1c

**USER TRAINING
CHECKLIST**

PAGE __1__ OF __1__
PROJECT NO. __028__
ORGANIZATION __ABC COMPANY__   PREPARED BY __J.JONES__
APPLICATION TITLE __LABOR DISTRIBUTION__   DATE __4-1__

DESCRIPTION OF ACTIVITY	INDIVIDUAL RESPONSIBLE	DEPARTMENT RESPONSIBLE	START DATE	COMPLETION DATE	APPROVED BY
1. USER PREPARATION	—				
2. INTERNAL NOTIFICATION					
EXECUTIVE ANNOUNCEMENT	R.ROE	PLANT MGR	4/1	5/15	
EMPLOYEE ANNOUNCEMENT	J.BLACK	ACCTG.	4/1	5/15	
3. EXTERNAL NOTIFICATION	—				
CUSTOMER CO-ORDINATION					
VENDOR CO-ORDINATION					
PUBLIC RELATIONS					
OTHER					
4. POLICY CONSIDERATIONS					
CORPORATE	J.BLACK	ACCTG.	4/1	5/1	
DIVISIONAL	J.BLACK	ACCTG.	4/1	5/1	
5. PROCEDURES					
INTER-DIVISIONAL	J.JONES	SYSTEMS	4/15	5/1	
INTRA DIVISIONAL	R.ROE	PLANT MGR	4/15	5/1	
DEPARTMENTAL	J.BLACK	ACCTG.	4/15	5/1	
6. JOB OUTLINES	J.JONES	SYSTEMS	5/15	5/30	
7. FORMS					
DESIGN	J.JONES	SYSTEMS	6/1	6/15	
INTERNAL PRINTING	—				
EXTERNAL PRINTING	J.JONES	SYSTEMS	6/1	6/15	
8. TRAINING AND ORIENTATION					
OUTLINES	J.JONES	SYSTEMS	6/1	6/15	
MANUALS	J.JONES	SYSTEMS	6/1	6/15	
TRAINING AIDS	J.JONES	SYSTEMS	6/1	6/15	
OTHER	J.BLACK	ACCTG.	6/15	6/30	
9. SPECIAL EQUIPMENT & FIXTURES	—				
DETERMINATION OF REQ'MTS.					
ENGINEERING DEPARTMENT					
SUB CONTRACTORS					
10. OFFICE EQUIPMENT REQ.	J.BLACK	ACCTG.	6/1	6/15	
11. FLOOR SPACE & LAYOUT	—				
12. SUPPLIES	J.BLACK	ACCTG.	6/1	7/1	
13. PERSONNEL					
RECLASSIFICATION	—				
HIRING	J.BLACK	ACCTG.	6/1	7/1	

APPROVED BY: _W W White_   _W Smith_
       SYSTEMS DEPARTMENT   PROJECT LEADER

Figure 9-2

SYSTEM TEST INCREMENTS

A major planning achievement in preparation for System Test calls for the designation of test units.   These are work increments—building blocks—established especially with test operations and functional feasibility in mind.   At this point, programs have been run and debugged individually. In System Test, the run/module and interrun relationships of data and file processing must be tested and validated.   The technique used, as illustrated in Figure 9-4, must be such that problems which come up are isolated and easily identified as they occur.   The planning and implementation of System Test on a unit basis is designed to start with the smallest, low-common-denominator building blocks of a system, combining these to structure tests for subsystems and the full system so that problem identification will be relatively straightforward any time a "blowup" occurs.

SYSTEM TEST CHECKLIST

Planning for the System Test activity also calls for preparation of a checklist of potentially required tasks and documents—like the one shown in Figure

USER TRAINING PLAN

PAGE 1 OF 1
PROJECT NO. 028
PREPARED BY J.JONES
ORGANIZATION ABC COMPANY
APPLICATION TITLE LABOR DISTRIBUTION
DATE 4-2

DESCRIBE THE FOLLOWING MAJOR ACTIVITIES IN TERMS OF SPECIFIC TASKS, ACTION STEPS, OR ITEMS TO BE ACCOMPLISHED:

INTERNAL NOTIFICATION	TRAINING AND ORIENTATION
EXTERNAL NOTIFICATION	SPECIAL EQUIPMENT AND FEATURES
POLICY CONSIDERATIONS	OFFICE EQUIPMENT REQUIREMENTS
PROCEDURES	FLOOR SPACE AND LAYOUT
JOB OUTLINES	SUPPLIES
FORMS	PERSONNEL

1.   INTERNAL NOTIFICATION
    A.   EXECUTIVE ANNOUNCEMENT
        R.ROE, PLANT MANAGER, WILL NOTIFY ALL DEPARTMENT HEADS AND SUPERVISORS WHO HAVE RESPONSIBILITY FOR DIRECT LABOR DEPARTMENTS.

    B.   EMPLOYEE ANNOUNCEMENT
        J. BLACK, CONTROLLER, WILL NOTIFY ALL TIMEKEEPERS AND ACCOUNTING DEPARTMENT PERSONNEL.

II.   EXTERNAL NOTIFICATION
        THERE IS NO REQUIREMENT FOR EXTERNAL NOTIFICATION INVOLVED WITH THIS SYSTEM

III.   POLICY CONSIDERATIONS
        J.BLACK, CONTROLLER, WILL INVESTIGATE CORPORATE AND DIVISIONAL POLICIES FOR CONFLICTS OR RESTRICTIONS CONCERNING THE WORKING HOURS OF TIMEKEEPERS AND DATA PROCESSING PERSONNEL.

IV.   PROCEDURES
        THE FOLLOWING ARE THE PROCEDURAL RESPONSIBILITIES OF THE SYSTEM:

PROCEDURE	RESPONSIBILITY
LABOR TRANSACTION PROCESSING	J.JONES, SYSTEM
ACCOUNTING DEPT.-LABOR REPORT	J.BLACK, CONTROLLER
LINE DEPARTMENTS - LABOR REPORT	R.ROE, PLANT MANAGER

APPROVED BY: B.BROWN   W.WHITE
USER DEPARTMENT   SYSTEMS DEPARTMENT

Figure 9-3

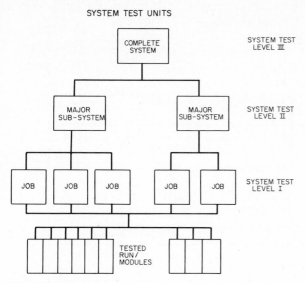

SYSTEM TEST UNITS

Figure 9-4

9-5.   Using this checklist as a guide, user and system managers designate specific people for the System Test tasks.   Start and completion dates for the System Test activity are also entered on this form.   Note that columns are provided for later entry of actual start and completion dates — and for approval sign-offs for the acceptance of System Test increments.

COMPUTER TEST PLAN

The Computer Test Plan establishes the operating descriptions and standards for the machine functions to be performed and accepted during System Test.   A copy of this form is shown in Figure 9-6.   Note that the test criteria are listed sequentially, in order of performance, and are described in short narrative sentences.

This test plan, as was also true for the System Test Checklist, is developed on a program module basis.   Note that full identification for the program increments involved and for the responsible programmer are incorporated within the form.

Again, this form will be carried forward as a guide to the completion and acceptance of this phase of System Test.

CONVERSION CHECKLIST

This document, illustrated in Figure 9-7, sets up responsibilities and schedule dates for the tasks involved in the Conversion activity in much the same

SYSTEM TEST CHECKLIST

PAGE _1_ OF _1_
PROJECT NO. _028_
PREPARED BY _J.JONES_
DATE _4-3_

ORGANIZATION _ABC COMPANY_
APPLICATION TITLE _LABOR DISTRIBUTION_

MODULE NO.	MODULE NAME	SCHEDULED START DATE	ACTUAL START DATE	SCHEDULED COMPLETION	ACTUAL COMPLETION	PROJECT LEADER
1	DAILY BATCH PROCESSING	6/1	6/3	7/30		W SMITH

DESCRIPTION OF ACTIVITY	INDIVIDUAL RESPONSIBLE	DEPARTMENT RESPONSIBLE	START DATE	COMPLETION DATE	APPROVED BY
1. COMPUTER TEST PLAN					
2. TEST PROCEDURES					
USER DEPARTMENT	J.BLACK	ACCTG.	7/1		
DATA PROCESSING OPERATIONS	J.JONES	SYSTEMS	7/15		
SYSTEMS & PROGRAMMING	J.JONES	SYSTEMS	7/15		
DATA PROCESSING CONTROLS	J.JONES	SYSTEMS	7/15		
3. FORMS					
INPUT TEST DATA	J.JONES	SYSTEMS	6/20		
FILE CREATION & MAINTENANCE	J.JONES	SYSTEMS	6/20		
4. CONTROLS					
USER DEPARTMENT	J.BLACK	ACCTG.	6/20		
DATA PROCESSING CONTROLS	J.JONES	SYSTEMS	6/15		
5. EQUIPMENT					
AVAILABILITY	J.JONES	SYSTEMS	6/15		
EMERGENCY SERVICE	J.JONES	SYSTEMS	6/20		
6. MANPOWER					
USER DEPARTMENT	J.BLACK	ACCTG.	6/15		
DATA PROCESSING OPERATIONS	J.JONES	SYSTEMS	6/15		
SYSTEMS & PROGRAMMING	J.JONES	SYSTEMS	6/20		
DATA PROCESSING CONTROLS	J.JONES	SYSTEMS	6/20		
7. SUPPLIES					
AVAILABILITY	J.BLACK	ACCTG.	6/1		
8. DATA					
CREATED & VERIFIED	J.BLACK	ACCTG.	6/15		
CONTROLLED	J.BLACK	ACCTG.	6/15		
9. FILES					
CREATED & VERIFIED	J.JONES	SYSTEMS	6/20		
CONTROLLED	J.JONES	SYSTEMS	6/20		
10. MISCELLANEOUS					

Approved by _J. Jones_

USER DEPARTMENT   SYSTEMS DEPARTMENT   DATA PROCESSING DEPARTMENT   PROJECT LEADER

Figure 9-5

way as corresponding checklist forms did for the User Training and System Test activities.

Note that this form covers the tasks within the Conversion activity in a broad, general way. Initially, there are three planning tasks. Then, attention is called to the need to convert existing files, design forms (if applicable), conduct parallel processing, establish a file conversion sequence, prepare conversion programs, and, as necessary, establish interface relationships with other systems.

As discussed earlier in this chapter, the Implementation Planning activity is a make-or-break point for effective Conversion planning. The checklist in Figure 9-7, in turn, serves as a tool which guides this important function.

CONVERSION PLAN

The Conversion Plan itself is recorded on a narrative-oriented form like the one shown in Figure 9-8. As can be seen, the heading on this form incorporates a checklist which serves as a guide for the Conversion Plan elements which must be performed during this activity. Note that this form provides a good deal of latitude for outlining the Conversion Plan to the full level of detail called for by the system under development.

FILE DATA ACQUISITION PLAN

An important part of the Implementation Planning activity lies in pinpointing sources and developing a working plan for the acquisition of all data elements to be incorporated in the files for the new system.

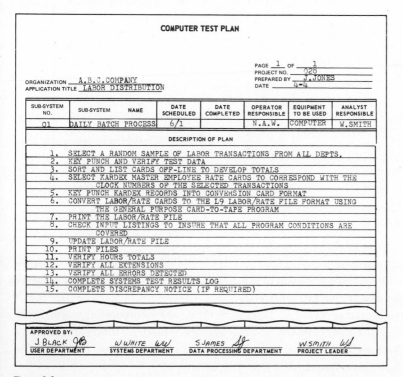

Figure 9-6

CONVERSION CHECKLIST

PAGE 1 OF 1
PROJECT NO. 028
PREPARED BY J.JONES
DATE 4-5

ORGANIZATION ABC COMPANY
APPLICATION TITLE LABOR DISTRIBUTION

DESCRIPTION OF ACTIVITY	INDIVIDUAL RESPONSIBLE	DEPARTMENT RESPONSIBLE	START DATE	COMPLETION DATE	APPROVED BY
1. CONVERSION PLAN	J.JONES	SYSTEMS	5/1	6/1	
2. FILE DATA ACQUISITION PLAN	J.JONES	SYSTEMS	5/1	6/1	
3. MANPOWER & EQUIPMENT PLAN	J.BLACK	ACCTG.	5/1	6/1	
4. FILES					
PURIFICATION OF RECORDS	J.BLACK	ACCTG.	5/15	7/1	
CODING REQUIREMENTS	J.BLACK	ACCTG.	5/15	7/1	
CONTROL	J.BLACK	ACCTG.	7/1	7/1	
CONVERSION	J.JONES	SYSTEMS	6/1	7/1	
MAINTENANCE	J.BLACK	ACCTG.	7/1	-	
5. FORMS	-	-	-	-	
DESIGN					
INTERNAL PRINTING					
EXTERNAL PRINTING					
CONVERSION					
6. PARALLEL PROCESSING					
PROCEDURES	J.JONES	SYSTEMS	5/1	6/1	
VERIFICATION REQUIREMENTS	J.BLACK	ACCTG.	5/1	6/1	
SCHEDULE	J.JONES	SYSTEMS	5/1	6/1	
7. CONVERSION SEQUENCE					
ORGANIZATIONAL SEQUENCE	J.BLACK	ACCTG.	5/1	6/1	
SCHEDULE	J.JONES	SYSTEMS	5/1	6/1	
8. CONVERSION PROGRAMS					
DEFINITION	J.JONES	SYSTEMS	4/1	5/1	
SPECIFICATIONS	J.JONES	SYSTEMS	5/1	6/1	
PROGRAMMING	W.SMITH	PROG.	6/1	7/1	
9. INTERFACE WITH OTHER SYSTEMS:	-	-	-	-	
FILES					
DATA					
PROGRAMS					

APPROVED BY:

J.BLACK
USER DEPARTMENT

W.WHITE
SYSTEMS DEPARTMENT

S.JAMES
DATA PROCESSING OPERATIONS

W.SMITH
PROJECT LEADER

Figure 9-7

The form used to control this task is illustrated in Figure 9-9. The working guide for the completion of this task is the series of File Definition forms like the one shown in Figure 8-3.

As indicated earlier, File Definition forms are incorporated in the *Technical Requirements Manual* and its cumulative predecessor documentation. The working plan for this task is to execute one acquisition plan form for each File Definition carried into this activity.

As can be seen from examination of the form layout, each data element (including those to be acquired as input to the new system) is accounted for numerically and through descriptions.

The use of data element numbers on the File Data Acquisition Plan form highlights a built-in quality control feature of structured project management. Specifically, data element identifications (numbers and mnemonic descriptions) are assigned early in the project and remain constant all the way through Conversion. This approach provides built-in continuity to be sure that all features specified for the system are, in fact, carried through.

CONVERSION PLAN

PAGE __1__ OF ___1___
PROJECT NO. ___028___
PREPARED BY___ J.JONES___

ORGANIZATION ___ABC COMPANY___
APPLICATION TITLE ___LABOR DISTRIBUTION___
DATE ____4-5____

DESCRIBE THE FOLLOWING MAJOR ACTIVITIES IN TERMS OF SPECIFIC TASKS, ACTION STEPS, OR ITEMS TO BE ACCOMPLISHED:

FILES	CONVERSION SEQUENCE
FORMS	CONVERSION PROGRAMS
PARALLEL PROCESSING	

I. FILES
   A. PURIFICATION OF RECORDS
      THE PRESENT EMPLOYEE RATE KARDEX RECORDS WILL BE REVIEWED
      INDIVIDUALLY BY THE ACCOUNTING DEPARTMENT TO VERIFY THE
      ACCURACY OF:
            DEPARTMENT NO.
            CLOCK NO.
            HOURLY RATE

   B. CODING REQUIREMENTS
      ALL KARDEX RECORDS WILL BE CODED AS TO THE ACTIVE OR INACTIVE
      STATUS OF EACH EMPLOYEE:
            1 = ACTIVE
            0 = INACTIVE

   C. CONTROL
      AN ADDING MACHINE TAPE OF ALL KARDEX RECORDS WILL BE RUN ON
      7/1 TO SUMMARIZE:
            CLOCK NUMBERS
            HOURLY RATES

   D. CONVERSION
      THE SYSTEMS DEPARTMENT WILL DEVELOP A CARD FORMAT INTO WHICH
      EACH KARDEX RECORD WILL BE PUNCHED AND A CONVERSION PROGRAM
      TO CONVERT THE REQUIRED CARDS TO MAGNETIC TAPE. THE CONVERSION
      PROGRAM WILL CONTAIN THE REQUIRED CONTROLS.

   E. MAINTENANCE
      ADDITIONS, DELETIONS AND CHANGES TO THE LABOR/RATE FILES WILL
      BE MADE ACCORDING TO THE OPERATIONAL INSTRUCTIONS FOR MAINTEN-
      ANCE TO BE DEVELOPED BY THE SYSTEMS DEPARTMENT

APPROVED BY:

| J.BLACK | W.WHITE | S.JAMES | W.SMITH |
| USER DEPARTMENT | SYSTEMS DEPARTMENT | DATA PROCESSING OPERATIONS | PROJECT LEADER |

Figure 9-8

FILE DATA ACQUISITION PLAN

ORGANIZATION ___ ABC COMPANY
APPLICATION TITLE ___ LABOR DISTRIBUTION

PAGE 1 OF 1
PROJECT NO. ___ 028
PREPARED BY ___ J.JONES
DATE ___ 4-6

FILE NO.	FILE NAME				RECORD CODES ON FILE			FILE MAINT. PROG. NO.	ANALYST RESPONSIBLE
	LABOR / RATE								J.JONES
								LD-040	J.JONES

ELE. NO.	ELEMENT NAME	FILE OR DOC. CONVERTED FROM	INPUT TRANS. CODE	INPUT RECORD NAME	INPUT RECORD CODE	FIELD NO. OR C.C.	CONV. PROG. NO.	DESCRIPTION OF OR REFERENCE TO METHOD OF ACQUISITION *
001	DEPARTMENT	EMPLOYEE RATE KARDEX	201	EMPL. RATE	401	4-7	NONE	PUNCH FROM EMPLOYEE RATE KARDEX RECORD INTO 201 TRANSACTION CARD
002	CLOCK NO.	EMPLOYEE RATE KARDEX	201	EMPL. RATE	401	8-11	NONE	SAME AS ABOVE
003 TO 009								ACCUMULATED FROM CURRENT INPUT
010	HOURLY RATE	EMPLOYEE RATE KARDEX	201	EMPL. RATE	401	12-16	NONE	PUNCH FROM EMPLOYEE RATE KARDEX RECORD INTO 201 TRANSACTION CARD

* REFERENCE MULTI-PURPOSE FORM NO.

APPROVED BY:.

J.BLACK
USER DEPARTMENT

W.WHITE
SYSTEMS DEPARTMENT

S.JAMES
DATA PROCESSING OPERATIONS

W.SMITH
PROJECT LEADER

Figure 9-9

Thus, in assigning numbers on the File Data Acquisition Plan form, the systems analyst checks all the way back to the *System Requirements Manual,* where data element numbers were established through use of a Data Element ID form, a Data ID form, and, as applicable, a data dictionary.

For each data element to be acquired, the source is identified on the File Data Acquisition Plan. Further, the transaction code number is listed, and the input record name and description are given. Further, the position of the individual data element within its file is identified according to character position or card column numbers. If Conversion programs are to be used to set up the new files, these are identified. Finally, for each data element, a description is entered for the method to be used in its acquisition.

In summary, this form is designed as a working guide for the project team personnel who will be responsible for setting up the data files of the new system during the Conversion activity.

MANPOWER AND EQUIPMENT PLAN

The form shown in Figure 9-10 is the final planning control document prepared in planning for the Conversion activity. This is used to stipulate and schedule the resources in both men and machines which must be allocated to the Conversion activity. Note that the general categories of manpower and equipment requirements are described in the column at the far left of this form. In succeeding columns, the systems analyst enters descriptions of skill levels for manual operations and the total hours required. Then the work requirements are spread over a monthly schedule set up in the remainder of the body of the form.

In effect, this form quantifies and schedules previously discussed Conversion documentation. Again, a good measure of the total success of the system hinges on the effectiveness of plans established for Conversion at this point in the project.

Because it is obviously a front line planning tool at the project level, the Manpower and Equipment Plan should be incorporated in the master Project Plan originated during the System Planning Study activity and carried forward and updated in succeeding activities. Obviously from its content, the Manpower and Equipment Plan has all the information necessary to serve as the basis for initiating the Conversion activity.

MANPOWER AND EQUIPMENT PLAN

PAGE _1_ OF _1_
PROJECT NO. _028_
PREPARED BY _J. JONES_
DATE _4-6_

ORGANIZATION _ABC COMPANY_
APPLICATION TITLE _LABOR DISTRIBUTION_

RESOURCE	SKILL LEVEL *	HOURS REQ'D.	MAY	JUNE	JULY	AUGUST		
					SCHEDULE			
1. USER DEPARTMENT ACCOUNTING	CLERICAL	200	50	150				
	MGMT.	20	10	10				
2. DATA CONTROL	CLERICAL	16			16			
3. DATA CONVERSION		100		100				
4. OUTSIDE SERVICES								
5. EAM EQUIPMENT	SORTER ORERATOR	20		20				
6. COMPUTER		20			10	10		
7. OTHER								

APPROVED BY:

J. BLACK
USER DEPARTMENT

W. WHITE
SYSTEMS DEPARTMENT

W. SMITH
PROJECT LEADER

* WHEN APPLICABLE

Figure 9-10

IMPLEMENTATION PLAN

The cumulative documentation created in the course of this activity is incorporated in a formal Implementation Plan. As indicated in Figure 9-1, the plan goes through an initial review with user management. At this point, the need for user commitment prior to the full-scale User Training activity which will follow immediately is emphasized. Unequivocal commitment at all management levels in the user organization must be secured as a prerequisite to the culmination of the Implementation Planning activity.

As the flow chart indicates, the Implementation Plan is revised and approved following the user review.

The Implementation Plan is then ready for diagnosis in a User/Technical Conference for which participants include programming, EDP operations, and technical services personnel.

After any modifications needed to satisfy the User/Technical Conference have been incorporated in the Implementation Plan, it is presented to the EDP Systems Planning Steering Committee—with a Management Summary affixed for management-level review.

The steering committee review, as indicated earlier, concentrates on exceptions or alterations between the Implementation Plan and previously presented schedules, costs, and commitments. In other words, this review is more of a stringent checkpoint than a full-dress reexamination of project status. If all elements of the Project Plan are still within the bounds indicated at the time of the last review, the committee action is fairly routine. However, as a matter of policy, any exceptions or changes should be scrutinized closely.

Obviously, the committee can terminate the project, reschedule it, or reevaluate at this point—based on the content of the Implementation Plan and the Project Plan. This review by the committee is important from a management-control standpoint because of the magnitude and expense of the three activities which will take place before the next scheduled review by the committee.

Once committee approval is granted, the project moves forward into the parallel activites of Programming and User Training. These, in turn, are followed directly by System Test. In other words, the next time the committee will look at the project again, it will have completed its Development phase and be ready for Implementation.

CHAPTER TEN

Programming

DEFINITION

Unlike other terms cited earlier and used with complete consistency, references to programs and programming have had varying meanings. This is virtually inevitable in a discussion of system project techniques. In the real world of system development, the terms are used loosely and inclusively. Therefore, for the purposes of this chapter and ensuing discussions, the terms will be defined and used generally.

A *program* is an identifiable sequence of instructions which can be executed as a single processing unit.

Programming is the skill of expressing generalized system requirements and logical functions in specific, machine-compatible terms. This is done through the rendering of generalized objectives into specific instructions, or coding, which control computer performance. The end product of programming is a program, or series of programs, depending on the individual task at hand.

The term "program," as used here, can apply to and be synonymous with the already-defined words "module" and "run." That is, a run or a module can also be described as a program. According to the definitions given in Chapter 8, runs and modules fit the description just accorded to programs in that they are executable sequences of instructions. A job, however, is larger in scope and stature. It would encompass two or more programs, modules, or runs.

Within this scoping of the terms, care should be taken never to confuse a program with a system. A system, as defined in Chapter 1, is a combination of people, procedures, equipment, and materials oriented toward achievement of specific objectives.

Considering this terminology from another viewpoint, the terms "program" and "programming" are used in their functional sense within this work. This is not to say that other uses of the terms are wrong. Rather, this discussion has been intended as a qualification of the context and concepts within this book and its accompanying volume, *Managing the EDP Function.*

ACTIVITY SCOPE

Whether programming is done in-house or by a subcontractor, no direct performance demands are made on either the system project leader and his staff or the user group. It is an independently conducted activity, whether it happens to be in-house or subcontracted.

ACTIVITY RESPONSIBILITY

Because of these basic characteristics of the Programming effort, this chapter—and this book—will not go into detail about how programs are designed, written, tested, debugged, or stored in libraries. Rather, this discussion will concentrate on the inescapable fact of life that, just as is the case with every other activity in the system project, the system project leader remains responsible. He is in charge. He must devise and implement working controls. All the stated and implied rules of management control apply even though there may be no "hands-on" involvement by system project personnel.

In terms of overall scope, therefore, the system project leader must have a complete schedule of work performance, assurance that schedules will be maintained, that programs will meet standards, and so on.

ACTIVITY WORK FLOW

With the Programming activity, as with all others, checkpointing and control are built into the work flow task sequence, which is diagramed in Figure 10-1.

As indicated, this activity begins with and is based upon a review and

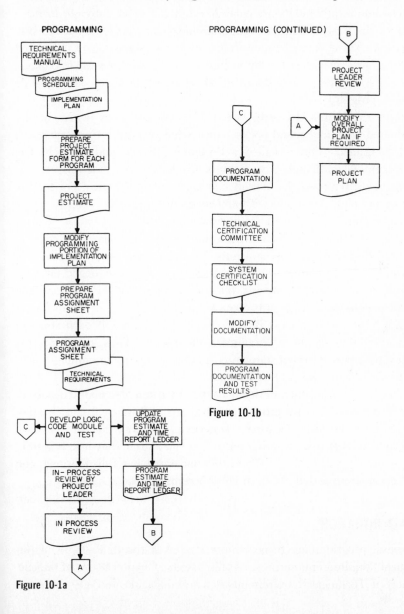

PROGRAMMING

TECHNICAL REQUIREMENTS MANUAL

PROGRAMMING SCHEDULE

IMPLEMENTATION PLAN

PREPARE PROJECT ESTIMATE FORM FOR EACH PROGRAM

PROJECT ESTIMATE

MODIFY PROGRAMMING PORTION OF IMPLEMENTATION PLAN

PREPARE PROGRAM ASSIGNMENT SHEET

PROGRAM ASSIGNMENT SHEET

TECHNICAL REQUIREMENTS

DEVELOP LOGIC, CODE MODULE AND TEST — C

UPDATE PROGRAM ESTIMATE AND TIME REPORT LEDGER

IN-PROCESS REVIEW BY PROJECT LEADER

PROGRAM ESTIMATE AND TIME REPORT LEDGER

IN PROCESS REVIEW

B

A

Figure 10-1a

PROGRAMMING (CONTINUED)

C

PROGRAM DOCUMENTATION

TECHNICAL CERTIFICATION COMMITTEE

SYSTEM CERTIFICATION CHECKLIST

MODIFY DOCUMENTATION

PROGRAM DOCUMENTATION AND TEST RESULTS

Figure 10-1b

B

PROJECT LEADER REVIEW

A — MODIFY OVERALL PROJECT PLAN IF REQUIRED

PROJECT PLAN

assimilation of the contents of the *Technical Requirements Manual.* From there, the work and documentation stream proceeds as follows:

- Using a quarterly programming work schedule updated to reflect commitments on this project during the Technical Requirements activity, the programming manager divides the project, from a programming standpoint, into work increments according to program modules. Schedule requirements are established on a Project Estimate form.
- From the Project Estimate, programming work assignments are prepared. These assign responsibility and time allotments to individual programmers within the department on a module-by-module basis. A separate Program Assignment Sheet is prepared for each module to be programmed.
- A control document is established which incorporates figures for estimated times and actual performance achievements in the preparation of programs. This is called a Program Estimate and Time Report Ledger. Even though programmers turn in separate time reports, this document becomes the overall management surveillance tool for the programming associated with any single given project.
- Programmers execute their assignments. As indicated in Figure 10-1, programming tasks within the project management concept under discussion are divided into three elements—logic, coding, and testing. Performance in each of these three areas is logged onto his assignment sheet. From this, the control ledger for the programming task is updated. For quality control throughout the life of the Programming task, an In-process Review form is signed off at each stage of every module by the programming supervisor. Thus, the In-process Review serves as a real status report between the programming manager and the system project leader.
- After all programs for a project have been written, documented, tested, and approved by the programming group, a Technical Certification Committee reviews the work. If necessary, further modifications are made. Certification of programs is done on a form known as a System Certification Checklist. When this document has full approval, the Programming activity is considered accomplished.

ACTIVITY INITIATION

In a sense, programming responsibility started in the final stages of the Technical Requirements activity. As discussed in Chapter 8, one of the end products of Technical Requirements is a schedule, like the one shown in

Figure 10-2, which commits the people and time slots needed to program the system under development. As indicated in Figure 10-2, one workable method for handling this scheduling task is to plan programming time on a quarterly basis. The schedule shown covers three separate planning and scheduling dimensions:

1. Programming for the individual project is charted and scheduled, module by module, workweek by workweek.
2. Programmers assigned to the project have their time allocations scheduled in terms of hours per week.
3. In the chart at the bottom of the form, time availabilities of the affected programmers are plotted in terms of 13-week periods.

As indicated, this type of schedule is updated and approved for the specific project during the Technical Requirements activity. However, because the commitments are for programming tasks and programming people, the programming group fills out these forms in coordination with the system project leader and the systems analyst responsible for the Technical Requirements activity. This schedule, along with the *Technical Requirements Manual*, becomes input to the Programming activity, as indicated in Figure 10-1.

PROJECT ESTIMATE

The Project Estimate form shown in Figure 10-3 is directly related to the programming schedule form. In practice, the Project Estimate is generally filled out along with and at the same time as the Project Schedule. Depending on the preferences of the individual programming manager, the Project Estimate can actually be used as a work sheet completed in direct parallel with the schedule.

As can be seen in Figure 10-3, this form provides areas to enter identifications for the programs (runs) and individual modules. Coordination between system designer, system project leader, and programming manager is necessary to agree upon the module breakdown and work time estimates represented on this form.

Note particularly that a system of standards has been set up for programming estimations. For each module entered on the form, the programming manager is asked to indicate whether it is available in the organization's library. If a yes answer is entered, the module is considered to be available and no programming time is entered.

Where programming will be required, the programming manager indicates a complexity rating. Four categories are provided on this form, in-

PROGRAMMING   ☒ DEVELOPMENT / ☐ MAINTENANCE   SCHEDULE

ORGANIZATION _ABC Company_
APPLICATION TITLE _Labor Distribution_

PAGE _1_ OF _1_
PROJECT NO. _028_
PREPARED BY _R. Bates_
DATE _4/9_

THIRTEEN WEEK PERIOD FROM _4/11/70_ TO _7/6/70_

THIRTEEN WEEK PLAN

SYSTEM REQUEST NUMBER	ORIGINATING DESIGN GROUP	PROJECT NAME	PROGRAMMER	ACTIVITY	1	2	3	4	5	6	7	8	9	10	11	12	13
028	Systems Development	Labor Distribution	M. Kirsch	LD 0105	8												
				LD 020	30	35	20	5	6								
				LD 030			3	3	10								
				LD 040				10	20	30	20	20	30	30	14		
			T. Martin	LD 050	30	20	25	30	15	25	20	30	10	5	5	10	
				LD 060				5	5	10		10	10	5	5	12	8
				LD 070													
				LD 080													

PERSONNEL AVAILABILITY (NET OF SCHEDULED HOURS AND LOST TIME)

	1	2	3	4	5	6	7	8	9	10	11	12	13
1. M. Kirsch	2	5	17	22	4	10	20	20	10	10	26	30	40
2. T. Martin	10	20	15	5	1	15	30	10	30	30	35	28	32
3.													
4.													
5.													
6.													
7.													
8.													
9.													
10.													
11.													
12.													
13.													
Total Net Available Hours	12	25	32	27	4	25	40	30	40	61	58	72	

Figure 10-2

PROGRAM NO.	PROGRAM NAME	TYPE	Freq	Mod. No.	MODULE NAME	Avail In Lib.	A	B	C	D	Prog.	SysTst	Total	Prog	SysTst	Recur.
							COMPLEXITY				MAN-EFFORT			COMPUTER TIME		
LD-040	UPDATE LABOR/RATE	D		01	COMPUTE I/O COUNT	N		X			32	4	36	4	1	—
				02	UPDATE LABOR/RATE	N			X		60	4	64	6	1	—
				03	PRINT UPDATE REPORT	N		X			24	4	28	3	1	—
				04	PRINT RECORD COUNTS	N	X				12	4	16	3	1	—
				05	READ LABOR/RATE	N			X		32	4	36	4	.5	.5
				06	WRITE LABOR/RATE	Y					—	4	4	—	.5	.5

ORGANIZATION ABC COMPANY
APPLICATION TITLE LABOR DISTRIBUTION
☐ SYSTEMS PLANNING   ☒ PROGRAM DEVELOPMENT
PROJECT ESTIMATE
PAGE 1 OF 1
PROJECT NO. 028
PREPARED BY R.BATES
DATE 9-10

PROJECT NAME LABOR DISTRIBUTION   TOTALS 1 1 2 1   160 24 184   20 5 1

APPROVALS 1._____ DATE _____
2._____ DATE _____
3._____ DATE _____

NOTE: 1. Man-Effort is in days for Systems Planning
2. Man-Effort is in Hours for Program/Development

COST SUMMARY	M-E	Man $	Computer Hours	Computer $	Total $	Hours Mo.	$/Mo.
	DEVELOPMENTAL					RECURRING	
PROGRAMMING	160	1140	20	400	1540		
SYSTEMS TEST	24	171	5	100	271		
TOTALS	184	1311	25	500	1811	22	440

Figure 10-3

dicated by four columns, A through D. Each of these ratings is standard-ized according to programming time requirements. As can be seen from entries on the sample form, an A rating in complexity indicates a 12-hour job, and a B rating indicates a 24-hour job.

As part of the project programming estimating process, time require-ments are totalled. This form, obviously, is then cross referenced with the programming schedule and with subsequent documentation which will be used in managing and controlling the Programming activity.

As discussed earlier, a general objective of programming management under the methodology discussed here is to limit individual work assign-ments to a maximum of ten days each. This minimizes exposure and poten-tial loss through inapplicable programming efforts and serves to help meet the objective of controlling a project on a tight, week-by-week basis.

Implementation of this program control technique begins with an initial subdivision of the overall System Requirements in jobs, modules, and runs —as discussed. For the purpose of programming work assignments, stand-alone program functions of the type which exist in all programs are isolated and identified on the work schedules as individual modules.

To illustrate, in a typical on-line inquiry program, there would be sepa-rate modules covering file search, transaction or inquiry identification, error control, output formatting, and so on. In addition, each program controlled in this manner would have one linkage module which tied all the others together.

This approach becomes particularly attractive for the writing of programs which will run in an operating system environment. Under software control, linkage modules can be implemented at execution time rather than as part of the source program, as was necessary in second generation programming.

In addition to being workable as a project development technique, this approach also gives the EDP organization an opportunity to build a library of program functions, some of which may be actively reusable within a number of applications. For example, a file search routine might be applicable within almost any on-line system developed for the computer using organization.

PROGRAM ESTIMATE AND TIME REPORT LEDGER

The Program Estimate and Time Report Ledger form, illustrated in Figure 10-4, is, clearly, a document designed to compare estimated against actual performance. The form begins with the entry of original estimates of working times. Then, as work is performed, appropriate entries are made,

PROGRAM ESTIMATE AND TIME REPORT LEDGER

DATE OPENED 5/10

PAGE 1 OF 1
PROJECT NO. 028
PREPARED BY R. BATES
DATE 4-11

ORGANIZATION ABC COMPANY
APPLICATION TITLE LABOR DISTRIBUTION

PROGRAMMING

Mod No MODULE NAME PROGRAMMER	START DATE	ORIGINAL ESTIMATE		5/15	5/22	5/29	6/5	6/12	6/19	6/26	7/3	7/10		TOTAL PROG	DUE DATE	Est., Systm Test
01 I/O COUNTS	PLAN: 5/29	LOGIC	13			13								PLAN: 32	6/5	4
		CODING	13			13										
M. KIRSCH	ACT: 5/29	TEST	6			6								ACT: 32	6/2	3
02 UPDATE	PLAN: 6/1	LOGIC	26			6	20							PLAN: 60	PLAN: 6/21	4
		CODING	26				20	6								
M. KIRSCH	ACT: 6/2	TEST	8					8						ACT: 60	ACT: 6/22	5
03 PRINT REPORT	PLAN: 6/19	LOGIC	10					10						PLAN: 24	PLAN: 6/26	4
		CODING	10					10								
M. KIRSCH	ACT: 6/20	TEST	4						4					ACT: 24	ACT: 6/26	4
04 PRINT COUNTS	PLAN: 6/26	LOGIC	5						5					PLAN: 12	PLAN: 6/30	4
		CODING	5						5							
M. KIRSCH	ACT: 6/28	TEST	2						5					ACT: 15	ACT: 6/30	4
05 READ L/R	PLAN: 5/15	LOGIC	13	10	3									PLAN: 32	PLAN: 5/26	4
		CODING	13		13											
M. KIRSCH	ACT: 5/15	TEST	6		6									ACT: 32	ACT: 5/26	4
06 WRITE L/R	PLAN: —	LOGIC	0											PLAN: —	PLAN: —	4
		CODING	0													
M. KIRSCH	ACT: —	TEST	0											ACT: —	ACT: —	4
	PLAN:	LOGIC												PLAN:	PLAN:	
		CODING														
	ACT:	TEST												ACT:	ACT:	
		TOTALS	160	10	22	38	20	20	34	19					ACTUAL 24	

SYSTEM TEST

PROGRAMMER	Plan Start	Actual Start	EST	7/3	7/10										Total Actual	Plan Comp Date	Actual Comp Date
M. KIRSCH	7/3	7/3	24	14	10										24	7/14	7/17

Figure 10-4

and comparative totals developed.   At a glance, the programming manager and system project leader can review this form and determine status in terms of both projected completion and actual expenditures as compared with estimates — on a week-by-week basis.

The ledger form shown in Figure 10-4, as its name implies, is both cumulative and historical, as is the case with accounting ledgers.   The use of this document is similar to that made of an accounting ledger.   That is, it serves as both a working document for performance accountability and as a basis for management status review for current position determination.

NOTE: All forms for programming management and control discussed up to this point — and those which follow — are set up according to weekly time modules.   In practice, it is usually recommended that the system project leader and programming manager hold reviews, based on these forms, on a weekly basis.

PROGRAM ASSIGNMENT

Along with the setting up and maintenance of project-level records, the programming manager must provide corresponding information, more detailed as necessary, to the programmer who will be responsible for each module.   Within the techniques under discussion here, the standard procedure is to prepare a separate Program Assignment Sheet, like the one shown in Figure 10-5, for each program module.

A separate sheet is used for each module, even in cases like the one which will be illustrated, where one programmer is assigned responsibility for more than a single module within the project.   Basic assignment information and work responsibility descriptions are entered on the Program Assignment Sheet by the programming manager.   The programming manager also enters scheduled hours and start and due dates for the assignment. The programmer himself enters the actual performance figures.

Note that separate entries have been made in Figure 10-5 for the logic, coding, and testing portions of the programming assignment.   Note also that these areas have been numerically coded so that cost and performance data can be computer processed.

It should also be understood that the form illustrated in Figure 10-5 also functions as a transmittal covering sheet.   That is, it is always accompanied by the documentation from the *Technical Requirements Manual* needed to perform the assignment at hand.   Spaces have been provided to check the designations for the documentation accompanying this form.   With the documentation described to this point, the programmer has all the back-

PROGRAM ASSIGNMENT SHEET

ORGANIZATION *ABC COMPANY*
APPLICATION TITLE *LABOR DISTRIBUTION*
PROGRAM NAME *UPDATE L/R*   PROGRAM NO. *LD-040*

PAGE *1* OF *1*
PROJECT NO. *028*
PREPARED BY *R BATES*
DATE *4-12*

PROGRAMMER   *J. JONES*

[X] NEW PROJECT   [ ] MAINTENANCE

Module Function or Maintenance to be Performed *UPDATE LABOR/RATE - MODULE 02 OF*
PROGRAM LD040 (UPDATE LABOR/RATE MASTER)

Documentation Attached

(X) Printer Layout   (X) Table Form   (X) Multi-Purpose Form
( ) File Definition   ( ) Decision Table   ( )

PLAN

Total Hours *60*   Start Date *6/1*   Due Date *6/21*

Time Reporting Control

Programming Work Unit			WE 6/2		WE 6/9		WE 6/16		WE 6/23		Total
Name	No.	Due Date	This Week	To Date	This Week	To Date	This Week	To Date	This Week	To Date	
LOGIC	01	6/8	6	6	14	20	—	20	—	20	20
CODING	02	6/19	—	—	—	—	20	20	6	26	26
TEST	03	6/21	—	—	—	—	—	—	8	8	8

*See Time Report For Programming Work Unit Codes.

TOTAL *54*

Figure 10-5

ground information and documentation he needs to undertake his assignment.

Similarly, the programming manager has the tools he needs to break down assignments into controllable segments.

THE PROGRAMMING TASK

As indicated in the entries on Figure 10-5, the programmer plans, executes, and keeps track of his working efforts in terms of the three component parts of his job — logic, coding, testing. Since this discussion will not get into the actual doing of programming, it is important to recognize, from a management standpoint, that this approach of separating work categories serves to reinforce the sense of both responsibility and pride needed to build and maintain the necessary feeling of professionalism in programming operations.

Figure 10-5, as indicated previously, is the reporting control document executed by the programmer in advising his manager and the system project leader on progress and status.

IN-PROCESS REVIEW

The In-process Review of programming status is generally conducted weekly at a management level—between the programming manager and the system project leader.   The basis for this surveillance is the In-process Review form shown in Figure 10-6.   As with the other reporting documentation discussed in conjunction with the Programming activity, this form is cumulative.   Spaces are provided for listing and approval sign-off for each of the modules within a program (run).   Sign-offs for each module are called for at four stages, each of the three working categories of the job and acceptance of test results.

Thus, when the senior programmer acting as a quality control reviewer has certified the results achieved at any of the four quality control checkpoints for each module, he presents his findings to the system project leader, who initials and dates the appropriate space to indicate his acceptance.

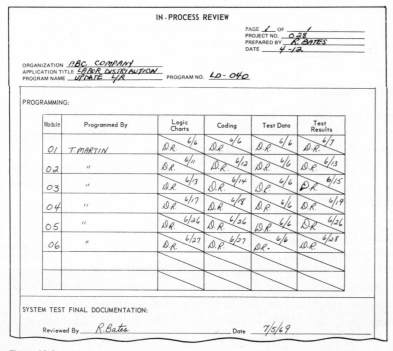

Figure 10-6

When all stages for every module have been signed off, the system project leader has "bought" the programs—at least up until the point of development within the scope of this activity. That is, the programs would still be subject to System Test and further evaluation during Conversion.

At this point in the project, however, the In-process Review form serves to stress the responsibilities and consequences involved. By calling for specific acceptances at each stage of development for every module, all managers involved are impressed with the consequences of their decisions.

OVERALL PROJECT PLAN IMPACT

Note that Figure 10-1 indicates a management task associated with the In-process Review which calls for modification of the overall Project Plan, as necessary, on the basis of the actual or forecast results of the Programming activity. Since Programming is entirely a technical activity, top-management reviews are needed only on an exception basis. Should modification be necessary, the chart shows that a modified plan is developed and the activity is suspended until it can be presented to and acted upon by operating management. Specifically, should developments during the Programming activity jeopardize either the overall project schedule or the budgeted costs approved by the steering committee, the matter should be referred back to the committee as soon as the situation comes to light.

PROGRAM DOCUMENTATION

The techniques and forms used for program documentation should be subject to standards developed, maintained, and enforced for each separate computer installation. Such standards are beyond the scope of this book. However, in reviewing the Programming activity, it should be stressed that formal, clearly stated standards should be established for every data processing department.

TECHNICAL CERTIFICATION

This task incorporates the final review, modification, and approval for the Programming activity. The review committee is made up of representatives from the programming, technical support (operations), and technical services groups. In addition, of course, the system project leader is part of this committee. The group assignment is to evaluate and approve the results of program testing.

The form used to control the technical certification of new programs is illustrated in Figure 10-7.   As the form shows, certification is done at three levels—documentation, technical quality, and management review and acceptance.   As appropriate, spaces are provided for certification signatures by responsible system maintenance or operations people.

At this point—prior to final approval within the Programming activity— the newly developed programs should have been run in their entirety, with all modules included.   Test data closely resembling the live information which will ultimately be processed should be executed.   Evaluations should be based on run timings as well as actual output results, error messages, and so on.   As indicated in Figure 10-1, a separate task should be established to perform any modification requirements uncovered by the

SYSTEM CERTIFICATION CHECKLIST

PAGE _1_ OF _1_
PROJECT NO. _028_
PREPARED BY _J JONES_
ORGANIZATION _ABC COMPANY_
APPLICATION TITLE _LABOR DISTRIBUTION_
DATE _7-1_

		MAINTENANCE		OPERATIONS	
DOCUMENTATION REVIEW:		Reviewed By	Date	Reviewed By	Date
	1. System Design Book	R. Bates	5/23		
	2. Program Specifications	R. Bates	7/4		
	3. Program Test Date and Results	R. Bates	1/10		
	4. System Test Plan and Results	R. Bates	1/22		
	5. Control Procedures			S. James	11/15
	6. Operating Instructions			S. James	1/15
	7. Run Books	R. Bates	1/22		
	8. Run Schedule			S. James	1/10
	9.				
TECHNICAL REVIEW:					
	1. Programming Standards	R. Bates	1/15	S. James	1/20
	2. Error Recovery Procedures	R. Bates	1/15	S. James	1/20
	3. File Handling Techniques	R. Bates	1/15	S. James	1/20
	4.				
MANAGEMENT REVIEW AND ACCEPTANCE:					
	1. Programming	R. Bates	1/23		
	2. Operations			S. James	1/23
	3. Accounting	J. Black	1/23		

Figure 10-7

Technical Certification Committee. The committee, then, should review and approve the programs for the entire system, including modifications. It is important that, after each modification, the entire system program test be performed again. It is not enough simply to test the modified segments of a program.

As indicated in Figure 10-1, the output of the Programming activity consists of the completed documentation and the accompanying test results. This documentation should be in a state of completeness so that it can be turned over to operations people who will support the System Test activity.

CHAPTER ELEVEN

User Training

ACTIVITY TIMING

Under the methodology proposed in this work, User Training takes place in direct parallel with Programming.

This is a departure from the sequence which was generally considered normal a few years ago and which is still practiced at many installations. Specifically, it is still fairly common to withhold User Training until after a system is converted and operational.

However, experience at many EDP sites has convinced the authors that, if the project team waits this long to begin training, it rarely gets done at all—never gets done to the degree and extent which should be considered necessary.

A system for which User Training is not carried out completely and at an early point in the project may find that this requirement becomes buried in good intentions and ineptness. If User Training is not performed until after System Test, the systems people are too busy to do the job properly. Users, for their part, are continually adjusting to strange procedures—or to a procedural void.

The reasons for positioning User Training at this point in the project have been touched on earlier. But they are worth stressing here:

- At this stage of the project, the timing is right for the parties concerned. The systems people associated with the project are not too busy because the Programming function does not occupy them fully. The user people are not fully occupied either. The Implementation Plan has been agreed to. They are, in large measure, waiting for the system to happen.
- With User Training completed at this point, users can perform System Test. System Test itself becomes more valid.
- By getting the users involved early, the project team gains an important opportunity to find bottlenecks and bugs in the manual and support procedures for the system. These cannot possibly come to light until the users are actually doing the work under conditions which are as realistic as possible.
- The timing proposed here keeps the users involved. There is no opportunity for interests or enthusiasm to wane while the user group waits around for Programming to happen.

The timing of the User Training activity, in turn, relates directly to the value inherent in user reaffirmation of and recommitment to the system goals during the Implementation Planning activity, as discussed in Chapter 9. If User Training did not follow directly behind Implementation Planning, it could well be difficult to secure full commitment at the Implementation Planning stage of the project. Without such a commitment, in turn, much of the discipline and meaning so important to system fulfillment would be lost.

ACTIVITY SCOPE

The User Training activity, as was noted in the discussion within Chapter 9 of its control forms (the User Training Checklist and the User Training Plan), takes in a comparatively broad scope. In effect, this activity is designed to handle all tasks necessary to get the user organization ready for system conversion. In addition to straightforward job training, several other critically important, preconversion requirements must also be met. For example:

- All personnel involved with the user-oriented, non-EDP portions of the system must be notified of system status, Conversion schedules, and their own impending changes in responsibility.
- Any major system will require reevaluation and change in many per-

sonnel and operating policies. The User Training activity is the place where the discipline necessary to finalize formulation of these policies is applied. Once the policies are determined, the affected people are advised.

- New, formal procedures must be developed and documented to cover changes to existing methods.
- Job outlines must be drawn for the functions and responsibilities which will be assigned to members of the user group under the new system.
- Forms and other business records to be incorporated within the manual portions of the new system must be designed, produced, distributed, and made ready for use.
- If the new system will require changes in physical facilities or equipment within the user area, the changes must be planned, laid out, and provided for during this activity.
- Other departments within the company which interact with the user department must be advised of projected changes.
- Provision must be made for notification of and coordination with persons and/or operations external to the sponsoring organization which may be affected by the new system. For example, if customer service is involved, provision must be made to advise customers of any changes which will be noticeable within the context of their normal transactions with the organization. In particular, if governmental or legal changes will be involved, preparations should also be completed in this area.
- Obviously, training materials must be prepared and administered. This requirement may involve interaction with and separate training of specialists from either the training or personnel department.
- If the new system will have public relations or advertising implications, these should be planned for at this point.

ACTIVITY RESPONSIBILITIES

Although the system project leader still has overall project responsibility and must keep himself cognizant of the status of this activity, actual performance of User Training tasks should be handled chiefly by user people. There are a number of reasons why user involvement should be heavy:

- User managers know their own people better than the systems staff can possibly hope to. They understand the operations at hand and the implications of transition. Since the system will ultimately belong to its users, this is the place for possession to begin.
- If users are handling the training, members of their own line organi-

zation will be more receptive and cooperative. A better basis for communication exists.

- If users perform the training, there is greater insurance that the user department will carry its share of responsibilities during System Test and Conversion. The likelihood of successful completion of training functions is greater if the work is carried out by and within the user organization.

- User personnel, who are not familiar with the developmental background of the system, will examine it with a fresh eye. They are more apt to uncover procedural problems and bugs.

In addition to users, several other departments or groups within the organization have important responsibilities associated with User Training activities. These include:

- The methods and procedures department, or the standards department, whichever has responsibility, should coordinate with the project team to be sure that all documentation generated conforms to overriding policies and practices within the organization.

- Similar coordination should be applied to make sure that any forms or business documents specified for the new system conform to applicable records management and design standards within the organization.

- Similarly, the personnel department should be brought into the picture for guidance and approval of content and format for job outlines developed in the course of this activity.

- Interaction should also be arranged between the purchasing and engineering departments in conjunction with equipment, materials, or procedures specified for the new system over which they may have cognizance.

ACTIVITY WORK FLOW

The work flow for the User Training activity is diagramed in Figure 11-1. Highlights include:

- The framework for the activity is established by documentation incorporated in the *New System Requirements Manual* and the Implementation Plan.

- User personnel are given task-force assignments within the individual groups involved in this activity.

- As necessary, the task force modifies the Implementation Plan to conform to its findings and requirements.

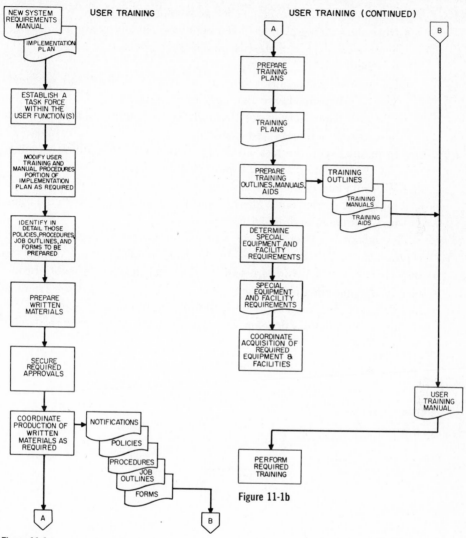

Figure 11-1a

Figure 11-1b

- The task force identifies its own working requirements for the development of policies, procedures, job outlines, and forms to be developed.
- The written materials identified in the previous task are prepared and/or are designed, as necessary.
- Approval is secured for all new forms, job outlines, policy statements, procedures, and so on.
- The task team arranges for and coordinates production and distribution for all the written materials associated with this activity.

- A detailed plan is developed for personnel training.
- Once the training plan has been approved, the necessary training outlines, manuals, text materials, audio-visual aids, and so on are brought together.
- Equipment and facility requirements are determined and specified. These system needs are thoroughly documented.
- The task team coordinates the ordering, expediting, and installation of needed equipment and materials.
- In parallel with the task involving equipment and facilities planning, the *User Training Manual* is produced and assembled.
- With all materials, equipment, and documentation ready, actual training can be carried out. This task includes, as necessary, both the training of trainers and actual user personnel.

Throughout the User Training activity, the system project leader is in continuous touch with progress on the Programming effort. Insofar as possible, the two activities are scheduled so that they are brought to completion at approximately the same time. Reviews for both User Training and Programming are completed within the system project team. Unless variances or exceptions develop, the project can move forward directly into System Test.

CHAPTER TWELVE

System Test

ACTIVITY SIGNIFICANCE

The System Test activity occurs at a highly critical juncture during the system project—it marks the end of the Development phase for the new system.

In terms of overall significance, the project is approaching a point of no return. If System Test is successful, the project and its sponsoring organization are committed to Implementation. If System Test is a failure, considerable loss and embarrassment are inevitable.

At the conclusion of System Test, the EDP Systems Planning Steering Committee makes its most sweeping and total commitment. If System Test documentation is approved, the committee commits the organization to the changes in its life-style and methodology implicit in any major functional alteration.

ACTIVITY SCOPE

The System Test activity is the equivalent of a shakedown cruise for a new ship. Before a new vessel is commissioned, it is checked out by its crew to be sure it is seaworthy and that all equipment functions properly.

At this point within the system development process, the new project is similarly berthed. It is built to completion and ready for service. But it needs to be tried out first.

Functionally, then, the scope of the System Test activity is total. It covers all aspects, every facet, of service and performance which will be expected of the final, operational system.

In terms of time frame and work requirements on the part of the system project team, System Test is a fairly compressed activity. It accounts for about 5 percent of the overall project expenditure. Elapsed time should be tied to schedules for bringing the new system into active use.

ACTIVITY RESPONSIBILITY

The system project leader is directly at the helm during System Test. However, this activity is highly interdisciplinary. The entire project team is involved in planning, supervising, and implementing System Test. However, this activity also involves a much larger group of personnel.

Specifically, the user personnel—who have now been trained in system operation—actually perform the System Test. Insofar as is possible, the System Test activity will be carried out under realistic operating conditions —except for inevitable exceptions. For example, if the new system replaces an already existing system, the old practices will still be in use. Therefore, in such a case, the test would have to be performed in a specially created environment. However, within this constraint, operations should be performed as normally as possible—allowing for the newness of the tasks and responsibilities for the people involved.

Specifically, user executives direct and manage the test activities. User personnel perform the jobs for which they have been trained. Programmers and other EDP professionals provide technical support services but do not become directly involved with users any more than is necessary to meet conditions as they evolve.

TEST PHILOSOPHIES

This approach to system testing is different from the methodology followed in many quarters. It has been common, for example, for EDP people to perform the complete System Test. Under this approach, user training generally does not take place until after the system has been tested. Then, the theoretically operational system is turned over to its users.

This approach has, in many actual, bitter instances, been the major cause for system failures of the type referred to at the outset of this book. As has been stated several times in this work, a system must belong to its users. System Test is a culmination for the workability of this approach and philosophy. If actual users do not test and buy off the system, there can be no assurance that it will really work when it goes live.

A variation of the approach under which System Test is performed by EDP people calls for use of casual employees to perform the clerical aspects of System Test. This has the added drawback of being wasteful in addition to failing to prove system workability. That is, with System Test performed by EDP people there is at least the advantage of having the experience within the organization. If casual employees are used, the greatest part of the experience of the test is lost.

Another underlying philosophy, or reason, for System Test is that procedures and conditions should be applied which make the system fail. Personnel should be instructed to overload the system, to make errors purposely, to present combinations of input records or documents which represent worst possible conditions. It is important to find out where a system will fail so that realistic boundaries can be set for normal operation.

THE IMPORTANCE OF TESTING

Paradoxically, although System Test is one of the most important activities within the project, it is also the activity which is most frequently abridged or skipped altogether. The rationale behind the shortcutting or elimination of system testing can be tempting.

Typically, a project is behind schedule, and user management, executive-level management, and maybe even the project leader, are looking for an opportunity to make up lost time. Under such pressures, opportunities to eliminate tasks within the System Test activity come to light all too readily. If pressures are great enough, strong arguments can be mounted in favor of skipping System Test altogether and going directly into Conversion. In such an approach, the project team members and company executives tell themselves they are taking a calculated risk. This approach should not be taken. *Such approaches court catastrophe!*

It is important that the facts of system development life be faced at this point: New computer-inclusive systems are going to have bugs. Revisions and modifications are going to be necessary. If these are not wrung out before Conversion begins, the organization can be demoralized, the users can be discouraged, and the probability of failure skyrockets. Further, cost estimates and budgetary planning go right out the window. If a system is not debugged before Conversion, costs of revision and correction increase at a geometric-or-greater rate.

As a further precaution, System Test within the developmental project should not be confused with or superseded by equipment tests performed by the manufacturer. All manufacturers have acceptance test specifications in their user contracts. Former practices called for performing these tests at the factory prior to shipment. Now, most testing of this type is done on the user premises as the equipment and peripherals are assembled. It is important that the system project leader make this distinction understood by his own management and members of the project team. A manufacturer's acceptance test should not, under any circumstances, be confused with the activity under discussion here—even if the equipment involved is to be dedicated to system fulfillment.

TEST CRITERIA

Allowing that one of the important purposes of System Test is to uncover, identify, and correct problems, procedures must be established for reporting and acting upon discrepancies which are discovered. A considerable portion of this chapter will be devoted to these techniques. However, separate emphasis should be placed on the fact that performance and acceptance standards should be developed and applied. Some of these date back to the initial statements of objectives, performance criteria, and stipulated benefits developed during the Planning phase of the project. These, as discussed, were reviewed and reconfirmed during the Implementation Planning activity. In addition, at every juncture, probabilities and consequences of substandard performance, service interruptions, partial failures, complete failures, and so on were dealt with as necessary contingencies.

These factors should be brought into focus and checked out during the System Test activity. Some of the elements within this category are listed below. However, it should be stressed that this list is neither inclusive nor universal. Performance criteria are individual for each system. Thus, the items below should be considered as something of a quality control checklist:

- *Turnaround.* This factor applies to both on-line and off-line systems. In effect, *turnaround* is a measure of the elapsed time between user input and realization or receipt of results. During System Test, it is important that all factors which bear on turnaround be measured and evaluated. Commonly, within an off-line system, it develops that required reports cannot be processed under stipulated schedules because of input bottlenecks or timetables. Within on-line systems, batch or low-priority processing is frequently delayed during peak hours of terminal inquiry or entry activity.

- *Service level.* Service level is a measure of the breadth and extent of user requirements which can be supported. Within System Test, the critical requirement is a determination of the impact of saturation. For example, within a batch system, report schedules have been known to slip during the days when month-end or year-end closings were being processed. Within an on-line system, certain low-priority terminals may be blocked out during peak hours. Typically, for example, an airline might stop processing inquiries from its accounting office or might not accept straightforward schedule status inquiries during busy travel hours. During System Test, measures of processing time utilization should be weighted and evaluations made to consider implications and alternatives of lowered service levels.

- *Backup procedures* should be tested as realistically as feasible. These will, obviously, vary widely with system type and size. With a batch system, backup plans might call for using alternate computers. If this is the case, trial runs should be conducted to verify that the new programs developed for the project will, in fact, run on the backup installation. This, of course, would not take place until the system had been debugged on its "home" computer. With on-line systems, testing of backup routines would call for realistic utilization of the off-line operating methods which would be used when on-line service is interrupted. Further, plans for backup procedures to handle interrupted service within on-line systems must be balanced by corresponding plans for restoration of service—restart plans—when service is restored. These procedures, too, should be tested.

- *Degradation plan.* This includes alternate methods used when computer systems are impaired but not disabled. With a batch system, for example, alternate procedures might be established for running on partial memory or without some of the system's peripherals. To illustrate, if a printer is down, the degredation plan might call for output to magnetic tape. If the system operates in an on-line environment, provisions must be made for dynamic reconfiguration of the system, for graceful degradation of service level on turnaround, and so on. Similarly, each degradation plan must have a counterpart plan for integration of equipment and procedures as service is restored.

- *Record and file protection plans.* These fall into two categories. One requirement might apply to vital records which are stored remotely for protection against disaster. The other would provide for reconstruction of files damaged through equipment malfunction. In this case, working files would have to be reconstructed from files for the previous period. Tasks should be established to confirm feasibility of such planning within the project under development.
- *Human factors.* Broadly, this includes all clerical, input/output, administrative, and personnel elements involved in the people side of the new system. Insofar as is possible during System Test, workability of personnel areas should be validated. This requirement covers the full range from lighting, to the comfort of new chairs, to the design of desks, to the adequacy of air conditioning, and so on.
- *Forms, methods, and procedures.* This is another catch-all type of category. It deals with the overall information flow within the system. For example, observations should be made on the convenience of entry for all hand-written forms. Then further checkout should be made to be sure that, if applicable, the data elements are arranged for keypunching convenience, and so on.

ACTIVITY WORK FLOW

The flow pattern for tasks and documents within System Test is diagramed in Figure 12–1. Highlights include:

- Input documentation to the System Test activity includes the Implementation Plan, the *System Specifications Manual,* and the *Technical Requirements Manual.* Note that programming documentation is not included here. Relevance, in this case, is determined by user involvement. Remember, users were involved in activities dealing with Implementation Planning, System Specification, and Technical Requirements.
- The first task is a review which includes modification and updating of the System Test Plan, as necessary, as well as orientation and work organization of the comparatively large staff involved in this activity.
- Test data is generated and/or collected. Insofar as possible, this should be live data.
- The system should be used—normally at first, then under conditions calculated to make it fail.
- Throughout the test activity, exceptions, discrepancies, and problems

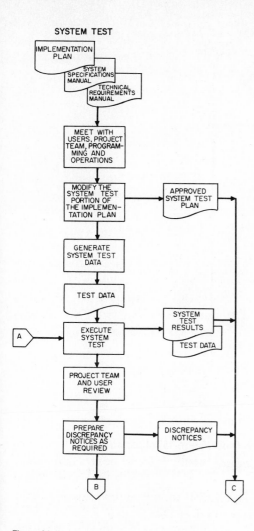

Figure 12-1a

should be noted and documented by all members of the project team. These are reviewed as a specific task within the activity.

- On the basis of reviews of problems, any necessary modifications or alterations are made.
- System acceptance is a formal task involving a definitive user commitment. This is based on an evaluation of System Test results, including results of modifications or alterations.
- At the conclusion of formal system testing, the Project Plan is reviewed

SYSTEM TEST (CONTINUED)

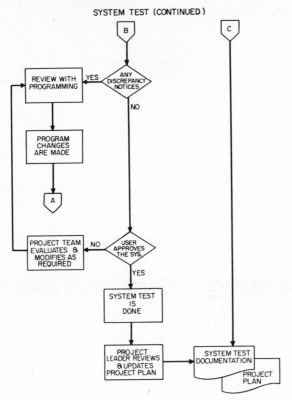

Figure 12-1b

again to determine whether time frame or other factors which have emerged during the test require modification in project implementation.

- End products of the System Test activity include System Test documentation and the updated, current Project Plan.
- This activity is followed by a final EDP Systems Planning Steering Committee review. If the System Test is successful, total buy-off is indicated and total commitment is mandated.

INITIAL PLANNING

The System Test activity calls for a reconvening of the full project team. This group worked as a tightly knit unit during the Implementation Planning activity. Then, the activities which followed became comparatively specialized, with the EDP people becoming technically involved while the user people concentrated on their training program. Now, at the initiation of System Test, the group must be reconstituted as a closely coordinated, working unit. Depending on schedules, the interdisciplinary group may actually have lost touch with each other. Morale may have sagged. Interest in the project may have waned. Recapturing the spirit and determination of the project team is an important management challenge which must be met by the system project leader. This is particularly important because of the critical timing and nature of the System Test activity.

The working documents for the initial planning task of System Test were initiated in the Implementation Planning activity. These are shown in Figures 12-2 and 12-3, with updated entries as they would typically be made during this review, planning, and scheduling task.

Figure 12-2 shows the System Test Checklist form which was introduced

SYSTEM TEST CHECKLIST

PAGE 1 OF 1
PROJECT NO. 028
PREPARED BY J. JONES
DATE 7-9

ORGANIZATION ABC COMPANY
APPLICATION TITLE LABOR DISTRIBUTION

TEST UNIT	TEST UNIT NAME	SCHEDULED START DATE	ACTUAL START DATE	SCHEDULED COMPLETION	ACTUAL COMPLETION	PROJECT LEADER
01	LABOR DIST.RPT.	5/15	5/15	6/1	6/1	W.SMITH

DESCRIPTION OF ACTIVITY	INDIVIDUAL RESPONSIBLE	DEPARTMENT RESPONSIBLE	START DATE	COMPLETION DATE	APPROVED BY
1. COMPUTER TEST PLAN	W.SMITH	SYSTEMS	5/15	5/20	Smith
2. TEST PROCEDURES					Smith
USER DEPARTMENT	J.BLACK	ACCTG.	5/15	5/20	
DATA PROCESSING OPERATIONS	S.JAMES	D/P	5/15	5/20	
SYSTEMS & PROGRAMMING	W.SMITH	SYSTEMS	5/15	5/20	
DATA PROCESSING CONTROLS	M.ROBERT	D/P	5/15	5/20	
3. FORMS					Black
INPUT TEST DATA	J.BLACK	ACCTG.	5/17	5/20	
FILE CREATION & MAINTENANCE	W.SMITH	SYSTEMS	5/17	5/20	
4. CONTROLS					White
USER DEPARTMENT	J.BLACK	ACCTG.	5/19	5/20	
DATA PROCESSING CONTROLS	M.ROBERT	D/P	5/19	5/20	
5. EQUIPMENT					White
AVAILABILITY	S.JAMES	D/P	5/20	5/20	
EMERGENCY SERVICE	-				
6. MANPOWER					Smith
USER DEPARTMENT	J.BLACK	ACCTG.	5/21	5/25	
DATA PROCESSING OPERATIONS	S.JAMES	D/P	5/21	5/25	
SYSTEMS & PROGRAMMING	W.SMITH	SYSTEMS	5/21	5/25	
DATA PROCESSING CONTROLS	-				
7. SUPPLIES					
AVAILABILITY	-				
8. DATA					Smith
CREATED & VERIFIED	S.JAMES	D/P	5/25	5/30	
CONTROLLED	M.ROBERT	D/P	5/25	5/30	
9. FILES					White
CREATED & VERIFIED	S.JAMES	D/P	5/25	5/30	
CONTROLLED	M.ROBERT	D/P	5/25	5/30	
10. MISCELLANEOUS					

Approved by
Joe Black — USER DEPARTMENT
White — SYSTEMS DEPARTMENT
James — DATA PROCESSING DEPARTMENT
W. Smith — PROJECT LEADER

Figure 12-2

in Chapter 9. Note that a separate checklist is prepared for each test unit. In this context, a test unit can be either a module which needs separate evaluation or a series of smaller modules which make up an integrated run. The same form is also used, as necessary, at the job and project level.

Within the form, ten separate categories of test areas and assignments are stipulated. Note that responsibility is pinpointed to departments and individuals in conjunction with these test items.

The form is designed for both scheduling and implementation. Dates for schedules and, later, actual test starts, are entered. Similarly, task completions are entered according to scheduled and actual completion dates. Each task must be specifically approved by the assigned task team member.

Figure 12-3 shows the Computer Test Plan. Note that this is presented in narrative form, on a step-by-step basis, and that approvals are required prior to initiation of the System Test activity.

TEST DATA

Responsibility is a critical factor in the selection of data to be used during System Test. The key point is that user acceptance is one of the end results of this activity. Therefore, since user values and user evaluations will set the standard, users should be held responsible for selecting, accumulating, and providing data which will test the system realistically. If at all feasible, the data should be generated during live operations. At very least, it is vital that the user group be aware of the requirements and that they assume responsibility for the validity of the data presented for System Test.

This, of course, does not alter the fact that the system project leader is still in charge and is still totally responsible. Further, during this activity, he assumes responsibility for the testing and validation of all programmable elements and conditions within the system.

Along with the test data entered into this activity, batch controls must be preestablished as a basis for validation. This is why the description above did not stipulate that the test use live, random data. Batching and preestablishment of totals are necessary, insofar as possible, even with on-line systems. Without controls, tests simply cannot produce acceptable results.

Where a project is aimed at developing an on-line system, it may be necessary to perform System Test before all the terminal and communica-

COMPUTER TEST PLAN

PAGE __1__ OF __1__
PROJECT NO. __028__
PREPARED BY __J.JONES__
DATE __7-9__

ORGANIZATION __ABC COMPANY__
APPLICATION TITLE __LABOR DISTRIBUTION__

SUB-SYSTEM NO.	SUB-SYSTEM NAME		DATE SCHEDULED	DATE COMPLETED	OPERATOR RESPONSIBLE	EQUIPMENT TO BE USED	ANALYST RESPONSIBLE
01	DAILY BATCH PROCESS		6/1	6/1	N.A.W.	COMPUTER	J.JONES

DESCRIPTION OF PLAN

1. SELECT A RANDOM SAMPLE OF LABOR TRANSACTIONS FROM ALL DEPARTMENTS AND INCLUDE WITH TEST DATA PREPARED DURING PROGRAM TEST PHASE.
2. KEY PUNCH AND VERIFY TEST DATA.
3. SORT AND LIST CARDS OFF-LINE TO DEVELOP TOTALS.
4. SELECT KARDEX MASTER EMPLOYEE RATE CARDS TO CORRESPOND WITH THE CLOCK NUMBERS OF THE SELECTED LABOR TRANSACTIONS.
5. KEY PUNCH KARDEX RECORDS INTO THE CONVERSION CARD FORMAT.
6. CONVERT LABOR/RATE CARDS TO THE LABOR/RATE FILE FORMAT USING THE GENERAL PURPOSE CARD-TO-DISC PROGRAM.
7. PRINT THE LABOR/RATE FILE.
8. CHECK INPUT LISTINGS TO INSURE THAT ALL PROGRAM CONDITIONS ARE COVERED
9. SORT DISC USING PROGRAM LD-010S
10. PROCESS PROGRAMS LD-020, 030,040,070,080
11. PRINT FILES LF-09, LF-03.
12. VERIFY HOURS TOTALS.
13. VERIFY ALL EXTENSIONS.
14. VERIFY ALL ERRORS DETECTED AND CONTROL TOTALS OF ERRORS.
15. COMPLETE SYSTEM TEST RESULTS LOG.
16. COMPLETE DISCREPANCY NOTICE (IF REQUIRED).

PROGRAM NO.	PROGRAMMER	PROGRAM NO.	PROGRAMMER	PROGRAM NO.	PROGRAMMER	PROGRAM NO.	PROGRAMMER
LD-020	M.KIRSCH						
LD-030	M.KIRSCH						
LD-040	M.KIRSCH						

APPROVED BY:

J.BLACK — USER DEPARTMENT   W.WHITE — SYSTEMS DEPARTMENT   S.JAMES — DATA PROCESSING DEPARTMENT   W.SMITH — PROJECT LEADER

Figure 12-3

tion interface equipment has been installed.   As a point of principle, terminals and communication equipment should be used if they can be made available in any way.   In some cases, terminals which have not yet been installed in user locations are assembled in a test environment specifically for transaction processing.   Where on-line equipment will not be available, test data should be encoded on tape or disc for entry and processing under conditions which are as realistic as possible.

SUBSYSTEM TESTING

Even though the objectives of this activity call for testing of the full system as a unit—and even though programs were tested and certified during the Programming activity—System Test should be performed progressively and cumulatively, building from modules to runs to subsystems to the full system.

The principle of attempting to make the system fail should be applied at each step in this cumulative process. It should be stressed for the benefit of all parties that the idea is to find and correct problems. Documentation and communication channels must be established for this purpose.

Figure 12-4 shows one form which has been used frequently and successfully for reporting and dealing with problems uncovered during System Test. This form is a Discrepancy Notice. This single document, which includes spaces for signatures by responsible parties, is used both to report

DISCREPANCY NOTICE

PAGE 1 OF 1
PROJECT NO. 028
PREPARED BY J. JONES
DATE 7-28

ORGANIZATION ABC COMPANY
APPLICATION TITLE LABOR DISTRIBUTION
TO ______ FROM ______

SYSTEM NAME LABOR DISTRIBUTION
OUTPUT/REPORT NAME LABOR DISTRIBUTION REPORT
(NOTE: Submit form in triplicate. One copy will be returned with an analysis of findings.)

ITEM NO.	DESCRIPTION OF DISCREPANCY DETECTED
1.	OVERTIME DOLLARS INCORRECTLY CALCULATED FOR ALL EMPLOYEES

ORIGINATOR'S SIGNATURE J. Doe

DO NOT WRITE BELOW THIS LINE

DATE REC.	PROJ. NO.	PROJECT LEADER	MODULE NO.	MODULE NAME	REPLY ASSIGNED TO	DATE OF REPLY
6/2	123	JONES	01	LABOR DIST. REPORT	W SMITH	6/2

ITEM NO.	DISCREPANCY ANALYSIS & CORRECTIVE ACTION TAKEN	PROGRAM NUMBER
1	HOURS OVER 8 NOT EXTENDED BY 150% OF HOURLY RATE — 15% IS BEING USED	LD-070
	PROGRAM LITERAL CORRECTED	

APPROVED BY

W.W. — SYSTEMS DEPARTMENT
SMITH — PROJECT LEADER

Figure 12-4

and take corrective action on each discrepancy. This completeness within each form is an important control factor. This approach also assures the system project leader that his documentation will be complete or that any uncorrected discrepancies will stand out at the final project review.

For control purposes, the EDP professionals associated with the System Test activity also keep a log of test results like the one shown in Figure 12-5. This is a complete, machine-oriented log used to record all test runs of system programs on the computer. An entry is made in this log for each run. Where critical incidents or discrepancies occur, they are recorded in the column at the far right. In the column second from right, a check mark is called for to verify that a Discrepancy Notice has been prepared to cover this condition.

TOTAL SYSTEM TEST

As its name implies, this task calls for running, force failure, discrepancy reporting, correction, and validation of the complete system as it will ulti-mately be implemented by its users. It is important that the test activity build up to a point of totality. Combinations of circumstances or conditions always arise when the full system is in operation, which simply do not take place in the running and utilization of individual increments.

Total test increments, as a rule, are built around system outputs. For example, in a typical batch system, each report, and all the programs and procedures needed in its development, represent total test increments. In an on-line system, a total test would center around application and user areas. With on-line systems, too, system tests are geared to individual out-puts. For example, in an on-line banking system, separate total tests would be performed for the programs involved in savings deposits, savings with-drawals, cash position inquiries, and so on. Typically, all such system tests

SYSTEM TEST ☒
IMPLEMENTATION ☐   RESULTS LOG

PAGE _/_ OF _/_
PROJECT NO. _028_
PREPARED BY _J. JONES_
ORGANIZATION _ABC COMPANY_
APPLICATION TITLE _LABOR DISTRIBUTION_   DATE _7-15_

DATE OF TEST	TIME OF TEST	MODULE NO.	OPERATOR RESPONSIBLE	ANALYST RESPONSIBLE	D/N √	RESULTS
						PROCESSED TO E.D.J.
6/1	0800	01	N. A. W.	W. SMITH	√	OVERTIME DOLLARS WRONG FOR ALL EMPLOYEES

Figure 12-5

would be logged and approved with specific sign-offs on a document like the one shown in Figure 12-6.

TEST APPROVAL

The approval form should be used as formal documentation in the relationship between EDP and user personnel. It can be regarded something like a marriage certificate. The user can speak up at the approval conference or learn to live with the system partnership into which he has entered.

The point is that acceptance and approval of System Test results should be treated with some formality and some gravity. By this point in a project, EDP and user personnel have established a close working rapport if the project has been well managed. Certainly, the group has learned to live together amicably. This is a point, however, where friendship should not cloud decisions. It is important that the system project leader make the consequences of approval fully known to the user group.

Once user and EDP management have approved a system—including all modifications in response to Discrepancy notices—the System Test can be considered complete.

PROJECT PLAN REVIEW

On the basis of System Test, the overall Project Plan should be reviewed and updated as necessary. Test activity findings might, for example, call for changes in Conversion procedures. If major discrepancies resulted, delays may be indicated, even though System Test is accomplished satisfactorily. For example, input documents or output report forms may have been redesigned in the course of System Test. The new documents may have been internally produced in the case of transaction records, or blank paper may have been used in the case of output reports. But, if it now be-

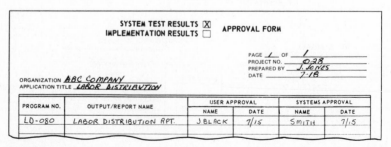

Figure 12-6

comes necessary to return to a vendor to have quantities of forms printed, this could impact Conversion schedules.

FINAL COMMITTEE APPROVAL

Once Project Plan determinations have been made, the system project leader and user manager are ready to go before the EDP Systems Planning Steering Committee for final approval. The presentation covering acceptance of test results is made by the user member of the committee. No narrative documentation is needed at this point, since the signatures on the approval forms speak authoritatively for themselves.

With committee approval, the Development phase of the system project comes to a close. Implementation can begin—under finalized schedules.

Implementation Phase

CHAPTER THIRTEEN

Conversion

IMPLEMENTATION PHASE OVERVIEW

To reestablish perspective for the system project cycle at the beginning of the Implementation phase, note that Figure 2-1, which diagrams a system project, has been repeated, with the Implementation activities highlighted. This chapter and the two which follow will discuss Implementation activities.

With the initiation of the Conversion activity, the project is in its home stretch—the Implementation phase.

Depending on how well the project has been managed up to this point, Implementation can be anywhere from traumatic to hectic. At very least, Implementation in general, Conversion in particular, is a time of long days and many sleepless nights.

The one important warning appropriate at this point is for the project team to remain in control. Assume at the outset of the Implementation phase that unforeseen incidents and problems will come up. Assume further that if a good working rapport has been created between systems and user people—and if management has been kept informed—everyone

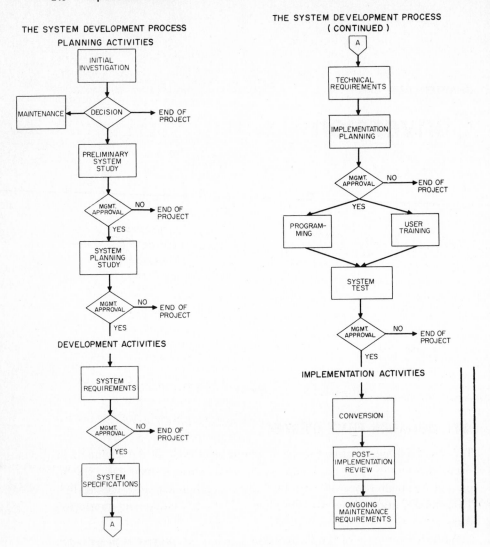

THE SYSTEM DEVELOPMENT PROCESS
PLANNING ACTIVITIES

INITIAL INVESTIGATION

MAINTENANCE ← DECISION → END OF PROJECT

PRELIMINARY SYSTEM STUDY

MGMT. APPROVAL — NO → END OF PROJECT
YES

SYSTEM PLANNING STUDY

MGMT. APPROVAL — NO → END OF PROJECT
YES

DEVELOPMENT ACTIVITIES

SYSTEM REQUIREMENTS

MGMT. APPROVAL — NO → END OF PROJECT
YES

SYSTEM SPECIFICATIONS

A

THE SYSTEM DEVELOPMENT PROCESS
(CONTINUED)

A

TECHNICAL REQUIREMENTS

IMPLEMENTATION PLANNING

MGMT. APPROVAL — NO → END OF PROJECT
YES

PROGRAM-MING   USER TRAINING

SYSTEM TEST

MGMT. APPROVAL — NO → END OF PROJECT
YES

IMPLEMENTATION ACTIVITIES

CONVERSION

POST-IMPLEMENTATION REVIEW

ONGOING MAINTENANCE REQUIREMENTS

involved will understand the problems which arise and will not demand miracles.

ACTIVITY OBJECTIVE

The main end product for the Conversion activity is an operational system which gains full user acceptance and performs up to the standards set and agreed to at the close of the System Requirements activity.

WORKING CONSIDERATIONS

Conversion is an emotion packed activity. No matter how well a project leader has planned or anticipated for Conversion events, change is absolute at this point. Things are different than they were. This, in itself, is cause enough for emotional and behavioral problems.

For the systems professional, therefore, Conversion is a time when cool heads and calm judgment must prevail. The system project leader must realize that he and his staff can only do so much and be in so many places. They can work long days. They can live in hotel rooms adjacent to the office. But, there are still limits to what can be accomplished by a finite number of people in a given number of hours, days, and weeks.

This adds up to another way of saying that the day may come when a conversion schedule has to slip. If this happens, the project leader should realize that his world, and his organization's world, will not come to an end. Allowing that the organization has been around for some time, and that it will continue to be around for some time to come, conversions involving a single system slipping for a few days, or even weeks, should not be assigned consequences which bring the situation out of proportion.

Although the Conversion activity is definitely a time for flexibility, there is one area in which rules and operations should remain rigid: The requirements established for the new system should not be changed during Conversion. This is not to say that a new system is locked in forever—that requirements cannot be changed or should not be changed. It is just that this is not the time to make changes in requirements. At this point, the system has been planned, developed, and tested to fulfill specifically stated, fully understood, accepted requirements.

Even though care has been taken at every step along the way, it is still not unusual to have a user report that a given system output is not really what he had in mind at all. Persons not versed in EDP systems will tend to ask for extensive output reformatting, supported by statements that they are only making small changes—really.

At this time, there are no small changes. A system either converts or it does not. Conversion is a full-time activity which must be built upon a foundation of firm, stable system requirements. If a system will not meet its requirements and/or objectives without eleventh-hour changes, the best course is to halt the project—at least temporarily.

Similarly, if the system itself cannot be brought into operational status without changes in requirements and/or objectives, the same course of action should apply: Halt the project until an orderly evaluation can take place and changes can be planned, developed, and tested before Conversion is resumed.

Actually, this high-impact nature of the Conversion activity is one of the important reasons why this book has recommended that system projects be kept within manageable proportions insofar as possible. The more controllable the scope of a project, the easier it will be to absorb the unavoidable impact of live startup.

IMPORTANCE OF TEAM SPIRIT

It is at this point in the project that the spirit and morale of the project team and the user organization, which have been nurtured, step by step, throughout the Planning and Development phases of the project, can pay really important dividends. The Conversion activity has been likened to a hard-fought athletic contest. Professional athletes today, particularly in sports like football and basketball, indicate that momentum is everything. It is common to hear experienced coaches talk about the importance of getting their teams "up" for a critical game.

This is exactly the situation, and the requirement, in the Conversion activity. The full team, including the entire user group, must be oriented toward success. Determination and cooperation can make the whole difference at this point. Indifference and/or lack of cooperation are the real enemies. It has been said that an average system can achieve excellence with determined user support, and an excellent system can be doomed to mediocrity by uncooperative or disinterested users.

Developing the intensive spirit necessary for successful conversion calls for special, conscious efforts. At this point in a project, an enthusiastic user organization will plan special dinners for users, parties or rewards for successful completion of conversion increments, buttons to be worn around the office with winning slogans, special ash trays, wall posters, and so on. If the situation warrants, the system project leader might do well to consult his organization's sales promotion department. These people are professionals at motivation. They run sales contests all the time. During Conversion, the project team has something to sell—success.

HANDLING PROBLEMS

Along with stimulating the flow of adrenalin which brings the activity to a high-interest key, the system project leader must be sure to establish close interaction and responsiveness for the handling of the problems which are bound to arise.   Discrepancy Notices like those discussed in the last chapter (Figure 12-4) in connection with the System Test activity should be filled out for any and all problems uncovered.   They should be acted upon with expediency.   Information on the follow-up or disposition of Discrepancy Notices should be communicated to users on a current basis.

The Discrepancy Notices initiated and acted upon during the Conversion activity should be recognized as providing the vehicle for the underlying strength and follow-through needed to make the effort successful.   It has already been stated that emotion tends to prevail during Conversion.   In an emotional environment, the only solid values readily available to the project leader are facts.   The Discrepancy Notices are vehicles of fact. Through their diligent use, the project leader can shore up the activity at times when it might otherwise falter.   The prompt handling of Discrepancy Notices creates an atmosphere of credibility.

SCHEDULING PROBLEMS

One important way to head off problems during Conversion is to avoid letting the project be rushed—stampeded in many instances—into untenable situations.   As a specific illustration, pressures frequently arise to start Conversion on time even though there has been schedule slippage during System Test.   There is only one answer to such requests: No.   Don't do it!

As far as schedule slippages are concerned, this is the place where they all come home to roost.   A tumbling domino effect sets in.   In a project which has slipped a little bit in several places, the whole impact strikes against the Conversion activity.   There is an inevitable temptation to try to make up for lost time during Conversion.   This simply cannot be done.

Making up lost time during Conversion is, literally, like trying to do twice as much in half the time.   Any expectations in this direction are unreasonable.   At this time the system is, in an operational sense, brand new.   It is in the infancy of its own efficiency.   A new system cannot make up lost time when it has not achieved its own full speed.   A new system must be developed to the point where it can do a day's work in one day before it is extended to do more than that.

FOLLOWING THE CONVERSION PLAN

During Implementation Planning, the project team planned the work of Conversion.   Now is the time to work the plan.   This should be done methodically, step by step.   Any temptation to operate a system before all the necessary files or controls, data input and validation procedures, and other requirements have been met simply courts disaster.

The analogy of implementing a Conversion on the same type of basis as a refinery which comes on stream bears repeating. No attempt should be made to get a new system off to a flying start. Conversion is an activity which must go forward in stages if it is to be completed successfully. The effective Conversion Plan includes definite stipulations about picking up one segment of the system at a time. Also included are schedules for parallel operations, audit trails, validations, and proofs of performance. These should not be regarded as nuisances. They are reassuring protection points for everyone associated with a new system.

If, despite the best efforts of everyone involved, a system does fall behind, it is best to avoid crash programs aimed at catching up. The fallacy of trying to catch up during Conversion has already been discussed. Everything said during the earlier reference to making up for slippages during previous activities goes equally—possibly even more so—for slippages which might occur during the Conversion activity itself. This is one place where lost time is absolute. It is far better to accept a schedule slip than to trigger almost certain disaster.

At the same time, bringing off a Conversion with relative smoothness can be a stimulating, invigorating achievement. No discussion of the consequences of Conversion should be considered complete without stressing the exhilaration of accomplishment which can be achieved. A good Conversion is a highly satisfying experience. It represents a degree of success which can make everything else worthwhile.

ACTIVITY WORK FLOW

The task and document sequence for the Conversion activity is diagramed in Figure 13-1. Most of the procedures and documents involved were introduced in Chapter 9, during the discussion of Implementation Planning. Also, some of the documents involved are identical to those discussed during the last chapter, on System Test. Therefore, this discussion will be brief, attempting to avoid as much repetition as is feasible:

- The activity begins with a review of its input documentation—the Project Plan, System Test documentation, and the Implementation Plan. Participants in this review include all interested parties, including users, project team members, programmers, and EDP operations personnel.
- As necessary, the Conversion portion of the Implementation Plan is

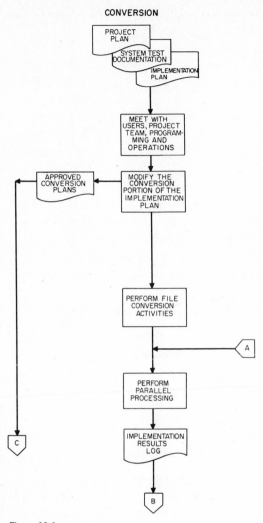

Figure 13-1a

modified and new schedules are agreed to. Major changes, of course, would be reviewed with the steering committee.

- File conversions are performed under control of documents prepared during the Implementation Planning activity.
- If applicable, parallel processing between elements of the old and new systems is initiated. If parallel processing is not being performed, the first increment of the conversion to the new system is initiated at the agreed time.

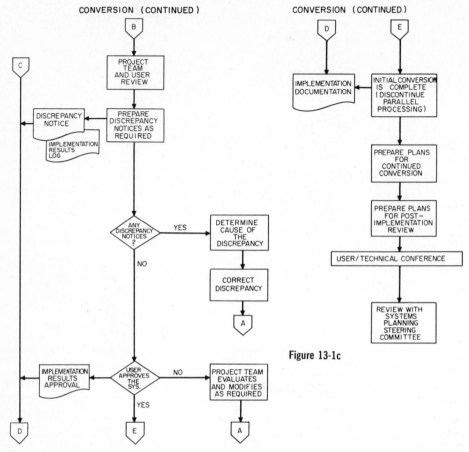

CONVERSION (CONTINUED)

CONVERSION (CONTINUED)

Figure 13-1c

Figure 13-1b

- In either case, results of all computer runs and operations for the new system are logged on a form like the one shown in Figure 13-2. As was the case in System Test, it is important that this log be updated with each applicable operation. Because of the importance of this log in system acceptance, it must be complete, inclusive.
- The scheduled frequency of reviews between the project team and users should be adjusted to the needs of each individual project. Generally, a full-dress review will be held after the first increment of the system has been converted. After that, depending on the situation, the people involved may well decide to wait until the conversion is fully implemented before a final review is held. However, this task should be considered as one with options open on either end. Reviews should be held as the people involved feel they are necessary. As the

flow chart indicates, the reviews serve as the formal point for presentation and consideration of Discrepancy Notice forms. A Discrepancy Notice is illustrated in Figure 13-3. The basic format and utilization are identical with the content and procedure discussed during the last chapter for the same form.

- As indicated in the flow chart, all Discrepancy Notices are reviewed and dealt with. Where modifications are called for, these are reentered into the system for routine processing, results logging, and consideration by the reviewing group.
- Similarly, if the reviewing group determines that any specific elements of a system are not acceptable, modifications and alterations are made as necessary. These, too, are processed and evaluated under the workflow cycle already discussed.
- On review/approval, the user formally accepts the system. System acceptance is noted on a form like the one illustrated in Figure 13-4. Note that approval is indicated at an individual run/module level. Again, the approval form illustrated in Figure 13-4 is the same basic document as was discussed in the last chapter. Note particularly that spaces are provided for two approvals for each program—one by the user and the other by the systems manager. The signature in the systems approval column certifies that the program involved is technically acceptable, that it meets technical specifications for its development, and that it conforms to all applicable standards established within the EDP organization.
- Note the emphasis in the flow diagram in Figure 13-1 on the detail applied to the initial Conversion task. This stresses that the first hurdle is the highest in the Conversion activity. Once this has been completed, additional Conversion steps, implementation documenta-

		SYSTEM TEST ☐ IMPLEMENTATION ☒	RESULTS LOG			

PAGE _1_ OF _1_
PROJECT NO. _028_
PREPARED BY _J JONES_
DATE _8-15_

ORGANIZATION _ABC COMPANY_
APPLICATION TITLE _LABOR DISTRIBUTION_

DATE OF TEST	TIME OF TEST	MODULE NO.	OPERATOR RESPONSIBLE	ANALYST RESPONSIBLE	D/N √	RESULTS
						ERROR FREE OPERATION
7/2	0800	01	J.E.W	W SMITH		

Figure 13-2

```
                              DISCREPANCY NOTICE
                                              PAGE __1__ OF __1__
                                              PROJECT NO. ___028___
                                              PREPARED BY __J.JONES__
ORGANIZATION  ABC COMPANY                     DATE _____8-30_____
APPLICATION TITLE  LABOR DISTRIBUTION

   SYSTEM NAME____LABOR DISTRIBUTION_____
   OUTPUT/REPORT NAME __LABOR DISTRIBUTION REPORT_____
              (NOTE: Submit form in triplicate. One copy will be returned with an analysis of findings.)
```

ITEM NO.	DESCRIPTION OF DISCREPANCY DETECTED
1	THE SHIFT BONUS HOURS FOR DEPARTMENT 4110 ON THE 7/2 REPORT DO NOT APPEAR TO BE CORRECT

ORIGINATOR'S SIGNATURE _____J. Doe._____

DO NOT WRITE BELOW THIS LINE

DATE REC.	PROJ. NO.	PROJECT LEADER	MODULE NO.	MODULE NAME	REPLY ASSIGNED TO	DATE OF REPLY
7/2	123	W.SMITH	01	LABOR DIST. RPT.	W.SMITH	7/2

ITEM NO.	DISCREPANCY ANALYSIS & CORRECTIVE ACTION TAKEN	PROGRAM NUMBER
1	THE ATTACHED TAPE OF THE SHIFT BONUS HOURS WAS TAKEN FROM THE 7/2 REPORT AND VERIFIES THE COMPUTER TOTAL	LD-070

```
APPROVED BY
      W.W.                 W.SMITH
SYSTEMS DEPARTMENT    PROJECT LEADER
```

Figure 13-3

tion, review, and approval routines are repeated until the entire system is operational.

- An important task near the close of the Conversion activity calls for the assembly of documentation needed to prepare for the Post-Implementation Review, which will form the next project activity.
- After Conversion is completed, a User/Technical Conference is held for a full, formal review. This task marks the assembly of the documentation and report which will be presented for review, analysis, and critique by the EDP Systems Planning Steering Committee.
- Following steering committee review, the new system is considered "up" and operational.

USER PHASE-IN

At each work increment within the Conversion activity, operations should proceed until the user is completely on his own. Systems people, who are very much in evidence at the outset, should withdraw gradually and gracefully. One of the end products of Conversion must be user self-reliance. This, necessarily, is best achieved on a step-by-step basis.

As Conversion increments are achieved, the systems members of the project team must be sure to monitor those Conversion steps still to be taken. Planning and resource allocation must be continuous within programs for providing user assistance during each successive stage of system conversion.

THE CONVERSION LEARNING CURVE

In conclusion of this discussion, it should be stressed that the Conversion activity, in particular, should be accompanied by a continuing learning process. The User/Technical Conference scheduled within this activity is intended specifically so that systems people can study problems and mistakes, thus accumulating experience which will make the entire organization more adept at bringing new systems to life.

Actually, one of the basic reasons for structuring the system development process on a project basis as has been recommended in this book is to provide a framework conducive to experience bench marks and proficiency development on the part of systems professionals. Much has been said in this book about the written portions of the project control system. These comments and discussions should not, however, be allowed to overshadow the important benefits to be derived from cumulative experience in an environment structured to enhance development of skills. In other words, the more systems they implement, the better the systems people become at bringing them to life.

Additionally, the greater the experience gained in system conversion, the greater the skills which will be acquired in planning and controlling the system development process.

Finally, skills in overall systems management are bound to be reflected, today, in more soundly run business and governmental organizations.

	SYSTEM TEST RESULTS ☐ IMPLEMENTATION RESULTS ☒	APPROVAL FORM	

PAGE _1_ OF _1_
PROJECT NO. _0.28_
PREPARED BY _J JONES_
DATE _9-1_

ORGANIZATION _ABC COMPANY_
APPLICATION TITLE _LABOR DISTRIBUTION_

PROGRAM NO.	OUTPUT/REPORT NAME	USER APPROVAL		SYSTEMS APPROVAL	
		NAME	DATE	NAME	DATE
LD-080	LABOR DISTRIBUTION RPT.	J BLACK	8/28	SMITH	8/28

Figure 13-4

CHAPTER FOURTEEN

Post-Implementation Review

ACTIVITY PURPOSE

Operational EDP systems are very quickly taken for granted. In a matter of weeks, they become part of the regular operating mainstream of a company. It is common for clerical and operating employees not to remember how the same functions used to be performed within a few months after a new system is operational.

But taking EDP systems for granted is a luxury in which management should not indulge itself. There are very few governmental or business organizations in which management men can say with certainty whether, and how, EDP operations are paying for themselves. Neither can most management men explain satisfactorily just what EDP is doing for an organization and how it is impacting operations and organizational structures.

Yet these are points of information which should be at the fingertips of all management people today. The same people who are vague about major business expenses like the cost of a computer and the results it produces would not consider shrugging off requests for information on how well a new factory is paying off, comparative output of a new piece of production machinery, or the impact upon a company's sales of a new branch or regional office.

It is generally true that computers are a necessity for large business and governmental organizations today. But, acceptance of computers as a necessity is a point of embarkation, not a matter of destiny. Degrees of management skill make for vast differences in EDP results. Therefore, review and evaluation—auditing, if you will—should be an integral part of EDP management continuity within any organization.

ACTIVITY OBJECTIVES

One way an organization's management can be sure to derive evaluations from operational EDP systems is to include a Post-Implementation Review procedure as an integral part of every system project structure.

Specifically, it is recommended that two Post-Implementation Reviews be held for each system project. One of these, it is felt, should take place six months after the initial cutover of the first conversion increment. Normally, this would be about three months after the average system is fully operational. The second Post-Implementation Review, it is suggested, should be scheduled about six months later—or approximately one year after initial cutover.

Experienced systems people within each organization will develop a sensitivity concerning the best, most logical time for Post-Implementation Reviews. Also, such factors as availability of qualified people, seasonal work loads, year-end closings, and other operating elements might impact the optimum date for scheduling a Post-Implementation Review. Therefore, the recommended schedule should be regarded as more of a target than a rule. Also, as has been the case throughout the project cycle, the rapport between users and systems people should be considered. Realistically, there comes a time in the life of every system when it can be considered to have passed its rough moments and be running smoothly. No Post-Implementation Review should be undertaken until a system has been operating routinely for some time.

The purpose of each Post-Implementation Review will be a thorough evaluation of the project according to three criteria:

1. The accomplishments of the system should be compared with requirements established at the outset of the project.
2. Actual project costs should be compared with initial estimates.
3. Ongoing operating costs should be compared with forecasts.

It cannot be stressed strongly enough that such reviews should be on an individual, project-by-project basis and that they should be an integral part of the system development process within each organization. Further, reviews should be applied to projects or systems as they exist currently within the organization.

In some companies, practices have evolved under which EDP reviews trace computer operations all the way back in history—to the days before the organization installed its first EDP system. Such studies are usually conducted under the guise of thoroughness. In practice, however, such historically oriented approaches prove nothing and can turn out to be highly disruptive within an organization's current operational structure.

One of the almost inevitable findings of such historic searches is that comparative data do not exist. This, in itself, reinforces the logic of planning EDP reviews on a current basis—building an information structure which will bring EDP into an organization's regular management loop.

To put this requirement in perspective, it appears best for management to consider its current EDP operations as an integral part of the business. Consider the business itself as a going concern and the existing EDP operations as part of this structure. Use the current EDP organization and operations as a base from which to build. This foundation will be firmer if it is not stirred up unnecessarily.

ALTERNATE REVIEW METHODS

As already indicated, the first Post-Implementation Review takes place about six months after initial cutover—when the system has been fully operational for an estimated three months or more. By this time, the system project team has almost certainly fulfilled its mission and been disbanded. Therefore, even though the review should be considered as a necessary part of the system project, special organizational and operational arrangements will obviously be necessary at this point.

For one thing, users involved in the project are now operating the new system or are engaged in other aspects of their department's line responsibilities. Their situation is different than it was during activities designed to bring the system into existence. Further, because the stated objective of the Post-Implementation Review is to derive as many lessons as can be learned from the recently completed project, this activity is of prime concern to systems professionals and management people.

Two alternatives are usually considered for the performance of Post-Implementation Reviews:

1. The EDP group can have a special team which performs this function. If this approach is used, the responsibility could well be given to the technical services group within the EDP department. Responsibilities in this case would be similar to those performed by internal audit functions within an organization's accounting department.
2. The EDP Systems Planning Steering Committee can form or appoint special task teams to perform individual Post-Implementation Reviews.

These alternatives are straightforward. They need no great amount of elaboration. However, some discussion about the makeup and functional philosophy of a Post-Implementation task team does seem to be in order.

REVIEW TEAM STRUCTURE

The Post-Implementation Review team should function in about the same way and under about the same ground rules as the project team did while the system was being planned, developed, and implemented. It should be headed by a qualified system project leader. This person can be the same one who ran the project—or a person with similar qualifications and experience.

The selection of the leader for the review team depends more on availabilities than any other single factor. That is, if he is available, there is nothing wrong with using the same person who directed the project itself. However, any other person with similar qualifications can also do the job.

Other members of the review team should include:

1. A qualified auditor.
2. An EDP operations man.
3. One or more systems analysts, as the scope of the activity requires.
4. Programmers or systems people, who are present largely for the learning potential inherent in the review process.
5. An operations manager from within the user group. This person should be selected for his intimate knowledge of previous procedures and the new system, as well as their impact on the user organization. He should also have enough perspective so that he can relate to the lessons to be derived for the overall system development process within the organization rather than being restricted to specifics of an individual project. Remember, fingerpointing and faultfinding are to be minimized during this review. It is more important to identify benefits for future projects than to place blame for past problems.

ACTIVITY WORK FLOW

The basic strategy which governs the work flow for a Post-Implementation Review is one of tracing and analyzing the analytical and thought processes which went into the development of the system project.

The work flow of the Post-Implementation Review, as diagrammed in Figure 14-1, very closely parallels the activities which went into the planning and benefit indentification portions of the project. The end result, hopefully, will be a greater awareness throughout the systems organization

POST-IMPLEMENTATION REVIEW

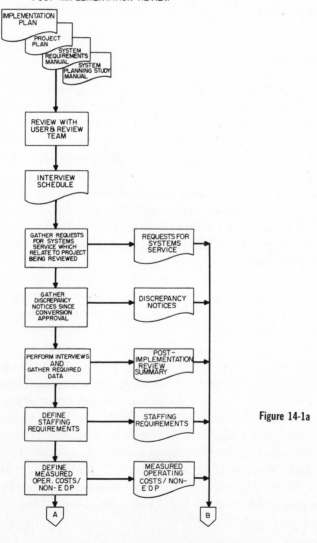

Figure 14-1a

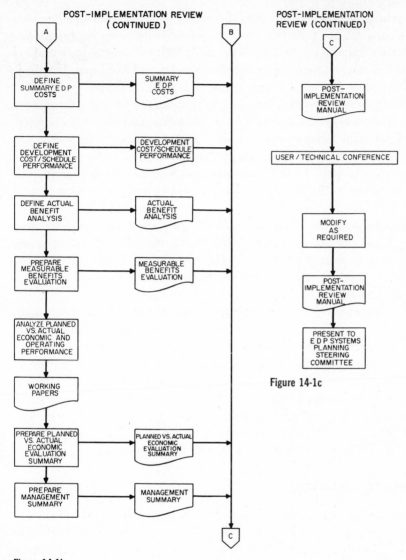

POST-IMPLEMENTATION REVIEW
(CONTINUED)

POST-IMPLEMENTATION
REVIEW (CONTINUED)

Figure 14-1c

Figure 14-1b

of the intangibles which lead to success in the formation, direction, and management of system projects.

In overview, the work flow moves along these lines:

- The activity is initiated with a review of the key planning documents for the project, including the *System Planning Study Manual,* the *New System Requirements Manual,* the Project Plan, and the Implementation Plan.

- As was the case in the activities which generated the key planning documents, the initiating study technique is interview-oriented information gathering. As a basis for this effort, the review team gathers and examines Requests for Systems Service and Discrepancy Notices filed after Conversion and system acceptance. Under the strategy used, persons who filed Requests for Systems Service and Discrepancy Notices will be among the primary interview subjects. Others interviewed will include persons largely at a management level who are using the outputs from the new system, are responsible for realizing the benefits targeted for the new system, or who may be in a position to contribute to future modification of existing systems or new system development projects.
- Succeeding review tasks deal with key cost/benefit aspects of the new system, including staffing requirements, non-EDP operating costs, EDP costs, overall cost and schedule performance factors, actual benefits realized, actual performance realized, and an overall economic evaluation.
- A Management Summary is prepared, and the accumulated documentation is incorporated in a *Post-Implementation Review Manual*. This is finalized at a User/Technical Conference, modified as necessary, and presented to the EDP Systems Planning Steering Committee as part of its surveillance responsibility and as a device for continuing EDP management education. For the committee itself, the *Post-Implementation Review Manual* serves an important accountability function. The user member of this committee, in earlier presentations, forecast benefits and cost results for the system project.

INFORMATION GATHERING

To structure the information-gathering effort within the Post-Implementation Review activity, team members can use an interview schedule like the one shown in Figure 14-2. This is similar in design and execution to inter-

INTERVIEW SCHEDULE						PAGE _1_ OF _1_
						PROJECT NO. _028_
ORGANIZATION _ABC COMPANY_						PREPARED BY _J. JONES_
APPLICATION TITLE _LABOR DISTRIBUTION_						DATE _1-3_
Interviewee/Title	Interviewer	Date	Time	Location	Topics to be discussed	Interview Summary Preparation Date
S. JAMES / D/P		1/10	10:00	404	LABOR/RATE FILE CONTROL EDIT CONTROLS TRANSACTION CONTROLS	1/15
W WHITE / SYSTEMS		1/10	11:30	404	PROGRAMMING	1/15
J. DOE / ACCOUNTING		1/10	2:30	404	USER INPUT USER PROBLEMS OUTPUT	1/16

Figure 14-2

PAGE _1_ OF _1_
PROJECT NO. _028_
PREPARED BY _J. JONES_
DATE _1-16_

ORGANIZATION _ABC COMPANY_

APPLICATION TITLE _LABOR DISTRIBUTION_

Interviewee: J. DOE	Position: ACCOUNTING CLERK	Organization:

SYSTEMS PERFORMANCE CHARACTERISTICS:
  A) DOES OUTPUT MEET STATED REQUIREMENTS?
  B) IS THE SYSTEM FUNCTIONING PROPERLY?
  C) HAVE OPERATING CONDITIONS (PROBLEMS) IMPROVED?
  D) HAVE MEASURED AND NON-MEASURED BENEFITS BEEN ATTAINED?
  E) WHAT IMPROVEMENTS ARE NECESSARY?
  F) WHAT IMPROVEMENTS WOULD BE NICE TO HAVE?

  A. DOES OUPUT MEET STATED REQUIREMENTS?-COMPUTER OUTPUT
      MEETS USER NEEDS.
  B. IS THE SYSTEM FUNCTIONING PROPERLY?-THE INQUIRY
      PROGRAM IS NOT FUNCTIONING PROPERLY; THE MASKING
      ROUTINE STILL HAS A BUG IN IT (THE ACCOUNTING DEPT.
      IS UNABLE TO ACCESS THE ENTIRE DATA RECORD)
C,D. HAVE OPERATING CONDITIONS (PROBLEMS) IMPROVED? HAVE
      MEASURED AND NON-MEASURED BENEFITS BEEN ATTAINED?
      MAINTAINANCE OF THE OLD MANUAL SYSTEM (DUE TO A LACK
      OF USER CONFIDENCE IN THE NEW COMPUTER SYSTEM) HAS
      AT LAST BEEN DISCONTINUED. THIS HAS ALLOWED US TO REDUCE
      PERSONNEL AS PLANNED. DUE TO ACCOUNTING RETENTION RULES
      ONLY HALF OF THE PLANNED STORAGE SAVINGS HAVE BEEN ATTAINED.
  E. WHAT IMPROVEMENTS ARE NECESSARY? CORRECTION OF THE
      SYSTEM BUG MENTIONED IN B. ABOVE WOULD SPEED INQUIRIES AND
      CUT USER CALLS TO THE SYSTEMS DEPT. ALSO, THE 4th COPY
      OF THE LABOR REPORT IS NOT USED AND SHOULD NOT BE PRINTED.
  F. WHAT IMPROVEMENTS WOULD BE NICE TO HAVE? CHANGE THE ON-
      LINE DISPLAY TO REVERSE THE PRESENT POSITIONS OF HOLIDAY
      HOURS AND OVERTIME HOURS.

Figure 14-3a

view schedules discussed earlier in this book. The purpose of the schedule, as was the case in other study tasks, is to determine how much work is to be done and to allocate it to available people. Also, a review of the schedule serves the management function of being sure that all the necessary sources are being covered.

Individual interviews are summarized on forms like the one shown in Figure 14-3. As was the case with earlier forms of similar design, a series of criteria or questions is listed in the heading as a guide for data gathering and interview performance. Note that the emphasis in Figure 14-3 is on results. Interviewers are asked to determine:

- Whether the output of the system meets stated requirements
- Whether the system is functioning according to specifications
- Whether operating conditions have improved
- Whether all the measured and nonmeasured benefits have been realized
- What improvements are necessary within the now operational system
- What improvements should be made as additions to the system

These questions serve to underscore the previously stated strategy of

POST-IMPLEMENTATION
REVIEW SUMMARY

PAGE __/__ OF __/__
PROJECT NO. __038__
PREPARED BY __J JONES__
DATE __1-16__

ORGANIZATION __ABC COMPANY__

APPLICATION TITLE __LABOR DISTRIBUTION__

| Interviewee: __J DOE__ | Position: __ACCOUNTING CLERK__ | Organization: |

SYSTEMS PERFORMANCE CHARACTERISTICS:
A.) DOES OUTPUT MEET STATED REQUIREMENTS?
B.) IS THE SYSTEM FUNCTIONING PROPERLY?
C.) HAVE OPERATING CONDITIONS (PROBLEMS) IMPROVED?
D.) HAVE MEASURED AND NON-MEASURED BENEFITS BEEN ATTAINED?
E.) WHAT IMPROVEMENTS ARE NECESSARY?
F.) WHAT IMPROVEMENTS WOULD BE NICE TO HAVE?

A. COMPUTER OUTPUT REPORT MEETS USER NEEDS

B. THE INQUIRY PROGRAM IS NOT FUNCTIONING PROPERLY; THE MASKING ROUTINE STILL HAS A BUG IN IT (THE ACCOUNTING DEPT. IS UNABLE TO ACCESS THE ENTIRE DATA RECORD)

CD. MAINTAINING OF THE OLD MANUAL SYSTEM (DUE TO A LACK OF USER CONFIDENCE IN THE NEW COMPUTER SYSTEM) HAS AT LAST BEEN DISCONTINUED. THIS HAS ALLOWED US TO REDUCE PERSONNEL AS PLANNED. DUE TO ACCOUNTING RETENTION RULES ONLY HALF OF THE PLANNED STORAGE SAVINGS HAVE BEEN ATTAINED.

E. 1) CORRECTION OF THE SYSTEM BUG MENTIONED IN B) ABOVE WOULD SPEED INQUIRIES AND CUT USER CALLS TO THE SYSTEMS DEPARTMENT

2) THE 4TH COPY OF THE LABOR REPORT IS NOT USED; IT SHOULD NOT BE PRINTED

F. CHANGE THE ON-LINE DISPLAY TO REVERSE THE PRESENT POSITIONS OF HOLIDAY HOURS AND OVERTIME HOURS.

Figure 14-3b

following the analytical process of system planning during the Post-Implementation Review.

STAFFING REQUIREMENTS

The Staffing Requirements information-gathering task—and the form illustrated in Figure 14-4—are relatively straightforward. In practice, the gathering of information shown on the Staffing Requirements form would follow the organization chart of the user group. All functional positions involved in operation of the system under study are listed, one line each, on the form. Expenses are summarized and projected in terms of numbers of employees and actual costs for current and several future accounting periods.

This summary, obviously, provides a measure of actual and forecast personnel requirements and expenses for the now operational system. As will be recalled, an almost-identical form was used in forecasting staffing requirements during the Planning phase of the project. Therefore, gath-

STAFFING REQUIREMENTS			☒ PRESENT ☐ PROPOSED				

PAGE _1_ OF _1_
PROJECT NO. _C-28_
PREPARED BY _J JONES_
DATE _1-30_

ORGANIZATION _ABC COMPANY_
APPLICATION TITLE _LABOR DISTRIBUTION_

JOB DESCRIPTION	SALARY (Annual)	SKILL LEVEL	PROJECTION BY PERIOD – COST/NUMBER OF EMPLOYEES									
			1		2		3		4		5	
ACCOUNTING CLERK	$7500	LEVEL 4	$7500	1	$7500	1	$7500	1	$7500	1	7500	1
TIMEKEEPER	6,000	LEVEL 1	24,000	4	24,000	4	24,000	4	24,000	4	24,000	4
PAYROLL CLERK	7,000	LEVEL 2	14,000	2	14,000	2	14,000	2	14,000	2	14,000	2
SUB TOTAL	$20,500		45500	7	45500	7	45500	7	45500	7	45500	7
FRINGE	2,100		4900		4900		4900		4900		4900	
TOTAL	$22,600		50,400	7	50,400	7	50,400	7	50,400	7	50,400	7

Figure 14-4

ering this particular information during the Post-Implementation Review provides a basis for directly applicable comparison.

MEASURED OPERATING COSTS—NON-EDP

The summary form shown in Figure 14-5 is also identical with Planning phase documentation. As can be seen from examining the form, it summarizes the detailed staff requirements analysis performed during the previous task.

MEASURED OPERATING COSTS/NON-EDP			☒ PRESENT ☐ PROPOSED							

PAGE _1_ OF _1_
PROJECT NO. _028_
PREPARED BY _J.JONES_
DATE _1-21_

ORGANIZATION _ABC COMPANY_
APPLICATION TITLE _LABOR DISTRIBUTION_

Categories	Unit	Rate	Quantity/Dollar Costs by Period									
			1		2		3		4		5	
1. Personnel (w/fringes)	—	—	7	$50,400	7	$50,400	7	$50,400	7	$50,400	7	$50,400
2. Equipment (non-EDP)	CALCULATOR	$200	1	$200		—		—		—		—
3. Operating Supplies	FORMS PAPER AND OFFICE SUPPLIES	$250	1	250	1	250	1	250	1	250	1	250
4. Services												
TOTAL				$50,850		50,650		50,650		50,650		50,650

Notes:

Figure 14-5

SUMMARY—EDP COSTS

The purpose of this task is to produce a summary of computer operation costs which is directly comparable with the projection created during the System Planning Study activity. Therefore, an identical form, like the one shown in Figure 14-6, is used.

DEVELOPMENT COST SCHEDULE—
PERFORMANCE SUMMARY

This task is performed through a detailed, audit-type review of the Project Plan, which was kept up to date from its initiation in the System Planning Study activity through Conversion. From the information in the Project Plan, review team members derive original estimates for costs and schedules of each activity. Alongside these figures are listed the actual completion dates, work time requirements, and costs. In effect, then, the form shown in Figure 14-7 becomes a variance analysis report between planned and actual expenses and performance for the project.

SUMMARY-EDP COSTS

PAGE __1__ OF __1__
PROJECT NO. __028__
ORGANIZATION __ABC COMPANY__
APPLICATION TITLE __LABOR DISTRIBUTION__
PREPARED BY __J.JONES__
DATE __1-23__

Cost Category	Units	Rate	Qty.	$	Qty.	$	Qty.	$	Qty.	$	Qty.	$
Computer Operation	OPERATOR	7000	1/2	3,500	1/2	3,500	1/2	3500	1/2	3500	1/2	3500
COMPUTER TIME	HOUR	$20	850	17,000	850	17,000	850	17,000	850	17,000	850	17,000
TERMINALS	RENTAL/HR	1200	4	4,800	4	4,800	4	4800	4	4800	4	4,800
DATA CONVERSION	OPERATOR	6000	1	6,000	1	6,000	1	6,000	1.5	9,000	2	12,000
Clerical	CLERK	6,000	1/3	2000	1/3	2000	1/3	2,000	1/2	3,000	1/2	3,000
Control	CLERK	6,000	1/3	2,000	1/3	2,000	1/3	2,000	1/2	3,000	1/2	3,000
Maintenance	PROG.	9,000	1/3	3,000	1/3	3,000	1/3	3,000	1/3	3,000	1/3	3,000
TOTAL				38,300		38,300		38,300		43,300		46,300

Figure 14-6

		DATE 1/20			DATE 10/1			
		ORIGINAL			ACTUAL			COMMENTS
NO.	ACTIVITY NAME	END DATE	PLAN HOURS	PLAN COST	END DATE	HOURS	COST	
1	PROJECT ORGANIZATION	2/1	56	$600	2/1	56	$600	
2	SYSTEM REQUIREMENTS	2/22	80	800	2/25	104	800	
3	SYSTEM SPECIFICATIONS	2/26	120	1200	2/26	120	1200	
4	TECHNICAL REQUIREMENTS	4/1	80	800	4/2	88	800	
5	IMPLEMENTATION PLANNING	4/8	80	1000	4/8	80	950	
6	PROGRAMMING	7/1	560	4000	7/15	672	5000	
7	USER TRAINING	7/8	80	800	8/1	85	850	
8	SYSTEM TEST	8/9	120	1200	9/1	120	1500	
9	CONVERSION	9/1	120	1200	9/15	120	1200	
10	ADMINISTRATION	9/1	80	1000	9/15	90	1100	

DEVELOPMENT COST/SCHEDULE
PERFORMANCE SUMMARY

PAGE 1 OF 1
PROJECT NO. ___
PREPARED BY J. JONES
DATE 1-28

ORGANIZATION ABC COMPANY
APPLICATION TITLE LABOR DISTRIBUTION

JOB NO.
PROJECT NO.
ACTIVITY NO.

PROJECT [X]
ACTIVITY [ ]

TOTALS 1,376 12,600   1,535 14,000

PART A
PREPARED BY   J. JONES
APPROVED BY

PART B
PREPARED BY   J. JONES
APPROVED BY

Figure 14-7

BENEFITS ANALYSIS

During the Planning phase of the project, considerable emphasis was placed on identifying, describing, and, where feasible, quantifying benefits to be derived from the system project. Similarly, one of the important tasks of the Post-Implementation Review is to measure benefits actually realized and compare them with those which were forecast.

This is done with a form like the one shown in Figure 14-8, with a series of questions and analysis factors listed as part of the heading to serve as a guide for narrative presentation.

The benefits which are quantitative in nature are then recapped on a summary form like the one shown in Figure 14-9. This provides a financial summary of benefits which are now being realized, together with a fore-cast of those projected at the time of the Post-Implementation Review.

ECONOMIC EVALUATION SUMMARY

It should be stressed that the Economic Evaluation Summary task incor-porates the really creative challenge within the Post-Implementation Re-

```
                              ACTUAL BENEFITS ANALYSIS      PAGE  1  OF    1
                                                            PROJECT NO.  028
                                                            PREPARED BY  J. JONES
                                                            DATE        2-3
        ORGANIZATION  ABC COMPANY
        APPLICATION TITLE  LABOR DISTRIBUTION


        DESCRIPTION OF BENEFIT

            HOW BENEFIT WAS ACHIEVED

            WHEN BENEFIT WAS ACHIEVED

            VALUE OF BENEFIT

            METHOD OF CALCULATION

            RESPONSIBILITY FOR ACHIEVING BENEFIT


            1) BENEFIT WAS ACHIEVED BY SELLING THE EXCESS
        FILING CABINETS AND THROUGH A REDUCTION IN RENTED STORAGE SPACE.
        FURTHER, BENEFIT WAS REALIZED THROUGH REDUCED PAYROLL
        PREPARATION CHARGES. THESE BENEFITS WERE REALIZED DURING
        THE FIRST YEAR THE SYSTEM WAS IMPLEMENTED
            2) BENEFITS AMOUNTED TO: $9,100 IN THE FIRST YEAR
                STORAGE SPACE SAVED (200 SQ.FT.)  $600
                EXTRA FILING CABINETS            $500
                REDUCED PAYROLL PREPARATION COSTS $8,000
            3) MR. J. JONES, SYSTEMS, AND, MR. J. DOE, ACCOUNTING, WERE
        RESPONSIBLE FOR THE REALIZATION OF THE PROPOSED BENEFITS.
```

Figure 14-8

view activity. Its title should not lead to confusion with routine accounting or audit-type economic summaries. Rather, where system projects are involved, evaluation summaries should stress the intangible and qualitative aspects of the project as well as recording basic numbers for comparison purposes.

Because of the need to analyze both quantitative and qualitative aspects of a system at this point, two separate forms are recommended. Figure 14-10 is a straightforward economic summary. It corresponds with a document included in the *System Planning Study Manual* as a guide to the development and implementation of the system, incorporating cash flow and return on investment projections. At this point, the projections are compared directly with actual performance.

Over and above these quantified data, this task also generates a narrative form like the one shown in Figure 14-11. As indicated, this form incorporates a series of criteria in the heading as a guide for value and judgment-related narrative descriptions. Factors to be covered are qualitative in

MEASURABLE BENEFITS EVALUATION

PAGE __1__ OF __1__

PROJECT NO. __028__

ORGANIZATION __ABC COMPANY__

PREPARED BY __J.JONES__

APPLICATION TITLE __LABOR DISTRIBUTION__

DATE __2-4__

BENEFIT DESCRIPTION	Cash Flow by Period					
	1	2	3	4	5	6
REDUCED FILING SPACE - 200 SQ.FT.	$ 600	600	600	600	600	600
SELL FILING CABINETS	500	—	—	—	—	—
REDUCED COST OF PREPARING INPUT FOR PAYROLL	8,000	8,000	8,000	8,000	8,000	8,000
TOTAL	$9,100	8,600	8,600	8,600	8,600	8,600

Figure 14-9

nature.   In execution, this document represents a summary presentation to management incorporating the judgment and recommendations of persons responsible for the Post-Implementation Review.   Topics include:

- Summaries of performance problems observed by the review team
- The number and nature of outstanding requests for modification
- The number and nature of outstanding Discrepancy Notices
- Recommendations of the reviewers

PLANNED VS ACTUAL
ECONOMIC EVALUATION SUMMARY

PAGE __1__ OF __1__

PROJECT NO. __028__

ORGANIZATION __ABC COMPANY__

PREPARED BY __J.JONES__

APPLICATION TITLE __LABOR DISTRIBUTION__

DATE __2-5__

Proposed System:	PLAN / ACTUAL	PLAN / ACTUAL	PLAN / ACTUAL	PLAN / ACTUAL	PLAN / ACTUAL	PLAN / ACTUAL
Development Costs	12,600 / 14,000	— / —	— / —	— / —	— / —	/
Operating Costs- Non EDP	50,050 / 50,850	50,650 / 50,650	50,650 / 50,650	50,650 / 50,650	50,650 / 50,650	
EDP Recurring Costs	36,900 / 38,300	36,900 / 38,300	36,900 / 38,300	36,900 / 43,300	36,900 / 46,300	
Measurable Benefits	(10,200) / (9,100)	(9,200) / (8,600)	(9,200) / (8,600)	(9,200) / (8,600)	(9,200) / (8,600)	
Gross Cost (Benefit) Proposed System	98,350 / 94,050	78,350 / 80,350	78,350 / 80,350	86,350 / 85,350	86,350 / 88,350	
Present System:						
Operating Costs - Non EDP	80,000 / 80,000	85,000 / 85,000	90,000 / 90,000	95,000 / 95,000	105,000 / 105,000	
EDP Recurring Costs						
Total Present System	80,000 / 80,000	85,000 / 85,000	90,000 / 90,000	95,000 / 95,000	105,000 / 105,000	
Net Savings (Cost)	(18,350) / (14,050)	6,650 / 4,650	11,350 / 9,650	8,650 / 9,650	18,650 / 16,650	

Figure 14-10

MANAGEMENT SUMMARY

PAGE __1__ OF _____1_____

PROJECT NO. _____628_____

PREPARED BY _____J.JONES_____

DATE _____2-8_____

ORGANIZATION _ABC COMPANY_

APPLICATION TITLE _LABOR DISTRIBUTION_

A. PROBLEMS
B. NUMBER AND NATURE OF OUTSTANDING REQUESTS FOR SYSTEMS SERVICE
C. NUMBER AND NATURE OF DISCREPANCY NOTICES
D. SUMMARY OBSERVATIONS — SYSTEM PERFORMANCE
E. RECOMMENDATIONS

A. DATA PROCESSING OPERATIONS HAS ENCOUNTERED PROBLEMS IN STAFFING THE EDP OPERATION ON SUNDAY NIGHTS. NONE OF THE CURRENT STAFF WANTS TO WORK ON SUNDAYS.

B. NO OUTSTANDING REQUESTS FOR SYSTEMS SERVICE.

C. THE ONLY OUTSTANDING DISCREPANCY IS THAT OF FAULTY CALCULATION OF THE SHIFT PREMIUM FOR A HOLIDAY.

D. SYSTEM PERFORMANCE HAS BEEN EXCELLENT AND ACCORDING TO PLAN.

E. IN ORDER TO RELIEVE THE EDP STAFFING PROBLEM IT IS RECOMMENDED THAT THIS JOB BE RUN ON FIRST SHIFT ON SATURDAY.

Figure 14-11

POST-IMPLEMENTATION REVIEW MANUAL

The accumulated documentation of the Post-Implementation Review activity is incorporated in a final report manual. This is scrutinized at a User/ Technical Conference, updated as necessary, and presented to the EDP Systems Planning Steering Committee—by that group's user member if feasible.

In summary, this activity is a constructive backward glance of the type which can be critically important in the management learning process.

CHAPTER FIFTEEN

Ongoing Maintenance Requirements

THE MAINTENANCE FUNCTION

Within an EDP context, systems maintenance is big business. It should be planned for and managed accordingly.

By the beginning of the decade of the seventies, it was common to find, in large EDP departments, that systems maintenance accounted for up to 50 percent of the overall work load. Further, the proportion of maintenance activity to the department total was still growing. Clearly, any single factor of a department's operations which grows to such proportions needs to be supported by management attention and control techniques.

The rate of growth in systems maintenance should not be considered alarming. On the contrary, this development is normal. It is to be expected. Actually, growth in maintenance requests is a sign of maturity for an EDP organization. When maintenance requests increase, this means a substantial portion of an organization's main line EDP systems are on stream and functioning smoothly enough so that they can be updated routinely rather than discarded and redeveloped.

THE NATURE OF SYSTEM MAINTENANCE

A system project, under the definition used here, is finite in its responsibilities and scope. It has a definite beginning and ending. When its objectives are achieved, the project is concluded.

EDP systems themselves, however, are continuous—never ending. Actually, it is one of the measures of soundness for an operational system that it can be expanded and modified dynamically to keep pace with the needs of its organization. Therefore, it is one of the basic requirements for continuity in the systems business that provision be made for ongoing maintenance.

In effect, maintenance activities pick up and continue where system projects leave off. Therefore, a maintenance effort can be considered as a miniature system project. Certainly, the same basic requirements for planning, management, and control exist in maintenance as they do in a full-scale project.

The discussion in this chapter will be directed toward maintenance requirements considered routine. That is, the maintenance needs to be discussed will be of the type aimed at expanding or improving existing systems. The implied assumption is that such requirements can be handled on a planned, fairly routine basis.

However, it should be mentioned in passing that maintenance requirements of an urgent, emergency nature can and do arise—all too frequently for most EDP professionals. This chapter will not get into discussions of what to do or how to handle situations where systems might blow up and require immediate, emergency maintenance, possibly in the middle of the night.

In passing, it should be noted, however, that each EDP department should recognize that this type of thing will happen. Provisions should be made to document both the occurrences and the remedies devised. Even if maintenance occurs on an emergency basis, it should be stressed that any changes to a system should be documented and incorporated in the appropriate system libraries.

The diagram in Figure 15-1 reflects this basic nature of the maintenance function. As is readily apparent, each maintenance project incorporates a series of activities similar to those within a system project. Structurally, the chief differences lie in magnitude. Because maintenance projects are relatively smaller than system projects, the regularly interspersed management committee reviews are not called for. Any individual maintenance project can be carried out between users and the EDP technical services

ONGOING MAINTENANCE REQUIREMENTS

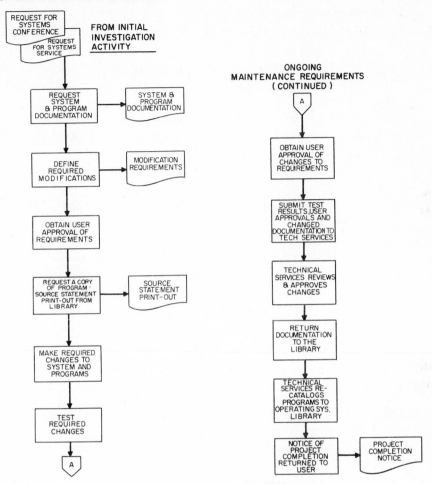

Figure 15-1a

Figure 15-1b

group, on their own cognizance, subject to the review and judgment of the systems manager and the manager of the affected user department or departments.

As Figure 15-1 indicates, documentation is very much a part of a maintenance project, just as it is for a system project. Further, the documentation generated through maintenance activities should be compatible with system project documentation—particularly considering that maintenance updates standard system libraries. Therefore, for the purposes of this discussion, it should be assumed that the same forms discussed in conjunction with system projects can be used, as appropriate, and correspondingly, in maintenance activities.

As a further basis for this discussion, it is assumed that all the documentation and support functions necessary to system maintenance are part of the routine work assignments, facilities, and operations of the technical services group which is responsible for system maintenance. These prerequisites include:

1. The systems library should include full documentation for all operational systems and system projects. Thus, the technical services group should have all its reference sources readily available. Further, documentation maintenance can be performed internally within this group.

2. The same would apply for programming libraries, with the additional stipulation that all source, as well as object, programs are stored and maintained under cognizance of this group.

3. The technical services group has responsibilities and procedures for screening all system modifications and verifying that they have been tested, converted, and approved before they are incorporated into the library. Procedures should be set up to provide assurance that all such changes or modifications are made within established standards for the department.

WORK FLOW

As indicated in Figure 15-1, a maintenance project is initiated by the documents generated from an Initial Investigation activity like the one described in Chapter 3 of this book. Remember, Initial Investigations are carried out by cognizant system project leaders. All requests are accorded Initial Investigations. Where the problem is of a maintenance nature, this is determined at the Initial Investigation Conference. A maintenance project stems from an Initial Investigation Conference decision agreeing that the requirements can be met through maintenance rather than requiring a new system project.

As the first activity within a maintenance project, the programmer/analyst is responsible for carrying through the project requests and reviews documentation for the system and its programs. In conference with the requester and/or other members of the user organization, the programmer/analyst defines the required modifications and obtains approval for them.

With these approved objectives as a guide, the programmer/analyst and any other technical services personnel assigned to the project obtain copies of the source program statements and written procedures for system operation. With the approved statement of requirements as their guide, the technical services people go through the development, testing and implementation of the maintenance changes, incorporating them within the operational system. Test and Conversion results are documented and approvals are obtained from responsible user personnel.

As indicated, before any changes are incorporated in the system library, they are completely reviewed under procedures established within the technical services group. Systems and programming libraries are updated and cataloged to reflect these changes. Then, after the libraries have been brought up to date, the user is notified with a copy of the project completion notice.

CHAPTER SIXTEEN

Conclusion

Although this book has gone into considerable specifics about work flows, documents, and practices for project management, it should be emphasized that the intent has been an enunciation of principles and requirements rather than the creation of a "cookbook" with recipes which can be concocted within any computer-using organization.

The authors do not envision, or recommend, that the management techniques discussed here be picked up bodily and applied literally. Rather, in conclusion, it should be stressed that every organization has individual characteristics and requirements. Every manager will approach his responsibilities and problems differently. Therefore, in the long run, the specifics of forms and procedures are less important than the evolution of workable controls within which individual managers feel comfortable.

The real attraction of the systems environment for talented people lies in the individuality of the challenges offered. Methodology must not infringe upon opportunity. This, as the authors see it, is what effective management is all about, at any level.

Electronic data processing is carried out in a highly technically oriented environment. However, the technicalities and associated terminologies of the EDP fraternity should not be permitted to obscure either the challenges or the requirements involved for management.

This happened in many cases during the sixties. Preoccupation with the technical side of EDP tended to obscure what computers were all about. The real challenge, as it has emerged through the formulation of criteria and techniques available to managers of the seventies, lies in harnessing the power of computers as a tool to assist management in running the business.

That is, management people need not concern themselves, today, with the technicalities of electronics, software, data communications, or procedural fine points within an EDP system any more than they must be expert in architecture and engineering to recognize that they need a new plant. The manager's job, rather, is to communicate with architects and engineers whose competence he relies on to create the results he wants.

EDP competence and technology can also be assumed. What must be mastered is an understanding of its capabilities and the techniques for its management. For management people, preoccupation with details of hardware, software, peripherals, or procedural details is a thing of the past. For the seventies, management of the EDP process is "all about" stating and communicating objectives, planning, and controlling resources which can now be assumed, relied on, and applied as a building block for meeting the challenges of the future. This book has, chiefly, been a statement of such a need and an enunciation of methods for meeting it.

Index

273